BASICS OF
LICENSING

Gregory J. Battersby
Danny Simon

Kent Press
▪ Norwalk, CT ▪

© 2010 Kent Press All Rights Reserved.

Printed in the United States of America

ISBN 978-0-9830963

To Susan – 40 years of marriage and now 30 books. I don't know how you withstood either, but I couldn't imagine life without you.

-Greg

To the things that mean the most – my wife Carey for her love and friendship, my daughter Jane who lights up my life, and my faithful stuffed champions Dorothy and Doggie Arf Arf for their steadfast support.

-Danny

ABOUT THE AUTHORS

Gregory J. Battersby is a senior partner in the intellectual property law firm of Grimes & Battersby, LLP with offices in Norwalk, CT and New York City. He has almost 40 years of experience in intellectual property and licensing law. Before founding Grimes & Battersby in 1982, he had been associated with two major New York City IP law firms and was senior counsel at Gulf & Western Industries (now Viacom). Greg has a degree in biology/chemistry from Seton Hall University and a law degree from Fordham Law School.

For the past 15 years, he has served as General Counsel for the International Licensing Industry Merchandisers' Association ("LIMA") and was recently inducted into its Hall of Fame. He has also been an officer and member of the Board of Directors of the New York Intellectual Property Law Association ("NYIPLA").

Greg is a prolific author, having written more than 25 books on various licensing and IP topics, including the seminal book on the law of merchandising entitled *The Law of Merchandise & Character Licensing*, which was originally published in 1985 and is updated annually through West Publishing. He is a founder and executive editor of *The Licensing Journal* and the *IP Litigator*, both published by Aspen and is the legal columnist for *Total Licensing*. He has written more than 50 articles on various licensing and IP topics and given more than 200 talks on the subject before a wide range of audiences, including the INTA, LES, AIPLA and other organizations.

He has been qualified as an expert in more than thirty actions on licensing related matters.

Greg turned a passion for baseball into a business, having invented a computerized video baseball/softball pitching simulator for which he has received 13 U.S. patents and numerous international ones. In his spare time, he created and now runs a company called ProBatter Sports, which manufactures and sells these simulators to a wide range of customers including a dozen Major League teams and more than 200 colleges and commercial training facilities.

Danny Simon is a thirty plus year veteran of the licensing industry with expertise in all phases of the merchandising and licensing process. Having built the licensing division for Lorimar Productions, 20th Century Fox and Carolco Pictures, he opened his own licensing agency in 1992 in Los Angeles, CA, called The Licensing Group, Ltd.

Danny has been a pioneer in the area of entertainment licensing, with a focus on material geared to the teen plus market. Beginning with the television program DALLAS, he was among the first to license adult, prime-time television entertainment and, with DYNASTY, he was the first to apply branding techniques to television shows. He also developed successful licensing programs for M*A*S*H, Fall Guy, Alf, Rambo, Terminator 2: Judgment Day, Mortal Kombat, Baywatch, U.S. Secret Service, Arnold Schwarzenegger and David Hasselhoff.

He has also succeeded in feature film development. With MORTAL KOMBAT, he produced the first ever film adaptation of a video game. He's a partner in an entertainment development company that sold the rights to the MATT HELM book series to DreamWorks, where it is currently in development as a motion picture.

For the past 18 years Danny has taught a continuing college level course on entertainment licensing at UCLA. He's a founding member of LIMA and has been its president and a two-time member of its Board. With Greg Battersby, he developed and serves as Co-Dean of LIMA's Certificate of Licensing Studies program.

Danny also is a regular lecturer on a variety of licensing topics around the world and serves as an international licensing consultant, providing consulting services to the Hong Kong Trade Development Council and other international groups.

He has been qualified as an expert witness on licensing issues in over 20 different litigations.

Over the years Danny has written many articles on the subject of licensing for various licensing magazines. He is a regular contributor to the book *Licensing Update*, published annually by Aspen, and also writes a monthly column on entertainment licensing for *The Licensing Journal.*

PREFACE

The licensing of brands, characters, sports team names, college logos and artwork, often called "merchandising," has become a huge business. While it may have begun as a fad, it has exploded into a $100+ billion industry at retail and generates more than $7 billion in royalty income for those property owners who are savvy enough to license their properties for a wide variety of consumer products.

While the roots of licensing can be traced back to the 1800's, the real growth of the licensing industry began in the 1970's with the explosion of such blockbuster motion pictures as STAR WARS and JAWS which were highly merchandised for a wide variety of products.

Although the entertainment industry was the genesis of licensing, it has expanded rapidly to include many different types of properties: entertainment/character, corporate/brand, sports, fashion, collegiate, art, music, non-profit, and publishing. As a result, licensing has evolved from its humble beginnings to that of a regularly accepted marketing strategy for owners of intellectual property rights. In fact, all around the world, many companies and corporate licensing divisions have been established solely for the purpose of representing marketable intellectual properties.

Some licensing programs are designed to take advantage of a current trend or fad sweeping the marketplace, and therefore have a relatively short lifespan, or appeal to a narrow segment of the public. Other licensing programs have the potential to remain relevant indefinitely, by virtue of their ability to attract interest from a wide and diverse range of consumers. Regardless of the type of licensing program or the industry that spawned it, merchandising has established itself as a viable and important form of marketing.

While licensing is attractive to property owners who see it as a way to help promote their underlying properties and generate licensing revenues in the process, it is similarly attractive to manufacturers as it permits them to leverage the value and popularity of a brand, character or sports entity to drive sales of their product. Under the right circumstances, licensing can be a win—win collaboration for all parties.

What has not kept pace with the growth of the licensing industry, in our collective opinion, is the availability of informative materials for persons who desire knowledge about the various practices of the licensing industry, or those seeking information that will help them to hone their licensing skills. We are of the opinion that the industry needs a

"How To" book appropriate for anyone who is interested in capitalizing on this potentially lucrative market. In satisfying this need, we were not content merely to cover the basics. Our objectives, thus, have always been two-fold: first, to develop a book for those entering the licensing field that will help chart their path to success and, second, to provide enough relevant and practical information in the book that it can be used by an experienced licensing professional when confronted with an issue that is new to them. With the product now in your possession, we feel that we have accomplished both objectives.

After providing the obligatory "dictionary" of licensing terms, we have included a detailed history of the merchandising industry for one express purpose, to put today's success into context. In order to understand what licensing has become, we believe it important to know and understand how it got to this stage. The history chapter details the industry's growth, and honors those whose work helped to transform the licensing industry into the big business it has become.

We then follow the history chapter with a series of chapters that are intended to provide property owners with a roadmap for the development of their property into a licensable commodity, and to furnish licensees with useful information that will be of value for licenses they have or will acquire. We begin with a discussion of the steps necessary to protect and clear a property, followed by a detailed discussion of how best to develop and administer a licensing program. The work also includes chapters on the all-important license agreement; the development of royalty rates, how best to use licensing agents and consultants, when and how to audit licensees, how to deal with counterfeiters, advice on marketing and promoting properties and the role that retailers play in licensing. We have concluded with an appendix containing a comprehensive and useful set of forms needed to commence a licensing program.

The preparation of any book of this type requires the input and efforts of a number of people and a preface is the ideal place to give recognition to their contributions and express our appreciation and thanks for their efforts. First and foremost is our editor, Rob Gessinger, who worked tirelessly on helping us pull this book together, interfacing with our publisher and keeping us on track all along the way. Most importantly, Rob helped us refine the work into something that can be readily understood by both the novice and experienced licensing professional.

It is also important for us to note that this book has been developed with the endorsement of the International Licensing Industry

Merchandisers' Association ("LIMA"), the central trade organization for this industry and who will participate financially from its sales. As such, the folks at LIMA deserve special mention, particularly Charles Riotto, LIMA's President. Charles provided us with great support and guidance at every step of the way.

Finally, a word of special thanks to an individual who we consider to be one of five nicest people in the entire world, LIMA's Vice-President of Member Relations and resident historian, Louise Caron. Her help in developing the chapter on the history of licensing is greatly appreciated.

We hope you find this book to be both an informative and useful guide to the business of licensing. Enjoy the read.

Greg Battersby & Danny Simon

INTERNATIONAL LICENSING INDUSTRY MERCHANDISERS' ASSOCIATION

Founded in 1985, LIMA has more than 1000 member companies representing over 35 countries from all areas of the licensing industry: Licensors, Licensees/Manufacturers, Agents, Consultants and support groups including Retailers, Accountants, Attorneys, Graphic Designers and more. Headquartered in New York City, LIMA has branch offices in London, Munich, Tokyo, Hong Kong and Shanghai with a growing number of international regional representatives in additional markets around the world.

By joining LIMA you become part of the global licensing community, with an ability to utilize the services that LIMA provides to enhance your business and/or your career. LIMA members have free access to a wide variety of print and electronic resources, information that helps you make informed decisions, find reliable resources and expand your business. Available to all LIMA members:

➤ Free access to LIMA's online licensing industry database with search capabilities

➤ Annual Harvard/Yale licensing industry statistical study

➤ Subscription to regular licensing industry newsletters & reports

➤ Discounted exhibitor and seminar rates at licensing trade shows

➤ Association discounts on business services and insurance

➤ Free access to webinars on timely licensing-related topics

➤ Participation in regional networking events

➤ Access to members-only meeting facilities at various trade shows

Join LIMA and become a member of the worldwide licensing community. For membership information contact:

Louise Caron, VP Member Relations
LIMA
350 Fifth Avenue, Ste. 4019
New York, New York 10118
212-244-1944 X 5
212-563-6552 (Fax)
Louise@licensing.org
www.licensing.org

TABLE OF CONTENTS

Chapter 1

Defining the World of Licensing

1.1   Definitions and Terminology

Over the years, the licensing industry has developed a set of terms that need to be familiar if one is to understand how the industry works.

1.1.1   Forms of Licensing

The term **"licensing"** typically means any transaction in which the owner of a piece of intellectual property grants another party the right to use such intellectual property, typically in exchange for some form of consideration or payment. Absent the grant of such a right or license, the other party's use of the intellectual property would be considered infringing use. Thus, the license constitutes a defense to infringement.

"Intellectual property" can take many forms including, for example, musical works, literary works, artwork, drawings, inventions, discoveries, designs, patents, trademarks, names, logos, legends, industrial designs, trade dress, celebrity rights, etc. Regardless of the type of intellectual property, the one constant is that it must be protectable under some form of intellectual property protection, e.g., as a patent, trademark, copyright, right of publicity or trade secret. Intellectual property is frequently referred to simply as **"IP."**

There are many types of licensing, virtually all of which will depend, in large measure, on the type of intellectual property involved. For example, when the intellectual property being licensed is technology or is covered by a patent, the licensing of such technology or patent is typically called **"technology licensing"** or **"patent licensing."** Similarly, when the property being licensed is computer software, the licensing of the software is normally called **"software licensing."** When a trademark is being licensed, it is typically referred to as **"trademark licensing."**

When a character from a book or motion picture is the property being licensed, such licensing is commonly called **"character licensing."** Similarly, when a corporate brand is the subject matter, it is typically called **"brand licensing."**

When one licenses a highly recognizable brand or character for goods or services in categories different from the one where the brand or

1

character had originally been popularized, such licensing is frequently called **"ancillary product licensing"** or simply **"merchandising."**

This book will focus primarily on merchandising, although at various times the terms merchandising and licensing may be used interchangeably throughout the work.

It should be appreciated that the term merchandising may have other meanings, particularly in the retail or marketing fields. In the retailing field, merchandising means something other than licensing, usually referring to some form of "sales promotion as a comprehensive function, including market research, development of new products, coordination of manufacture and marketing, and effective advertising and selling."

1.1.2   Contractual Terms

The grant of a license to a manufacturer is typically done pursuant to a written **"license agreement"** or **"licensing agreement."** While oral licenses can occur, the vast majority are granted under formal license agreements.

In the context of licensing, the owner of the IP that is granting the license is commonly called a **"property owner"** or **"licensor"** while the party receiving the license to use the intellectual property on their product is typically called a **"licensee."**

The intellectual property being licensed is normally called a **"property"** or, more accurately, **"licensed property,"** while the products for which the license is being granted are typically called **"licensed products** or **licensed articles."** If the intellectual property is being licensed for use in conjunction with a service, e.g., for advertising services, those services would be called **"licensed services."**

It is quite common to include **"schedules"** in a license agreement to more accurately and completely define both the licensed property and the licensed products or licensed services.

There are a number of different types of license grants. An **"exclusive license"** is one in which the licensee is the only party receiving the right to use the licensed property for the licensed products. There may be some instances, however, in an exclusive license where the licensor reserves the right to use the licensed property itself for such products, but that would have to be specifically stated.

A **"non-exclusive license"** is one in which the licensee is granted the right to use the licensed property for the licensed products on a non-exclusive basis so that the licensor may make similar grants to other parties.

In the licensing area, many licenses are of the non-exclusive type, even where the licensor may have no intention of granting a similar right to anyone else. This is done primarily to protect the licensor in the event that the licensee should declare bankruptcy. In such event, the licensor might be able to find others to step into the shoes of the bankrupt licensee during the pendency of the bankruptcy proceeding.

Virtually all licenses are granted for a defined period of time, e.g., three (3) years or for so long as the licensee continues to sell licensed products. The length of a license grant is typically called its **"term."** In many cases, a licensee is given an **"option"** to renew the term of the license upon meeting certain conditions. In such cases, the initial period may be called an **"initial term"** and the renewal period may be called a **"renewal term."**

Most licenses will restrict the licensee's use of the property to a particular geographical area, e.g., North America or the European Union, and this is typically called a **"licensed territory."**

Similarly, a licensor may want to restrict the licensee's sales of the licensed products to a specific market or channel of trade, e.g., "mass market" or "Internet." Such distribution limitations are commonly referred to as **"channels of distribution."**

Licensors may want to exclude certain rights from the license grant, either to give it the freedom to exploit those rights itself or to be able to grant such rights to others. Many licensors will exclude from a license grant the right to use the property as a **"premium"** or in conjunction with a **"promotion."** The reason for such an exclusion is that premiums and promotional products are not typically sold as merchandise through the normal channels of distribution but, instead, are given away to the public to promote the sale of another property, e.g., McDonald's BAKUGAN Happy Meal Program, in which BAKUGAN toys were given away by McDonald's to help promote the sales of its restaurant services.

The most common form of compensation in licensing is the payment of a **"royalty"** to the licensor, which is most often based on a percentage of the licensee's **"net sales"** of the licensed products. "Net sales" is almost always a defined term in any license agreement and will vary from license agreement to license agreement. It is often defined as the licensee's gross sales of licensed products, less certain agreed upon

<u>deductions or credits</u>, usually referred to as **"discounts and allowances**.*"*

At the time it enters into a license agreement, a licensee is typically required to pay the licensor an <u>**"advance"**</u> against its future royalty obligations. In most instances, the advance is creditable or deductable against the licensee's future earned royalty obligations. Thus, if the licensee paid a $100,000 advance, it would normally not need to pay any additional royalties until its earned royalty obligation had exceeded $100,000.

In the licensing area, most licensors require that the licensee pay a **"guaranteed minimum royalty,"** often referred to as simply a **"minimum"** or **"guarantee."** Guarantees are intended to protect the licensor in the event that the licensee's net sales prove to be lower than anticipated. As the name would imply, the licensee is actually guaranteeing that it will pay the licensor a certain minimum amount of royalties over a given period during the term of the license.

Although there are a number of ways to apply this guaranteed minimum royalty obligation, in most instances it only applies when the licensee's earned royalties fall below a certain minimum amount for a particular period. In such case, the licensee is obligated to supplement its earned royalty payments to meet the guarantee for that period.

In addition to the payment of a royalty, many licensors require their licensees to also contribute to the licensed property's <u>**"marketing fund"**</u> which is to be used by the licensor to support and promote the property and the licensing program. These payments are often called a **"marketing royalty"** because they are frequently calculated as a percentage of the licensee's net sales of licensed products for a particular period in much the same manner that the royalty is calculated.

While most licensees are allowed to use third parties to manufacture the licensed products for them as **"approved manufacturers,"** there is a difference between such practice and <u>**"sub-licensing,"**</u> which is almost always prohibited. In sub-licensing, the licensee actually grants a third party the same rights that it had received from the original property owner or licensor, not simply the right to manufacture products for it.

1.2   Types of Properties

There are a number of different types of properties that can be merchandised or licensed, although the vast majority of them constitute words, names, titles, symbols, designs, character or personality images or likenesses that have acquired a wide degree of public recognition through mass media exposure. Licensing properties typically fall into a number of different categories, including:

- Art
- Celebrity
- Collegiate
- Corporate
- Entertainment
- Fashion
- Music
- Non-Profit
- Publishing
- Sports

1.2.1 Art

Art properties can be virtually any image or other piece of artwork. In the case of prominent artists such as Thomas Kinkade, Warren Kimble or Mary Engelbreit, the artist's name can also be included as part of the licensed property.

It's been said that in art licensing, "it's all about the image." Consumers are purchasing the licensee's products primarily because of the artwork or image that appears on the products and manufacturers are licensing the artwork for the same reason. Licensing the artwork of an outside artist lowers the licensee's development costs which makes it very attractive. While artwork is licensed for a host of different types of licensed products, including apparel and printed matter, it is also extensively licensed for use in advertising and on packaging.

While publishers and manufacturers have been using other people's artwork and images for decades, the actual licensing of artwork has been a more recent trend. In the "early days," artwork was typically purchased by a manufacturer for nominal sums of money, rather than licensed on a royalty-bearing basis.

As the licensing business grew, however, artists (and their agents) recognized the shortfall of selling off all rights in the artwork to publishers and manufacturers who would then reap far greater profits from its use. Consequently, many artists started declining to sell their artwork outright and, instead, turned to licensing as a way to potentially share in the merchandising profits that the artwork generated.

As art licensing grew in popularity, so too did the sizes of the advances and guarantees that a publisher or manufacturer would be willing to pay for the right to use the artwork. In many instances, these advances and guarantees were significant and frequently were never earned off by the licensee.

As a result, the business model changed…again. While most artwork is still licensed rather than simply sold or assigned, the current trend is towards smaller advances and guarantees. Though the artist may still be able to ride the crest of a very successful licensed product, these smaller advances and guarantees protect the licensee if the licensed products do not sell up to the expectations of the parties when the agreement was negotiated. In short, business sanity has set in.

According to the 2010 LIMA Survey of the Licensing Industry, the three largest categories of licensed products for art properties were gifts & novelties, home décor, and housewares.

1.2.2   Celebrity

Undeniably, we live in a world in which people are fascinated by the lives of celebrities. Magazines such as *People* and *In Touch* have generated subscriber bases in the millions and huge web followings simply because people want to closely follow the lives of their favorite celebrity figures. It should not, therefore, come as any surprise that when a celebrity elects to put their name on a product or otherwise associate themselves with that product, more people will want to buy that product. The celebrity licensing category functions according to this basic premise.

In a nutshell, celebrity licensing is the licensing of a celebrity's name, image or likeness for use on a licensed product, or in association  with the advertising or promotional material for that product, to enhance the sales of such product. The value of the license is tied directly to the popularity and standing of the celebrity which, unfortunately, can change over time or, in some cases, very abruptly.

In the early days, the celebrity might actually be required to act as a spokesperson for or even to endorse the licensed product, e.g., appearing in an infomercial on television or in print ads extolling the virtues or benefits of the licensed product and telling consumers why they should buy it. It has, however, evolved into one where the celebrity often simply licenses the right to use their name or image on the licensed product in a more classic licensing style.

In some instances, the celebrity might be required to make a promotional appearance or two with selected retailers, appear on the Home Shopping Network or to wear the licensed product on the "Red Carpet" before a Hollywood event, but the promotional support required is usually fairly minimal.

Ironically, the celebrity doesn't even have to be alive to be successful. The licensing of deceased celebrities has become big business and as a result there are licensing agencies that specialize in this particular niche area. For example, it has been reported that the estates of such deceased celebrities as Elvis Presley and Michael Jackson continue to derive significant revenue from licensing their names and likeness despite their passing.

A manufacturer needs, however, to be careful when taking a celebrity license of a living celebrity since their fame and public image can be fleeting. If the celebrity's personal life doesn't go the way everyone expected, not only will the celebrity's career suffer, but so will the sales of their licensed products. For example, after evidence of Tiger Woods' marital infidelity hit the media, not only did his golf game suffer but so did the sales of TIGER WOODS licensed products.

According to the 2010 LIMA Survey of the Licensing Industry, the three largest categories of licensed products for celebrity properties were gifts & novelties, home décor, and housewares.

1.2.3   Collegiate

Over the past two decades, collegiate licensing has become a very important part of the licensing industry, as colleges and universities now regularly license the right to use their names, logos or mascots for a host of  different types of licensed products. The royalty income generated by such licensing programs is used by these schools to support a wide variety of their athletic, academic and other quality of life programs.

While sales of collegiate licensed products were initially confined to college bookstores and alumni catalogs, distribution channels for such products have greatly expanded as collegiate brands continue to grow in popularity. Today, a significant amount of collegiate licensed products are carried by major retailers on a national basis.

As one might expect, the success of a college licensing program is frequently tied to the success of its athletic teams. If a college wins a national football championship or makes an appearance in the NCAA's Final Four basketball tournament, the college will almost certainly enjoy a meteoric rise in the sale of its licensed merchandise with a corresponding jump in the royalty revenue that it receives—a double win.

An example of how athletic fame and fortune can translate into increased royalty revenue is BOISE STATE's experience. When it decided to change its logo and take its football program onto a national stage, the college experienced a ten-fold jump in its royalty revenues over a six year period. More significantly, the sale of its licensed products expanded from local stores to national retailers.

The viability of a college brand is not just limited to success on the athletic field. Schools such as Oxford, Harvard and Princeton have developed strong licensing programs on the strength of their academic reputations.

Interestingly, even colleges with unique or "catchy" names or from popular geographical regions have found success in the marketplace, e.g., SLIPPERY ROCK UNIVERSITY and UNIVERSITY OF HAWAII.

Not to be outdone by its member schools, the NCAA has even jumped into the licensing arena, developing licensing programs based on the names of its various tournaments, e.g., the FINAL FOUR. Similarly, the various football bowl games, e.g. the ROSE BOWL, have licensed such names for a variety of different products.

The collegiate licensing marketplace is an interesting one because almost half of the colleges and universities use the same agent, i.e., The Collegiate Licensing Company ("CLC"), which is now owned by IMG. Another significant portion of the schools use a second agent, the Licensing Resource Group ("LRG") while the remaining schools are independent and conduct their own licensing programs.

According to the 2010 LIMA Survey of the Licensing Industry, the three largest categories of collegiate licensed products were apparel (by a large margin), software and video games and accessories.

1.2.4 Corporate

In the early years of licensing, the corporate world watched with great interest as the entertainment industry jumped in and found it to be an excellent way of promoting their brand names and underlying products, while generating additional revenue at the same time.

It is, therefore, no surprise that corporations would eventually follow suit and use licensing as a means of both increasing their bottom lines and further enhancing their brands' identities. Today, more and more major corporations with highly recognizable brands and trademarks have turned to licensing.

While the prospect of generating additional revenue is always important to most corporations, many have developed licensing programs for other reasons. For example, some have found it to be a cost-effective vehicle for diversifying their product lines and entering product categories that they had not previously explored.

For example, in the early 1980's Winnebago Industries was mired in a depressed recreational vehicle market. While sales of RV's were down dramatically due to the gas crisis, the WINNEBAGO mark was still a widely known and respected brand. Capitalizing on the public awareness of its name, Winnebago decided to diversify into the exploding camping market by licensing the WINNEBAGO mark for a line of sleeping bags, tents and other outdoor products. It was a classic example of how licensing can permit a company to leverage the power of its brand into other markets for little or no capital investment or risk.

Other corporations have entered the licensing arena to help strengthen their underlying trademark rights. For example, the Coca-Cola Company decided to pursue licensing opportunities at the suggestion of its trademark attorneys who were concerned about the company's ability to enforce their valuable trademark rights against individuals who were selling a variety of COKE products in categories and on goods that were totally unrelated to soft drinks.

Coca-Cola proceeded by setting up what has become one of the largest corporate licensing programs in the world, with more than 300 different licensees manufacturing thousands of such diverse licensed COCA-COLA products as beach towels, boxer shorts, baby clothing, jewelry and even fishing lures. The company opened up a number of COCA-COLA stores around the world carrying a wide array of licensed products, many of which express a nostalgia theme based on early COKE advertising campaigns.

More significantly, the Coca-Cola licensing program has been financially successful beyond anyone's wildest imagination and the revenue that it generates adds directly to the bottom line. At one point, it was reported that the program netted at least $70 million in annual profits or about 0.3% of its total net operating revenues—all while strengthening the company's trademarks in the process. It also does not hurt, of course, that the wide spread sale and distribution of licensed COCA-COLA merchandise continues to help promote (and some may say advertise) the primary COKE soft drink products.

Some companies, particularly those in the alcohol and tobacco industries, have relied on licensing for promotional purposes since governmental regulations significantly restrict their ability to advertise through conventional media channels. Licensing permits these companies to still convey their marketing messages through the sale of licensed products which bear their marks, while also serving as a lucrative revenue producer.

According to the 2010 LIMA Survey of the Licensing Industry, the three largest categories of licensed products for corporate brands were food & beverage, apparel and housewares.

1.2.5   Entertainment

Entertainment and character properties are, of course, the most visible of all types of licensing properties and always produce the largest revenues in the industry.

Entertainment properties come from virtually all segments of the entertainment industry, although the largest source of such properties is Hollywood through its motion pictures and television shows. For example, the SPONGEBOB character featured in Nickelodeon's hit television show *SpongeBob SquarePants*, has become a major force in children's licensing, as well as the subject of dozens of promotional programs for virtually all of the major retailers and fast food chains.

Similarly, the *Sesame Street* characters, ELMO, BIG BIRD and OSCAR THE GROUCH, have become licensing legends due, in large measure, to the constant exposure that these properties receive every day on television. Such children's characters as MICKEY MOUSE, WINNIE THE POOH, BUGS BUNNY and PETER RABBIT found their origins in various media formats in the early 20th century, and remain popular today as a result of their continued media exposure.

Blockbuster Hollywood motion pictures have produced some of the most successful licensing programs in the industry, the best example being the Star War films. In recent years there has been a string of motion pictures based on superheroes, e.g., SPIDERMAN, HULK, BATMAN, and SUPERMAN, that have spawned successful licensing programs. The tremendous licensing success of such characters has resulted in the studios creating their own "Consumer Products Divisions", a/k/a licensing departments, responsible for the licensing of their properties.

Highly popular toys and video games have also been successful incubators for entertainment properties. BARBIE started out as a popular fashion doll for Mattel and, through licensing, has become a franchise. Similarly, the BRATZ line of dolls by MGA Entertainment and the GI JOE action figure by Hasbro have both been extensively merchandised for a wide array of products. MARIO was the featured character in an early Nintendo video game called Donkey Kong and was not only extensively licensed, but even became Nintendo's official "mascot."

Interestingly, this category has expanded with the growth of technology. Software, video games and mobile phones have made significant use of entertainment properties as the basis for games, wallpaper and even accessories such as game controllers or mobile phone cases.

According to the 2010 LIMA Survey of the Licensing Industry, the three largest categories of licensed products for entertainment properties were toys & games, software and video games and apparel.

1.2.6 Fashion

Fashion or designer properties have been a staple of the licensing industry for years due, in large measure, to the wide variety of different properties available and the vast number of products for which they are licensed. One need only walk through the clothing section of any department store or, for that matter, look at the different fashion brands in his or her own closet to see the impact that these properties have had. The reason for their success is very simple and one that retailers readily understand: the presence of a fashion brand on a product *sells*.

POLO
RALPH LAUREN

Consumers have come to expect seeing a fashion brand—any fashion brand—on an article of apparel since it conveys the impression that the underlying product is better designed and of a higher quality than the generic version. Irrespective of whether that proposition is true or not, in fashion licensing, perception becomes reality and, as a result, a vast number of clothing products and related accessories today carry some fashion brand—either that of a real designer or a "house" brand to convey the same impression.

Designers such as PIERRE CARDIN, ANNE KLEIN, BILL BLASS, OSCAR DE LA RENTA, and CALVIN KLEIN clearly started the trend and paved the way for the next generation of designers, including TOMMY HILFIGER, DONNA KARAN and VERA WANG. Spin-offs or extensions of these properties, such as TOMMY or POLO, have enjoyed enormous popularity in their own right.

Fashion brands don't always have to be a designer's name. They can, instead, convey a certain lifestyle image, e.g., NAUTICA, FUBU, TOMMY BAHAMA, GUESS? and HANG TEN. Many retailers have developed their own fashion brands, e.g., the ROUTE 66 apparel line at K-Mart, or Wal-Mart's FADED GLORY brand.

The names of some of the famous design houses are also licensable, as demonstrated by the success of the CHANEL and LOUIS VUITTON lines of licensed products where good design prevails.

Some of the top catalogs have not only branded their own products, but licensed out their names for ancillary products such as the EDDIE BAUER line of SUV's by Ford. That said, some fashion designers are uncomfortable with the idea of licensing, since they would like the public to believe that all products bearing their brands are actually produced by their company, not by a third party licensee.

At the end of the day, however, fashion licensing is all about design and quality. Fashion properties that feature good design and offer quality and value will ultimately prevail and bring the consumer back, year after year.

According to the 2010 LIMA Survey of the Licensing Industry, the three largest categories of licensed products for fashion properties were apparel, accessories and health and beauty products.

1.2.7 Music

The music industry rocks when it comes to producing hot licensing properties. Such bands and performers (alive or dead) as the BEATLES, ELVIS PRESLEY, MICHAEL JACKSON, BRUCE SPRINGSTEIN, BILLY JOEL, CHER, MADONNA, CELINE DION, the DOORS, KISS and OZZY OSBOURNE

Jennifer Lopez

have not only sold a vast amount of merchandise at their concerts and while on tour (called "venue sales"), their licensed products have also found their way into traditional channels of retail distribution.

The JESSICA SIMPSON brand has proven to be enormously successful at retail, most notably through the sale of licensed shoes, handbags and accessories, selling hundreds of millions of dollars in licensed products over its first five years. USHER has licensed his name (and persona) for a wide range of products, including cologne and aftershave lotion. Similarly, the total concert merchandise sales of BRITANY SPEARS' licensed products have been in the tens of millions of dollars, the BRITTANY SPEARS' line of cosmetics for Elizabeth Arden and JENNIFER LOPEZ's line of toiletries have all sold well.

Rock bands have likewise come to recognize the power of their brand. At their height, the all-female British group ATOMIC KITTEN even created its own branded line of clothing called AK BRANDS. The use of music videos has proven to be an excellent way to sell branded merchandise for rock stars, as Australian pop star KYLIE MINOGUE proved when she appeared in a music video that successfully promoted her licensed line of lingerie for Agent Provocateur.

1.2.8 Non-Profits

Foundations, organizations, charities and associations regularly use licensing as a means to both convey their message to the public as well as a source of fund raising. Non-profit organizations, such as the American Society for the Prevention of Cruelty to Animals ("ASPCA"), have embraced licensing for these purposes. Revenue generated from the ASPCA's licensing program helps fund its national humane initiatives while promoting brand recognition in the minds of consumers.

Similarly, the World Wildlife Fund ("WWF") works closely with companies and individuals in marketing partnerships, where licensees are permitted to use its PANDA logo and WWF name. Again, such programs serve the important dual function of not only generating royalty income for the WWF but also of building awareness for its activities. In addition, the WWF engages in cause-related marketing promotions and sponsorship programs.

Some associations even set up their own related entities to directly engage in licensing. For example, the American Association of Retired People ("AARP") created AARP Financial Inc. to license and endorse credit cards, insurance products and financial services. The AARP name appears on mutual funds, IRAs, CD's, and a group that provides financial advice to its members. New York Life sells AARP Life Insurance policies and annuities; The Hartford sells AARP-branded auto and home insurance to AARP members; and other "partners" sell AARP motorcycle and mobile-home insurance. An AARP Visa credit card is offered by Chase Bank.

According to the 2010 LIMA Survey the three largest product categories carrying Non-Profit Properties were apparel, publishing and gifts & novelties.

1.2.9 Publishing

Many of the most popular entertainment properties trace their roots back to the publishing industry, particularly the children's book market.

There is, of course, a fine line between pure publishing properties and entertainment properties since many entertainment properties actually came from the publishing industry and vice-versa. For example, the PEANUTS and GARFIELD characters grew out of syndicated comic strips of the same name while the popular characters PETER RABBIT and WINNIE THE POOH first appeared in books. Many of the superhero characters that became enormously popular as a result of blockbuster motion pictures originated in comic books, including SUPERMAN, BATMAN, and SPIDERMAN.

According to LIMA's 2010 Survey of the Licensing Industry, the three largest categories of licensed products bearing publishing properties were publishing, accessories and stationery products.

1.2.10 Sports

For decades, sports properties have consistently been among the most popular licensing properties due, no doubt, to the worldwide passion for athletics. Sports licensing is a global business and, with few exceptions, appeals to a very wide group of potential consumers. While the popularity of certain sports such as soccer, basketball, cricket and hockey transcend geographical boundaries, others such as baseball and football are enormously popular mainly in the United States.

The major professional sports leagues in the United States, i.e., Major League Baseball, the National Football League, the National Basketball Association and the National Hockey League, all have strong licensing programs that are run by the "Properties" divisions of their respective league offices. These entities control the licensing rights for all of their team logos and properties. Thus, if a company wants to take a license to use, for example, the NEW YORK GIANTS logo, on its product, it would need to coordinate this through NFL Properties. The same is true for each of the other professional sports leagues.

Team names and logos are not the only type of licensable sports properties, certain individual players are themselves equally popular. Professional athletes, such as MICHAEL JORDAN, LEBRON JAMES, PEYTON MANNING and DEREK JETER, are all featured in very prominent and successful licensing programs.

In professional sports, the licensing rights for individual players are typically handled by the player or their agent, while "group licensing rights" are typically handled through the respective players association for that sport, e.g., the NFL Players Association.

Since sports licensing will frequently involve the licensing of both teams and players, it can get complicated. For example, if someone wanted to run a promotion featuring all members of the Los  Angeles Dodgers that also included the DODGERS mark, they would need to apply for a group license from the MLB Players Association for the names and likenesses of these players *and* to MLB Properties for the right to use the DODGERS mark.

Professional sports leagues and players are not the only sources of sports properties. The United States Olympic Committee ("USOC") has long relied on its licensing and sponsorship programs to generate revenue to help underwrite its costs. Licensees regularly pay royalties to the USOC to use the OLYMPICS LOGO, while sponsors pay sponsorship fees and provide goods and services for the right to be called an "Official Sponsor" of the program. Some of these fees are substantial because of the esteem that a sponsor gains through its ability to associate itself with one of the strongest and most recognized marks in the world.

The International Federation of Association Football ("FIFA"), which is the international governing body for soccer and who oversees the FIFA World Cup tournaments, also relies extensively on licensing to support its efforts.

Tennis and golf stars such as MARIA SHARAPOVA and TIGER WOODS, look to licensing as a major source of their income. Not to be outdone, the governing bodies for these sports, e.g., the PGA, LPGA, and USTA, all regularly license out the use of their names and logos to raise money thereby help to support the growth of their respective sports.

According to the 2010 LIMA Survey of the Licensing Industry, the three largest categories of licensed products for sports properties were apparel, gifts & novelties and software and video games.

1.3   Types of Licensed Products

In the early years of licensing, the majority of licensed products were low end products, typically called "buttons, badges, and posters." That has changed dramatically as the industry has grown and become more established. Today, licensing has expanded into almost every imaginable product and service category including those that feature high-end luxury goods and services.

If one simply reviewed the Classification List published by the United States Patent & Trademark Office, they would find that there is at least some licensing activity in more than 30 of the 42 different classes.

According to LIMA's Annual Survey of the Licensing Industry, the following categories of licensed products generate most of the licensing revenue in the industry:

- Apparel: (Adult, Kids)
- Accessories: (Head Wear, Jewelry & Watches, Etc.)

- Food/Beverage: (Beverage, Candy, Etc.)
- Footwear: (Adult, Kids)
- Home Decor: (Furniture, Home Furnishings)
- Gifts/Novelties: (Collectibles, Gift, Etc.)
- Health/Beauty: (Health, Cosmetics, Etc.)
- Housewares: (Kitchenware, other Houseware Products)
- Music/Video
- Infant Products (Apparel, Furniture, Accessories, Etc.)
- Publishing (Novels, Story Books, Calendars, Etc.)
- Sporting Goods (Apparel, Equipment, Etc.)
- Paper Products/School Supplies (Art, Greeting Cards, Lunch Boxes, Bags/Totes, Etc.)
- Toys/Games: (Dolls/Action Figures, Games, Pre-School, Etc.)
- Software/Videogames: (Handheld, Software, Accessories, Etc.)

Of these possible categories, the three categories that recorded the most sales were apparel, toys & games and software and video games. A chart illustrating estimated revenues by product category for 2009 is as follows:

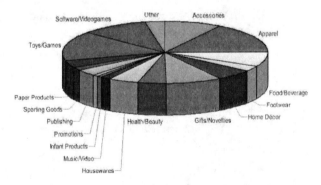

While the industry has come to expect licensed toys and t-shirts, there have been some "non-traditional" licenses granted over the years that one prominent licensing agent categorized as, "What Were You Thinking???" Examples of these "non-traditional" licenses include NORMAN ROCKWELL boxer shorts, a WIZARD OF OZ Menorah, MICKEY MOUSE full sized toilet seats, a PACMAN diamond bracelet and DALLAS barbecue grills. *Time* magazine recently published an article on the "Top Ten Oddball Celebrity Branded Products," which included: HULK HOGAN's Pastamania, SHAQUILLE O'NEAL's Shaq-Fu video game, STEVEN SEAGAL's Lightning Bolt energy drink and DANNY DEVITO's Limoncello.

1.4 ⭐Reasons for Its Popularity

What makes licensing so popular? The obvious answer to this question is that *it sells products*. From a property owner's perspective, there is little doubt that the opportunity to generate additional royalty income is the primary motivating factor behind setting up a licensing program. Furthermore, though, property owners have also come to realize that licensing provides a number of secondary benefits, including:

- Reducing the cost of product development;

- Providing additional exposure for the licensor's underlying products or services;

- Allowing the licensor to better leverage its advertising expenditures;

- Providing a hedge against the normal fluctuations of a licensor's basic business model;

- Allowing the licensor to achieve a high return on a minimal investment;

- Permitting the licensor to expand into new markets and test different new product areas;

- Allowing the licensor to further promote products of a type where there are governmental restrictions on what can be said; and

- Strengthening the licensor's underlying trademark rights by expanding the breadth of the goods or services on which the brand is used.

For the manufacturer, or licensee, the advantages that licensing provides include:

- Creating instant credibility through the use of a well-known, trusted brand or property;

- Providing a shortcut to the marketplace without the time and cost of building a brand from scratch;

- Allowing the manufacturer to create a product line that will have instant recognition and appeal to retail buyers; and

- Giving the manufacturer the ability to compete against larger, more established, companies.

Chapter 2

History of Licensing

2.1   The Properties

2.1.1 The Beginning

Although there is little historical documentation establishing exactly when the licensing of famous brands or characters actually began, it is believed that its origin traces back to the Middle Ages when it was reported that the Roman Catholic Popes  granted licenses to local tax collectors for the right to be associated with the Church in exchange for the payment of "royalties" to the Vatican. It is believed that this practice continued for a number of years and formed the basis for what would eventually become modern day licensing.

The practice of paying royalties for the right to use another's name or likeness is believed to have begun in the 18th Century when two British ladies of nobility were reported to have permitted (or licensed) a cosmetics manufacturer to use their name on its products and, in exchange, would receive a percentage of the revenues generated from the sale of such products.

Licensing, as we know it today, began in earnest in the 1870's when it is believed that Adolphus Busch allowed manufacturers to use the name **BUSCH** on a wine key that included a small blade, foil cutter and a basic cork screw in order to enhance sales of the key.

 One of the most famous licensing characters of all time, **PETER RABBIT**, traces its origins back to 1901 when Beatrix Potter designed and patented a soft toy based on the PETER RABBIT character that had appeared in a book she wrote and self-published in 1901. In 1902, Ms. Potter entered into an agreement with the British publisher, Frederick Warne & Co., who then published a color version that same year. It is believed that PETER RABBIT was the first licensed character.

In 1902, New York Herald cartoonist, Richard Outcault, created the **BUSTER BROWN** character as part of a comic strip and, two years later, began licensing the rights to the character to more than 20 licensees. One of the licensees used the character on a shoe that was introduced in the 1904 World's Fair.  That same year, the Brown Shoe Company purchased the licensing rights to the BUSTER BROWN property, reportedly for $200.

 Former President, Theodore "Teddy" Roosevelt, is associated with the creation of the name **TEDDY BEAR,** which actually started out as a licensing property before becoming the generic name for a particular type of toy product. It was reported that after his presidency, Roosevelt had gone on a bear hunt in Mississippi but, despite spending three days in the woods, never saw a single bear. The story goes that Roosevelt and his guide then came upon an old, injured bear, but Roosevelt could not bring himself to shoot it, ordering it instead to be put down to end its suffering.

After hearing the story, a political cartoonist, Clifford Berrymore, published a political cartoon about the episode in a number of the newspapers of the day. It was reported that a shopkeeper, Morris Michtom, saw the cartoon, contacted the former President and asked for permission to call a pair of stuffed bears that he had in his store window, **TEDDY BEARS.** The store would ultimately become the Ideal Novelty and Toy Company and the name TEDDY BEAR was eventually licensed to toy companies with the royalties used to establish the National Parks.

The **GIRL SCOUTS** (originally named Girls Guides of America) organization was founded in 1912 and soon, thereafter, began licensing its name for a line of "Official" GIRL SCOUTS products. It is believed that over the years, the mark has appeared on more than 1800 different products,  including the famous GIRL SCOUTS cookies.

The **RAGGEDY ANN** character was created in 1915 by Johnny Gruelle as a soft doll and, three years later, was introduced as part of a book entitled *Raggedy Ann Stories*. In 1920, her brother RAGGEDY ANDY, who dressed in a sailor suit and hat, was introduced as a sequel to that work. RAGGEDY ANN was inducted into the National Toy Hall of Fame in 2002 and her brother joined her in 2007.

LITTLE ORPHAN ANNIE was created by Harold Gray in 1924 and first appeared as a comic strip in the *Chicago Tribune*. The comic strip was published for more than 80 years by Tribune Media Services until the final installment appeared on June 13, 2010. In 1924, a LITLLE ORPHAN ANNIE radio show was launched with Ovaltine as its sponsor.

In 1926, A.A. Milne published in England the first of what would become a series of books on the adventures of **WINNIE THE POOH**. The books met with moderate success but when a U.S. based licensing agent, Stephen Slesinger, acquired the U.S. and Canadian licensing, television and recording rights to the character in the early 1930's, a licensing legend was born. Slesinger, a licensing pioneer, immediately launched an aggressive licensing program around the character that would reportedly generate more than $50 million in licensing revenues. In the 1940's, POOH became the first Sunday morning television cartoon series. Disney acquired all rights to the character in 1961 and, soon thereafter, entered into one of the first direct to retail licenses with Sears for the property. Today, POOH is a global icon and thousands of different POOH licensed products are sold around the world. POOH was the winner of LIMA's License of the Year Award in 1996.

Possibly the most famous licensing character of all time, **MICKEY MOUSE**, was created by Walt Disney and Ub Iwerks on November 28, 1928 as a replacement for another Disney character, OSWALD THE LUCKY RABBIT. The character was based on a cartoon called STEAMBOAT WILLIE that had appeared earlier that year. Disney  didn't waste any time in licensing the character for a variety of merchandise, including a license to Waldburger, Tanner in Switzerland for MICKEY & MINNIE handkerchiefs. MICKEY MOUSE would go on to become a corporate icon for Disney and is recognizable in virtually every country in the civilized world.

 **BUCK ROGERS** (originally named Anthony Rogers) first appeared in a comic strip in 1929 and then, later, in a series of motion pictures and television shows. Created by Philip Francis Nowlan, the character was an immediate hit as a licensing property and pioneered character-based, licensed merchandising. One of the most popular BUCK ROGERS toys was the Rocket Pistol that was introduced at the 1934 Toy Fair in New York and which sold out of Macy's in less than three hours after it was introduced.

LOONEY TUNES started out in 1930 as an animated cartoon series produced by Harman-Ising Pictures. In 1944, Warner Bros. purchased the rights and library and continued production through the 1960's. It was the first animated theatrical series and would ultimately serve as the cornerstone of  Warner Bros. licensing group, the **LICENSING CORPORATION OF AMERICA**, headed by **JOE GRANT** another of the industry's pioneers. The series featured such highly recognizable characters as BUGS BUNNY, DAFFY DUCK, PORKY PIG, ELMER FUDD, SYLVESTER, TWEETY, WILE E. COYOTE, ROAD RUNNER, YOSEMITE SAM, and SPEEDY GONZALES.

1932 was a historic year in character licensing—it was the year that **KAY KAMEN**, affectionately known as the "Father of Modern Licensing," joined the Walt Disney Company. Kamen promised a Disney product in every home in the United States—and actually came close. By 1935, he oversaw a licensing program that produced almost a thousand different types of MICKEY MOUSE products. It has been reported that at the height of the Depression, General Foods paid Disney $1 million for the right to put Mickey Mouse cut-outs on the back of its cereal boxes. Kamen recognized that licensing was mutually beneficial for all parties. It was reported that Disney's watch licensee, Ingersoll Waterbury, was able to stave off bankruptcy on the strength of its MICKEY MOUSE license—selling a record 11,000 watches in one day at Macy's in New York.

The child actress, **SHIRLEY TEMPLE**, began her career in 1932 and watched it immediately skyrocket. In 1935, she received a special Academy Award and would go on to star in such blockbusters as *Curly Top* and *Heidi*. Her licensing program quickly followed. She was reported to have made more than $100,000 in royalties before 1935 and her licensing income for

1936 was reportedly more than $200,000. Ideal Toy produced the first SHIRLEY TEMPLE doll in the 1930's and it is believed that more than $41 million of these dolls were sold by 1941.

SUPERMAN, a fictional, super-hero created by Jerry Siegel and Joe Shuster, was created in 1932 and, in 1938, the rights were eventually acquired by Detective Comics, Inc. (now DC Comics). With the distinctive costume having a large "S" on his chest and cape, SUPERMAN was perhaps the first super-hero character and would eventually be licensed for a host of different products from comic books to licensed capes. The earliest reported licensed SUPERMAN product was a 1939 button signifying membership in the Superman Club of America. By 1942, sales of SUPERMAN comic books surpassed 1.5 million copies and the Navy Department even provided copies of the comic books as part of standard supplies for U.S. Marines. The SUPERMAN property remains popular today, fueled by the release of blockbuster motion pictures by Warner Bros.

One of the major licensors, **DC COMICS,** was created in 1934 as National Allied Publications. It would ultimately become one of the largest and most successful comic book publishers, developing and popularizing such characters as SUPERMAN, BATMAN, WONDER WOMAN, GREEN LANTERN, CAPTAIN  MARVEL, and CATWOMAN. DC Comics is now the publishing division of DC Entertainment Inc., a Warner Bros. subsidiary.

 **HOPALONG CASSIDY,** played by William Boyd, first appeared on the big screen in 1935 and achieved immediate success. The character was originally created in 1904 by Clarence E. Mulford as part of a series of books, but it was Boyd's film version in 1935 that would popularize it. Boyd appeared on the covers of *Look, Life,* and *Time* and, reportedly, earned millions of dollars from licensing and endorsement deals. It is believed that HOPALONG CASSIDY was the first character ever licensed for a child's lunch box and more than 600,000 licensed lunch boxes were reportedly sold in the first year of sales. By 1950, there were more than 100 HOPALONG CASSIDY licensees selling more than $70 million in licensed products.

In 1938, Stephen Slesinger and Fred Harman introduced the western comic strip, **RED RYDER,** and it was immediately syndicated by Newspaper Enterprise Association. Slesinger, of POOH fame, developed a successful licensing program based on the property, with licenses for comic books, novels, rodeos and various products. RED RYDER BB guns were first produced in 1938 under license by Daisy Outdoor Products and are  still in production today, making it the longest continuous licenses in the history of licensing.

MARVEL COMICS, which would ultimately become a major force in licensing, was formed in 1939 by Martin Goodman. Its first publication, entitled *Marvel Comics #1*, appeared in October 1939 and introduced a number of new superheroes, including, the HUMAN TORCH. Marvel would go on to develop some of the most famous superhero characters in the industry, many of which were extensively licensed and adapted for motion pictures and television. Some of its most famous superhero characters include SPIDER-MAN, IRON MAN, the X-MEN, WOLVERINE, the HULK, FANTASTIC FOUR, CAPTAIN AMERICA, and GHOST RIDER.

The **BATMAN** character, created by Bob Kane and Bill Finger, also debuted in 1939, when it first appeared in a DC Comics publication. BATMAN's secret identity was Bruce Wayne, a successful American playboy who would put on a bat costume and working with his partner, Robin, fight crime in Gotham City. It spawned a number of memorable characters, including the JOKER, PENGUIN and BATGIRL and the character's popularity increased in 1989 after the release of the *Batman* motion picture. *Forbes* magazine estimated the BATMAN character to be the 9th "richest" fictional character in history, with revenues of at least $5.8 billion.

2.1.2 The 1940's

The 1940's represented not only the end of the Great Depression but the creation of some of today's most popular properties.

The **ARCHIE** property, created by John Goldwater, Vic Bloom and Bob Montana, made its first appearance in December 1941 in *PEP Comics #22* and, the following year, would become the basis of its own publication. Archie Comics has developed some of the most recognizable characters in the industry, including JUGHEAD, BETTY & VERONICA, JOSIE & THE PUSSYCATS and SABRINA THE

TEENAGE WITCH. These characters have all translated well into motion pictures and television shows and have been heavily licensed along the way.

THOMAS THE TANK ENGINE, a fictional locomotive, first appeared in 1946 in a series of books by Rev. W. Awdry and his son, Christopher. The property would lay somewhat dormant, however, until 1979 when a British producer named Britt Allcroft discovered it and invested all of her life savings to turn the character into a television series called *Thomas*  the *Tank Engine and Friends* (later, *Thomas and Friends*, with Ringo Starr as the narrator). The television series and resultant licensing program were immediate hits and THOMAS has been licensed for a wide range of products ranging from toy trains to videos, books, apparel and toys. It was LIMA's License of the Year for 1993.

The **HOWDY DOODY** show was one of the most popular children's television shows from 1947 until 1960. Created by E. Roger Muir, it featured a red-headed, freckled face puppet named HOWDY DOODY and host Buffalo Bob Smith. It was one of the first shows to be broadcast in color and, because of its enormous popularity, was heavily merchandised. In 1955, for example, its producers published a 24-page catalog that featured such licensed products as puppets, toys and clothing, comic books and other publications.

In 1947, Bill France, Sr. created the National Association for Stock Car Auto Racing (**NASCAR**). It would eventually become the largest sanctioning body of stock car racing in the world and the sponsor of the three largest racing series. NASCAR currently sanctions over 1500 races in more than 100 race tracks throughout the United States, Canada, Japan, Mexico and Australia. Its 75 million fans purchase over \$3 billion of licensed NASCAR products every year, most notably apparel and die-cast autos.

2.1.3   The 1950's

The decade commenced with the creation of **PEANUTS**, which would become one of the most popular licensing properties of all time.

Based on a syndicated comic strip created by Charles M. Schulz, it featured **CHARLIE BROWN, SNOOPY** and **LUCY**. The strip ran for almost 50 years until Schultz's death in 2000, with 17,897 strips published during that period. At its peak, the comic strip had a readership of 355 million in 75 different countries in 21 languages. It was reported that the strip and the related licensing earned Schulz more than $1 billion. PEANUTS characters have been licensed for virtually every product imaginable on earth....and beyond. NASA's Apollo 10 lunar module was named SNOOPY and the command module was named CHARLIE BROWN.

In 1952, we saw the first musician get into the licensing arena, when jazz guitarist, **LES PAUL** joined forces with Gibson Guitar to produce a LES PAUL branded guitar. The product was a joint collaboration between the two, which debuted to much fanfare and over the years has acquired somewhat iconic status as the instrument of choice for many leading guitarists,

including Slash, formerly of Guns 'N Roses, and Trey Anastasio the front man for Phish. Versions of the guitar are still produced today.

The first **PLAYBOY** magazine was published in 1953 by Hugh Heffner with Marilyn Monroe on the cover and as its centerfold. Not only did the magazine set the world on its heels, but it spawned a host of licensed PLAYBOY products, the first being a pair of PLAYBOY cufflinks that was introduced in 1959 and worn by all of the Playboy Bunnies at its clubs. It has been reported that the company currently derives about 10% of its revenues from its licensing division, Playboy Enterprises, which licenses the PLAYBOY name, the RABBIT HEAD design and a host of images. One of its more interesting licensed products is a case of wine featuring images of classic Playmates.

In the 1950's, ABC Television popularized the American frontiersman, **DAVY CROCKETT**, in a series of television shows and a motion picture starring Fess Parker. While the show and movie were moderately successful, the sales of licensed DAVY CROCKETT products sold extraordinarily well. At its peak, it was reported that DAVY CROCKET coonskin caps were selling at the rate of 5,000 per day. More than $300 million of licensed products were sold by 1955 and by 2001, licensed sales topped $2 billion.

The public's fascination with western sagas continued in 1954, when a television series, staring Gail Davis, debuted about western legend **ANNIE OAKLEY**. She was a female sharpshooter who regularly performed in exhibitions such as *Buffalo Bill's Wild West* show. The ANNIE OAKLEY character was licensed for a wide range of children's products, including toys, trading cards and apparel.

The **JAMES BOND 007** character was created by writer Ian Fleming in 1953 and was later featured in twelve novels and 22 motion pictures, the longest running of which was the 1962 feature *Dr. No*. The JAMES BOND 007 character was heavily licensed, particularly for toys, comic books and video games. The first video game was published in 1983 by Parker Brothers for the Atari, Commodore and Colecovision platforms. Other JAMES BOND video games have been produced by Electronic Arts and ActiVision based on GoldenEye 007.

Without question, one of the most extensively licensed properties of all time is **ELVIS PRESLEY.** ELVIS hit the world stage in 1954 and would go on to redefine the meaning of success for a celebrity license—both before and after the singer's death. Called the "King of Rock and Roll" ELVIS PRESLEY became a pop icon and is the best selling solo artist in history. His licensing program has been equally successful. Elvis Presley Enterprises licenses all ELVIS related properties, including his name, image and voice, song titles such as *Blue*

Suede Shoes, *Jailhouse Rock* and *Hound Dog* and words and phrases that have become associated with ELVIS, including GRACELAND, TCB and KING OF ROCK AND ROLL. It's been reported that Elvis Presley Enterprises' licensing revenues in 2009 (more than 30 years after his death) were $24.3 million.

Jim Henson's **KERMIT THE FROG** was first introduced in 1955 as a five-minute spot for WRC-TV's *Sam and Friends*. KERMIT would ultimately become the host of his own show, *The Muppet Show*, as well as appear regularly on *Sesame Street*. In 1970, KERMIT would star in *The Muppet Movie* and his single, The Rainbow Connection, would reach 25th on the Billboard Hot 100. The character has been used extensively in advertising programs and KERMIT is recognizable throughout the world. Not surprisingly, sales of licensed KERMIT merchandise have remained strong over the years.

Sports licensing really began to take hold in the 1960's due, in large part, to the efforts of Pete Rozelle who in 1956 became General Manager of the then Los Angeles Rams. Rozelle recognized the licensing potential of the **LOS ANGELES RAMS** name and logo and aggressively sought licensees for a variety of different licensed products—to both help promote the team and to raise additional revenue. Rozelle's genius was quickly recognized and, in 1959, he would become Commissioner of the National Football League. Rozelle oversaw the development of one of the most successful professional sports leagues in the world, with a licensing program that quickly emerged as a model for all other sports to follow.

HANNA-BARBERA CARTOONS was formed in 1957 by animation directors William Hanna and Joseph Barbera, in partnership with Columbia Pictures. Hanna-Barbera Productions would go on to dominate American television animation for fifty years,

producing such successful cartoon shows as the FLINTSTONES, SCOOBY-DOO, YOGI BEAR SHOW, JETSONS and the HUCKLEBERRY HOUND show.

The **SMURFS** property was first introduced as a comic strip in a Belgian magazine, *Spirou*, in 1958 by cartoonist Peyo and would soon grow to become a comic and television franchise. The comic strip was translated into English and later became a television series, produced by Hanna-Barbera Productions. Licensing of SMURF figurines commenced in 1959 by Dupuis Animation Studios. Schleich, a German toy company, became the largest producer of SMURF figurines, many of which were given away as promotional items. It has been reported that since their introduction, more than 300 millions SMURF figures have been sold.

PADDINGTON BEAR, that polite fictional bear with a hat and suitcase who loves marmalade sandwiches, made his first appearance in 1958 in the first of a series of books written by Michael Bond and illustrated by Peggy Fortnum. The books would eventually be published in more than 30 languages and sell more than 30 million copies. Over the years, it is reported that more than 265 licenses were granted for PADDINGTON products in virtually every civilized country in the

world. The character was so popular in England that the character was featured on a coin and postage stamp.

The 1950's closed out with the launch by Mattel of the first **BARBIE** doll at New York Toy Fair in March 1959. BARBIE was designed by Ruth Handler and was marketed as a "Teenage Fashion Model." The reception was extraordinary, as product literally flew off retailers' shelves. Mattel sold more than 350,000 units in the first year after introduction. BARBIE would go on to become a cultural icon—a section of Times Square in New York City was named Barbie Boulevard for a week and Andy Warhol created a painting of the character. It has also become a licensing franchise and the BARBIE property has been licensed for virtually every conceivable type of licensed product. There are even pop-up BARBIE stores in cities around the world.

2.1.4 The 1960's

The 1960's opened with the debut of the
FLINTSTONES, an animated television sitcom
produced by Hanna-Barbera which ran from
September 1960 until April 1966. It portrayed a
working class, stone-age family headed by Fred
Flintstone, his wife Wilma, and their neighbors,
Barney and Betty Rubble. Many believe that it

was an animated satire of the Honeymooners and was one of the first
television shows to be broadcast in color. The FLINTSTONES licensing
program pursued new and different types of licensed products. For
example, Miles Laboratories developed a line of children's
FLINTSTONE vitamins in the shape of the show's characters and Post
Foods sold a line of PEBBLES cereals that are still being sold today.

1960 was also the year that John Lennon,
Paul McCartney, George Harrison and Ringo Starr
joined forces in Liverpool, England to form the
what would become the most successful rock group
of all time—the **BEATLES**. Almost immediately,
the group was a household name, both musically
and in licensing. Their opening song, *I Want to
Hold Your Hand*, sold more than 2.6 million copies
in the United States during a two week period and
their initial appearance on *The Ed Sullivan Show*
had a 40 percent market share. BEATLES
merchandise sold as fast as did the group's music. It was estimated that
Americans spent $50 million in 1964 for licensed BEATLES
merchandise. Remco Toys ramped up to manufacture 100,000
BEATLES dolls but received orders for an additional 500,000, while
Lowell Toy sold BEATLES wigs at the rate of 35,000 per day. Some
considered BEATLES licensing as the biggest marketing opportunity
since Disney created MICKEY MOUSE.

In 1963, the National Football League formed a
wholly owned subsidiary called **NFL PROPERTIES**
and charged it with the responsibility for licensing the
name and logos of its teams and related properties,
including the soon to be created SUPER BOWL. It
was the first licensing division of any professional
sports league. In time, NFL Properties would become

one of the most dominating sports licensing groups in the world, with retail sales of licensed NFL products believed to top $3 billion. The other sports leagues soon followed suit—MLB Properties was formed in 1966 and NBA Properties was formed in 1967.

Scholastic Books published the first of what would become the **CLIFFORD THE BIG RED DOG** book series in 1963. Written by William Bridwell, the series was at least partially responsible for launching Scholastic as a major publisher. The featured character, CLIFFORD, entered life as the runt of the litter but would grow to over 25 feet long because of his owner's love. CLIFFORD would be featured in videos, as a television series and on a host of different licensed products.

The popularity of American folk heroes continued throughout the decade. In 1964, the television series *Daniel Boone* debuted, featuring Fess Parker as the main character, **DANIEL BOONE**. The show also starred country western singer Jimmy Dean and former football star, Roosevelt Grier and would remain

on the air through 1970. Like the other shows involving folk heroes, it was heavily licensed.

G.I. JOE was introduced by Hasbro in 1964, originally as the Adventures of G.I. Joe, but later as simply G.I. JOE in order to downplay its war theme. The toy would go on to create the "action figure" category of toys. While G.I. JOE characters are not superheroes, *per se*, they all have special skills in martial arts, weapons and explosives.

The character has been used and licensed extensively by Hasbro and has evolved into comic books, motion pictures and video games.

ANPANMAN, a fictional character created by Takashi Yanase, was introduced in Japan as a series of books in 1968. The character would ultimately become one of Japan's most popular animated children's cartoon series of all time. By 2006, more than 50 million ANPANMAN books have been
sold in Japan and it was made into a television series. It is Japan's most popular fictional character and has been licensed for a variety of products, including apparel, video games, toys and snack foods.

One of the longest running children's television shows of all time, **SESAME STREET**, premiered in 1969. Produced by Sesame Workshop (originally Children's Television Workshop), it has been a pioneer of contemporary educational television and was the first preschool educational television program to base its content on laboratory and formative research. The show has developed and licensed such characters as OSCAR THE GROUCH, BIG BIRD, BERT, ERNIE and, of course, ELMO, all of which have become household names. SESAME STREET's first licensee was Western Publishing which, in 1971, published the first of what would become more than 600 individual titles based on the characters. SESAME STREET's biggest impact on licensing has been in the toy area, initially with Tyco Toys and subsequently with Mattel and Hasbro. SESAME STREET remains one of the strongest licensing brands of all time, reportedly with licensed product sales in excess of $1.5 billion.

2.1.5   The 1970's

The decade started off in a big way when New York fashion designer, **RALPH LAUREN** created his soon to be famous, POLO brand, as part of a
line of women's suits that he had designed. In 1972, he introduced a short sleeved, mesh shirt with the POLO logo on it and a fashion industry fad was born. The shirt gained fame when it appeared in the motion picture, *The Great Gatsby.* By 2009, the RALPH LAUREN empire grew to more than $5 billion and it paved the way for other

fashion designers such as **PIERRE CARDIN, CALVIN KLEIN, GLORIA VANDERBILT** and **TOMMY HILFIGER**.

In 1972, American Greetings introduced the **HOLLY HOBBIE** character which had been created by writer and illustrator of the same name who lived in New England and who had previously written a series of children's books called *Toot and Puddle*. American Greetings bought her artwork that depicted a cat-loving, rag dress-wearing, little girl in a giant bonnet and a licensing legend was born. HOLLY HOBBIE was featured by American Greetings in a line of greeting cards and, in 1974, Knickerbocker Toys marketed the first licensed HOLLY HOBBY product—a rag doll.

The animated series Science Ninja Team Gatchaman, or simply **GATCHAMAN**, was first produced in Japan in 1972 by Tatsunoko Productions. It involved a group of teens who helped protect the planet from an alien invasion. The property was adapted into a number of English language versions, including one by Sandy Frank Entertainment named the **BATTLE OF THE PLANETS**. The series would become a worldwide television hit and is rumored to

have had an influence on George Lucas' development of the STAR WARS property.

HELLO KITTY, a fictional character designed by Yuko Shimizu, was first introduced in Japan by Sanrio in 1975 as a vinyl coin purse and, a year later, found its way into the United States. HELLO KITTY proved to be an immensely popular licensing property and more than $1 billion of licensed products are sold annually, ranging from dolls to stickers, greeting cards, apparel, accessories, school supplies, dishes and home appliances. There are currently two HELLO KITTY theme parks in Harmonyland and Sanrio Puroland, Japan.

By the mid-1970's, Hollywood studios had discovered the power of licensing as a means to generate additional revenue while helping to promote a motion picture or television show. Paramount Pictures was a leader

in this area, having developed licensing programs for virtually all of their television series, including **HAPPY DAYS, LAVERNE & SHIRLEY** and **MORK & MINDY,** as well as such motion pictures as **STAR TREK** and John Travolta's first three motion pictures, **SATURDAY NIGHT FEVER, GREASE** and **URBAN COWBOY.** These programs all generated significant amounts of revenue for Paramount and created a model for other studios to follow. Much of Paramount's licensing was handled by the colorful **ED JUSTIN,** who was known to his friends as simply **Honest Ed.** Ed was another one of the early pioneers of the licensing industry, having previously overseen the licensing departments at Columbia Pictures and NBC.

The 1970's also saw the emergence of **MARY ENGELBREIT** who would go on to pioneer the art licensing category. Engelbreit started out as a greeting card designer and illustrator in the 1970's working for an advertising agency in St. Louis. Her first success was a greeting card featuring a girl looking at a chair piled high with bows with the saying, "Life Is Just a Chair of Bowlies." She granted her first

art license later in the decade and has endured as a licensing success ever since, winning LIMA's Art License of the Year in both 2001 and 2003.

STRAWBERRY SHORTCAKE was created in 1977 by Muriel Fahrion while working as a greeting cards illustrator for American Greetings. Each of the characters had strawberry scented hair and lived in a world called Strawberryland. When American Greetings presented the concept to Bernie Loomis at Kenner Toys, a licensing phenomenon emerged. The success of the property led American Greetings to create its own licensing group, called

THOSE CHARACTERS FROM CLEVELAND.

Throughout the 1980's, the character was licensed extensively and was the basis of several television specials. It was re-introduced with a different look in 2002 and, once again, became quite popular, particularly on toys, DVD's and video games.

When the first **STAR WARS** motion picture was released on May 25, 1977 by Twentieth Century Fox, it set the licensing industry on its ear. Created by George Lucas, the STAR WARS film franchise would ultimately total six in number—each one of which

was a blockbuster. Total box office revenues for the six motion pictures were in excess of $5 billion, which made the series the third highest revenue producer of all time. While the movies were hits, the licensing success was unmatched by any property, either before or after. Bernie Loomis and Kenner Products were, once again, at the center of the licensing program, as the STAR WARS licensee for toys and action figures. When first introduced, Kenner could not manufacture product fast enough to meet consumer demand and it resorted to giving coupons to consumers for later redemption. From 1977 to 1985, Kenner sold more than 300 million STAR WARS action figures and its success paved the way for other studios and toy companies to produce their own line of licensed action figures. In an industry where the word "franchise" is overused, the STAR WARS property is truly a franchise.

The **GARFIELD** character was born out of a comic strip of the same name that was first published by Jim Davis in 1978. It featured a quirky, but lovable, cat named after Davis' grandfather as well as a dog called **ODIE**. By 2007, GARFIELD was syndicated in more than 2500 newspapers and journals and is considered the most widely syndicated comic strip of all time. GARFIELD has been featured on television shows, in motion pictures and adapted for host of licensed products, most notably toys, plush and apparel products.

The **CABBAGE PATCH KIDS** were created by Debbie Morehead and Xavier Roberts in 1978. The dolls were originally sold at local craft shows in Cleveland, Georgia until Roger Schlaifer of Schlaifer Nance & Company stepped in. He renamed them the CABBAGE PATCH KIDS, licensed the rights to Coleco Toys, and watched them become the hit of the 1982 holiday season.  Stores could not keep sufficient inventory to meet demand. Lines actually formed outside of many stores that announced that they had received a shipment. After Coleco's bankruptcy, Mattel, Hasbro and Play Along each marketed their own versions with modest success. It was reported that at its peak, there were over 150 CABBAGE PATCH licensees for products ranging from diapers to cereal to apparel. In 1984 alone, it was reported that more than $2 billion of CABBAGE PATCH products were sold at retail and, over its lifespan, retail sales were at least $4.5 billion.

 The **DALLAS** television series was first aired in the fall of 1978 and would run through 1991. Produced by Lorimar Productions and starring Larry Hagman as J.R. Ewing, it was a primetime soap opera about an affluent Texas family in the oil and cattle ranching business. DALLAS was one of the first adult properties ever to be licensed and demonstrated that entertainment licensing was not all about children's themes. The show paved the way for other adult merchandisable properties such as KNOTS LANDING, FALCON CREST and DYNASTY.

2.1.6   The 1980's

The **CARE BEARS** property was created by Elena Kucharik in 1981, originally for use on a line of greeting cards by American Greetings. Two years later, Bernie Loomis and Kenner Toys developed and began selling a line of plush products based on the characters and the licensing program was off to the races. A television series based on the characters ran from 1985 until 1988 and it was also featured in three motion pictures. The characters were re-introduced as toys in 2002 by

PlayAlong Toys with modest success. The **CARE BEARS** property ushered in a new era in licensing— the birth of the half-hour, animated, syndicated television series which was distributed to local television channels across the United States and abroad. Previously, the dominant platform for children's programming was Saturday morning television that only aired weekly. Syndication of half-hour animated shows, aired five times a week in after school time slots and provided greater exposure for their properties. The gamble with syndication paid off for a number of properties, including **MASTERS OF THE UNIVERSE** and **MY LITTLE PONY** and fueled the licensing industry for most of the 1980's. The bubble would, however eventually burst, unfortunately at great cost to the producers.

In a bizarre twist, a 1982 court decision finding that Champion Products' production of non-licensed **UNIVERSITY OF PITTSBURGH** clothing did *not* constitute trademark infringement, produced

the exact opposite result. At the time of the decision, Champion was selling more than $100 million of apparel bearing the logos of as many as 10,000 different schools and colleges. Instead of destroying any hope for the colleges to license out their names and logos, reasonable minds prevailed and a business solution was reached. Champion fell in line, recognized that these schools and colleges had valid rights, and began to take licenses to use their marks on its products. Thus, the collegiate licensing industry was born.

Shortly before the *Pitt* decision, a former football coach from Alabama, Bill Battle, formed the **COLLEGIATE LICENSING COMPANY** ("CLC"), that would go on to represent almost half the colleges in the emerging collegiate licensing industry. It was reported that in 2009, CLC, now a part of IMG, generated more than $200 million of royalty income for the colleges.

The 1980's also saw the creation of a trade association for the licensing industry. In 1982, Arnold Bolka (who was the then-owner and editor of *The Licensing Letter*) started the first industry association called The Licensing Association ("LIA"). LIA was composed primarily of licensors  and a former LCA executive, Murray Altchuler, became its Executive Director. It would eventually enter into an agreement with Expocon to sponsor the Licensing Show. Not to be outdone, the licensee community got together and organized its own association—the Licensing Merchandisers' Association ("LMA") which would be headed by Jerrold Robinson. For at least one, somewhat confusing year, both groups elected to stage their own "Licensing Shows" at the same time in adjacent Sheraton Hotels in New York. In 1985, the two associations merged and formed the Licensing Industry Merchandiser's Association ("**LIMA**") with Altchuler as its first Executive Director. Upon Altchuler's retirement in 1997, Charles Riotto became the LIMA president and would go on to oversee its growth into a truly global association.

E.T. was the blockbuster movie of 1982. Produced and directed by Steven Spielberg and written by Melissa Mathison, it was about a lonely boy who befriended an extraterrestrial called E.T. Box office sales skyrocketed, and, for a period, **E.T.** was the most financially successful motion picture of its time. While the E.T. character was heavily merchandised, it is perhaps best known for creating a concept called product placement, where a product is featured in the movie for the express purpose of promoting it. In E.T.'s case, that product was Hershey's Reese's Pieces which was portrayed as E.T.'s favorite candy.

In 1982, Crown Publishers published the first **MARTHA STEWART** book entitled *Entertaining*, and an empire began. Ms. Stewart then collaborated with Time Publishing in 1990 to develop a magazine called *Martha Stewart Living* which would eventually enjoy a circulation of 2 million readers. That led to a series of successful television shows and specials and, ultimately, the creation of the company, Martha Stewart Living Omnimedia, which would go public in 1999. Kmart has carried her licensed line of home furnishing products for decades and a licensed MARTHA STEWART line of paint is sold through Sears.

POUND PUPPIES was created in 1983 by Mike Bowling, a former Ford factory worker, when he saw the look of love on the face of his young daughter for one of her dolls and remembered that same feeling from his own childhood after going to the pound to pick out a pet. The first POUND PUPPIES doll was marketed in Canada in 1984 by Irwin Toys and, a year later, Tonka began marketing it in the United States. It would eventually generate more than $300 million in sales in 35 different countries and spawn a wide range of licensed products.

The **TEENAGE MUTANT NINJA TURTLES** was a joint collaboration between Kevin Eastman and Peter Laird. Using money from a tax return, they formed Mirage Studios in 1984 and published a comic book that featured these characters as a parody of Marvel's superheroes. It became enormously popular, principally because of the efforts of their licensing agent, Mark Freedman, who developed a licensing program with Playmates Toys. Throughout the 1980's and 1990's, TURTLE's licensees produced a wide range of licensed products and it was LIMA's License of the Year in 1991.

By the mid-1980's, licensing properties were coming from every imaginable source. A 1986 commercial for the California Raisin Advisory Board spawned a property that would receive LIMA's award for the Most Impactful Property of the year in 1988—the **CALIFORNIA RAISINS**. These characters were featured in the commercial dancing to the Marvin Gaye song, "I Heard It Through the Grapevine." With Applause as its primary toy licensee, sales of licensed products exploded. It was the first time that a commercial formed the basis for a licensing program.

Not to be outdone, Arby's restaurants launched a licensing program based on the catchy phrase **WHERE'S THE BEEF**. The phrase was licensed for a line of apparel and even found its way into the 1984 Vice-Presidential debate. The trend of licensing out catchy advertising slogans or characters has continued to this day, as evidenced by the licensing program conducted by former LIMA chairman Brian Hakan, for the **TACO BELL CHIHUAHUA**, who had been featured in advertisements for the restaurant. Similarly, the Mars Corporation regularly licenses the **M&M's** characters that are featured in Mars' television and print ads for its line of M&M's candy products.

In 1986, Scholastic published the first of what would become a series of children's books called the **MAGIC SCHOOL BUS.** These books were written by Joanna Cole and illustrated by Bruce Degan and featured an elementary school teacher, Mrs. Frizzle, who would take their readers on field trips to interesting places aboard a magical school bus. The books would eventually lead to a television series, a series of traveling museums and a very successful licensing program.

In 1987, Sheryl Leach of Dallas, Texas created the character **BARNEY** while overseeing production of a series of home videos entitled *Barney and the Backyard Gang* starring Sandy Duncan. While the DVD's were modestly successful, the character would ultimately be modified and became the basis for a PBS series that debuted in 1992 called *Barney & Friends*. The show was popular, however, its related licensing program was a real hit, particularly in the plush and toy areas. BARNEY won LIMA's License of the Year award in 1994.

It was during the 1980's that major corporations began testing the water, having recognized the advantages that licensing offered. Licensing assisted some companies in expanding the breadth of their trademark protection, while helping others promote the sale of their underlying products. Regardless of the reason for getting involved in licensing, all welcomed the additional revenue that it brought to their bottom line. Corporations with well known brands such as **COCA-COLA, HARLEY DAVIDSON, PEPSI, COORS** and **JOHN DEERE** all began to explore licensing activities with a significant amount of success. It was estimated, for example, that the COCA-COLA licensing program generated more than $70 million in net royalty income during its peak.

THE SIMPSONS, an animated television series created by Matt Groening, debuted on Fox in 1989 and is still on the air, which makes it the longest television show of all time. Featuring the characters **HOMER, MARGE, BART, LISA** and **MAGGIE**, it is a spoof on American family life. *The Simpsons Movie* was released in 2007 and grossed more than $525 million. Its enormous popularity has made it a licensing and media franchise, with the characters appearing on virtually every conceivable type of licensed product. By 2003, it was reported that there were more than 500 SIMPSONS' licensees worldwide. In the first 14 months after release of the motion picture, it is believed that more than $2 billion of licensed merchandise were sold. A Fox executive called the SIMPSONS, "without a doubt, the biggest licensing entity that Fox has had, full stop, I would say from either TV or film."

2.1.7 The 1990's

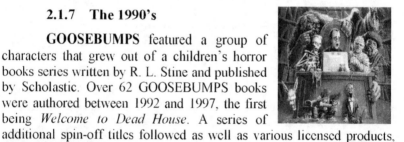

GOOSEBUMPS featured a group of characters that grew out of a children's horror books series written by R. L. Stine and published by Scholastic. Over 62 GOOSEBUMPS books were authored between 1992 and 1997, the first being *Welcome to Dead House*. A series of additional spin-off titles followed as well as various licensed products, including at least three board games by Milton Bradley and video games by DreamWorks Interactive. GOOSEBUMPS won LIMA's License of the Year award for 1993.

TERMINATOR 2: JUDGMENT DAY or simply **T2**, a science fiction motion picture directed by James Cameron and starring Arnold Schwarzenegger, was released in 1991 as a sequel to the original Terminator movie from 1984. It was one of the first "R" rated motion pictures to ever

spawn a licensing program and has become the most successful licensed "R" rated film of all time. The licensing program, conducted by former LIMA President and co-author, Danny Simon, was led by Kenner Toys and Acclaim Entertainment. Universal Theme Parks also developed a licensed T2-3D attraction.

The **MIGHTY MORPHIN POWER RANGERS**, which was based on a popular Japanese property called Kyōryū Sentai Zyuranger about four teenagers who were selected to fight evil, hit the television screens in 1993 as a live-action television series. It was produced by Haim Saban and

immediately became an overnight hit—both as a TV show and licensing property. The series ran for three years and "morphed" into a feature motion picture called *Mighty Morphin Power Rangers: The Movie.*

The **POKÉMON** property was created by Satoshi Tajiri in 1996 and launched by Nintendo that same year as a role-playing video game. It would become the second most successful video game-based franchise of all time, behind Mario Bros., selling more than 200 million copies. Under the watchful eye of LIMA Hall of Fame member Al Kahn at 4Kids Entertainment, it would also grow into a very strong licensing property, with licenses for trading cards, apparel, books, and other media forms. POKÉMON was LIMA's licensed entertainment character of the year in 2000.

Comedy Central first broadcast its animated sitcom called **SOUTH PARK** in 1997 and, since its introduction, it has consistently earned the highest rating of any basic cable program. Created by Trey Parker and Matt Stone for an adult audience with satirical humor, it focuses on four children and their

adventures in a Colorado town. It is reported to generate several million dollars a year in royalties and licensed products include a pinball machine by Sega and games and puzzles by Fun 4 All. In 1998, SOUTH PARK T-shirts were the largest selling specialty T-shirts in the United States.

Another true legend of licensing, **HARRY POTTER**, was introduced in June 1997 when J.K. Rowling's first novel (of what would become a series) entitled *Harry Potter and the Philosopher's Stone* was published. It described the exploits of a young wizard, Harry Potter, and his friends at the Hogwarts School of Witchcraft and Wizardry. Over 400 million copies of these books would be sold in 67 different languages making Rowling perhaps the only billionaire author. The Warner Bros. motion pictures have each achieved blockbuster status and are among the highest grossing films of all time. As one would expect, licensing has been extensive, particularly in the toy, game, video and costume areas and a *Wizarding World of Harry Potter* theme park was opened in Orlando, FL.

1997 also saw the **TELETUBBIES** property emerge. Created by Anne Woode and produced by Ragdoll Productions, it debuted in a BBC children's television series of the same name. The program was aimed at pre-school viewers, although it drew a large number of adult viewers because of its humor. A total of 365 episodes of the show were run in both the UK and the United States.  The show received a number of broadcasting awards and the property won LIMA's Best Overall License of the Year award in 1999.

DORA THE EXPLORER, an animated television series featuring Dora Marquez, first aired in September 1999 on Nickelodeon. The show, which was created by Chris Gifford, Valerie Walsh, and Eric Weiner, would continue until 2006 and be heavily merchandised along the way with DORA action figures, play sets, DVDs, cosmetics, hygiene products, ride-on toys, books, board games, plush dolls, apparel, handbags, play tents, and play kitchens.

The animated CGI character, **BOB THE BUILDER**, was created by Keith Chapman and first appeared on the BBC in 1999. BOB is a building contractor who takes on various building projects, including renovations, construction and repairs. The show's theme song, *Can We Fix It*, sold more than a million copies in the UK. The show has been extraordinarily popular and is aired in virtually every television market around the

world and its licensing program, managed by HIT Entertainment, has been equally successful. The property was named as LIMA's Entertainment/Character License of the Year in 2002.

Another potentially classic property was introduced in 1999, when Nickelodeon launched the animated television series, *SpongeBob SquarePants*, created by Stephen Hillenburg. **SPONGEBOB** lives in an underwater city called Bikini Bottom. The show would become Nickelodeon's top rated show and a feature film based on the character was released in 2004. Sales of licensed SPONGEBOB merchandise have been very strong. It was reported that in 2002, sales of SPONGEBOB dolls sold at the rate of 75,000 per week. Other licensed products include cereal, video games, clothing and electronics. The character has also been used extensively in promotional programs for virtually every fast food and convenience store chain and by virtually all of the major retailers.

2.1.8 The 21st Century

Licensing in the New Millennium has tended to focus more on Hollywood's "blockbuster" motion pictures, many of which were based on characters developed in the prior century. For example two **HULK** motion pictures, based on the Marvel superhero, were released, the first in 2003 and the sequel in 2008. The 2003 release earned $62.1 million in its opening weekend and would go on to gross almost $250 million worldwide. The

sequel, *The Incredible Hulk*, out-grossed the original, with worldwide box office receipts of more than $263 million, and another $60 million in

DVD sales. As would be expected, the sales of licensed products based on both motion pictures were strong.

Sony Pictures released three different **SPIDERMAN** motion pictures in the decade, all based on the original Marvel characters. The original **SPIDERMAN** motion picture was released in 2002, **SPIDERMAN 2** was released in 2004 and **SPIDERMAN 3** in 2007. The trilogy grossed almost $2.5 billion at the box office and won multiple awards. All three motion pictures were heavily merchandised by Sony and SPIDERMAN and SPIDERMAN 2 received LIMA's Best Overall License of the Year award for 2003 and 2005.

LIMA's award for the Best Overall License of the Year for 2006 went to **STAR WARS: Episode III Revenge of the Sith** which was released in 2005 and would be the last episode of the STAR WARS movies. All of these motion pictures were written and directed by George Lucas and produced by Lucasfilm Ltd. The film broke a number of box office records and would ultimately gross almost $850 million, placing it behind only the highest grossing film of 2005,

Warner Bros.' blockbuster, **HARRY POTTER and the Goblet of Fire**. Both motion pictures continued their history of strong licensing programs.

Disney's blockbuster motion pictures, **PIXAR CARS** and **HIGH SCHOOL MUSICAL 2,** won LIMA's Entertainment License of the Year awards for 2007 and 2008, respectively. PIXAR CARS was directed by John Lasseter and Joe Ranft and featured the voices of prominent Hollywood actors, including Paul Newman and Michael Keaton. **PIXAR CARS** premiered in May 2006 at Lowe's Motor Speedway in North Carolina and the related licensing program was nothing short of sensational. It was reported that retail sales of licensed merchandise, including scale models of its cars, broke records for a Disney-Pixar film with more than $5 billion of licensed products sold.

The *New York Daily News* reported that sales of its licensed merchandise were $600 million just two weeks after its release.

HIGH SCHOOL MUSICAL 2, which was the sequel to the Disney Channel Original Movie, **HIGH SCHOOL MUSICAL,** debuted on the Disney Channel in 2007 to 17.3 million viewers-- about 10 million more than for the original movie. That made it the most highly viewed Disney Channel movie to
date. Ultimately, **HIGH SCHOOL MUSICAL 3: SENIOR YEAR** was released the following year in theatrical distribution.

The Hollywood Blockbuster formula of superhero movies continued throughout the decade. In 2008, Warner Bros. released a sequel to its 2005 *Batman Begins* motion picture, entitled the **DARK KNIGHT,** which was written and directed by Christopher Nolan. It set box office records everywhere and would become the seventh largest grossing movie of all time which, no doubt, contributed to its success as a licensing property.

The trend of licensing blockbuster movies continued into 2009, first with the release of Paramount's **TRANSFORMERS: REVENGE OF THE FALLEN** which brought in more than $400 million at the domestic box office followed by Fox's release of **AVATAR** in 2009 which produced more than $750 million at the box office. Both motion pictures have generated strong licensing programs. It was reported that Hasbro, which owned the rights to TRANSFORMERS, had over 220
licensees for products across virtually all categories while Fox had over 125 licensees for the AVATAR property across at least four major categories, including video games, toys, apparel and publishing.

The decade was not, however, all about movie licensing. The **BRATZ** doll, introduced by MGA Entertainment in 2001, proved to be not only a very successful doll but a strong licensing property as well. Trendy and cutting edge, it was reported that more than 125 million BRATZ dolls were sold in its first five years and, by 2005, global sales of all BRATZ products topped $2 billion. From 2001 through 2010, it is believed that MGA had produced or licensed more than 550 different BRATZ dolls and products. BRATZ was the winner of LIMA's License of the Year award for 2004.

In 2002 artist Jim Benton came on the licensing scene in a big way with a smiling bunny called **HAPPY BUNNY**. Complete with catchy sayings, Carole Postal and COP Corp. developed a strong licensing program for the property covering a broad array of products, including key chains, computer mouse pads, energy drinks, school supplies, clothing, etc. HAPPY BUNNY was named LIMA's Art Licensing Property of the Year in 2006.

BAKUGAN, a Japanese animated television series produced by TMS Entertainment and Japan Vistec, debuted in 2007 in Japan and soon became popular in the United States and Canada. Not surprisingly, it spawned a line of licensed games led by SpinMaster as its major toy licensee. Other licensed products included branded digital cameras, alarm clocks and other electronic products. BAKUGAN was selected by LIMA in 2009 as the Best Overall Licensed Program of the Year.

The New Millennium also saw the emergence of a plethora of celebrities who licensed their names, images and likenesses for a wide variety of licensed products, some with extraordinary success. One of the most successful celebrity programs of the decade was the **JESSICA**

SIMPSON brand program which, through the efforts of her business manager, David Levin of DLE Entertainment in New York, and master licensee, the Camuto Group (headed by Vince Camuto of NINE WEST fame), is on its way to becoming a billion dollar brand at retail. After quickly establishing itself as one of the leading brands for women's shoes, lines of licensed JESSICA SIMPSON apparel, accessories and fragrances followed with similar success.

The **OLSON TWINS**, Mary Kate & Ashlee, are not waiting to become a billion dollar brand – they have already achieved it, mostly through their line of classic licensed apparel and accessory products. Only in their 20's, these celebrities are believed to be worth a combined

sum of $300 million due, principally, to the licensing empire that they have helped establish through the efforts of the Beanstalk Group. Other celebrities, including JACKIE SMITH, JENNIFER LOPEZ, BRITANY SPEARS, DAVID BECKHAM, CINDY CRAWFORD, LADY GAGA, have all entered the licensing arena with varying degrees of success, mostly good.

Perhaps the two best known celebrity licensors of all time are former basketball player **MICHAEL JORDAN** and golfer **TIGER WOODS**. While MICHAEL JORDAN continues to remain a licensing heavyweight, principally because of his relationship with Nike, the TIGER WOODS experience demonstrates the risks of celebrity licensing. WOODS, who reportedly earned almost $100 million in endorsement and licensing deals in 2009 and 2010, saw his golf score rise sharply while his licensing income fell precipitously after charges of his marital infidelity were made public. Other prominent sports stars

who earn significant sums through licensing and endorsements include fellow golfer, PHIL MICKELSON, baseball star ALEX RODRIGUEZ, tennis player ROGER FEDERER, soccer star DAVID BECKHAM and baseball star ICHIRO SUZUKI.

The property **PLEASANT GOAT AND BIG BIG WOLF**, a Chinese animated television series, was launched in China in 2005. Created by Huang Weiming, Lin Yuting and Luo Yinggeng, it is broadcast on more than 40 local television stations and almost 1000 episodes have been aired. The first motion picture based on the television series was released in 2009 and set a box office record in China for a Chinese animated film, earning more than $8 million during the opening weekend. A second movie was released in 2010. It is one of the most popular licensed characters in China.

2.2   LIMA License of the Year Award Winners

The following Properties were named LIMA's "Licenses of The Year" since 1989:

1989	CALIFORNIA RAISINS
1990	BATMAN
1991	TEENAGE MUTANT NINJA TURTLES
1992	THE LITTLE MERMAID
1993	THOMAS THE TANK ENGINE
1994	BARNEY & FRIENDS
1995	LION KING
1996	WINNIE-THE-POOH
1997	GOOSEBUMPS
1998	RUGRATS
1999	TELETUBBIES
2000	POKEMAN
2001	POWERPUFF GIRLS
2002	BOB THE BUILDER
2003	SPIDERMAN
2004	BRATZ
2005	SPIDERMAN 2
2006	STAR WARS

2007	PIXAR CARS
2008	HIGH SCHOOL MUSICAL
2009	BAKUGAN
2010	THE TWILIGHT SAGA: NEW MOON

2.3   The Major Licensors

It's virtually impossible to determine with any degree of accuracy which property owner has generated the largest amount of licensing revenue over time, let alone who would fall into the top ten of all-time revenue producers since many licensors consider their actual licensing revenues a closely guarded secret. Thus, any attempt to create such a list would be nothing more than pure speculation.

That said, *License!* published a list of Top 100 Licensors in 2009 based on what they estimated to be total sales of retail of their licensed products. The top ten in that list were:

1.	Disney Consumer Products ($30 billion)
2.	ICONIX ($6.5 billion)
3.	Warner Bros. Consumer Products ($6 billion)
4.	Marvel Entertainment ($5.7 billion)
5.	Nickelodeon & Viacom ($5.7 billion)
6.	Major League Baseball ($5.1 billion)
7.	Philips-Van Heusen ($5 billion)
8.	Sanrio ($5 billion)
9.	Collegiate Licensing Company ($4.28 billion)
10.	Cherokee Group ($4 billion)

Chapter 3

The Licensing Industry Today

3.1 Size and Scope of the Industry

It's unlikely that any of the exhibitors and attendees who gathered in the basement of a New York City hotel for the first Licensing Show in 1981 would have ever imagined that they were witnessing the birth of an industry. That first show, which was produced by Expocon Management Associates and its president, Fred Favata, had a couple of dozen tabletop exhibits and less than a thousand attendees. Thirty years later, that same show would morph into a Las Vegas extravaganza with almost 20,000 people from all segments of the industry in attendance.

It is also unlikely that any of the attendees in 1981 would have ever believed that it would spawn almost a dozen licensing shows outside the United States, many of which are significantly larger than the original New York Show. Brand Licensing Europe, held every fall in London, is perhaps the largest of these international shows and drew more than 6,000 attendees and exhibitors in 2010.

Other international licensing shows include the Brand Licensing & Merchandising Show in India, the Shanghai Licensing Pavilion, the Licensing Mart and the Day of Licensing in Germany, Licensing New Europe in Croatia, the Dubai Character and Licensing Fair, the Hong Kong International Licensing Fair and the Creative Market in Tokyo.

In addition there are licensing events or pavilions taking place at other industry-specific trade shows such as, the Bologna Book Fair in Italy and MIPCOM in France, as well as a number of other trade shows that feature licensed products such as the Magic and CES shows.

Likewise, few of the attendees at that first licensing show could have envisioned that the licensing industry would grow to a size that supports more than half a dozen trade publications devoted exclusively to licensing, including *The Licensing Letter*, *Total Licensing*, *License! Global*, *The Licensing Book*, *Royalties* and *The Licensing Journal* as well as publications in Spain (*Licencias Actualidad*, based in Barcelona), Germany (the *Licensing Press*, based in Rodermark), France (*Kazachok*, based in Paris) and India (*License India*, based in New Delhi). In addition, licensing topics are regularly covered in industry-specific publications, including *KidScreen, Brand Week, Billboard, Variety* and *Women's Wear Daily.*

Similarly, it is difficult to imagine that those who attended the Licensing Show in 1981 would ever believe that the "licensing industry" could actually support a trade association with more than 1,000 corporate members—the International Licensing Industry Merchandisers Association "("LIMA"). LIMA was formed in 1985 through the merger of two separate organizations: the Licensing Industry Association ("LIA"), which had only licensor members, and the Licensed Merchandisers Association ("LMA"), whose members were primarily licensees. The "licensing industry" also supports another trade association directed exclusively to collegiate licensing, the International Collegiate Licensing Association, which has almost 500 members.

Since 2000, LIMA has sponsored and published an annual Licensing Survey conducted by professors in the business schools at Harvard & Yale Universities that reports on licensing revenues received by licensors through the sale of licensed products in North America. The Survey breaks down the revenues by property type and product category. These Licensing Surveys not only report on the industry for the present year, but also compare the results with prior years to identify trends.

For every year since the inception of the Survey in 2000, these Licensing Surveys show that licensors received more than $5 billion in licensing revenues from their licensees as a result of the sale of licensed products in North America. Total licensing revenues actually reached a peak of more than $6 billion in 2006, but this figure has decreased in subsequent years due largely to a slowing of the worldwide economy and, of course, the recession that began in 2008. According to LIMA's 2010 Survey, licensors received $5.65 billion in licensing revenue in 2009 from the sale of licensed products in North America by their licensees. This was 8.7 percent lower than they had received in 2008, again attributable to the recession.

Attempting to translate total licensing revenue to actual retail sales of licensed products is challenging because retail markups and discounts vary. Nevertheless, the Harvard/Yale professors estimated that such licensing revenue would have corresponded to retail sales of approximately $92 million in licensed products for 2009.

Past Surveys are available at no cost to LIMA members and are accessible through the LIMA website at www.licensing.org. The results of the 2010 LIMA Survey for all of North America were the following:

Property Type	Estimated Licensing Revenue (in million dollars)										% Revenue	% Change
	2000	2001	2002	2003	2004	2005	2006	2007	2008	2009		
Art	$141	$147	$161	$167	$170	$175	$182	$175	$154	$136	2.63%	(11.7%)
Characters	$2588	$2484	$2580	$2502	$2565	$2626	$2680	$2710	$2605	$2400	46.47%	(7.8%)
Collegiate	$182	$175	$182	$203	$201	$203	$203	$201	$208	$200	3.87%	(3.8%)
Fashion	$980	$911	$892	$848	$814	$822	$830	$810	$775	$705	13.65%	(9.0%)
Music	$138	$117	$119	$113	$122	$128	$132	$125	$117	$110	2.13%	(6.0%)
Non-Profit	$36	$38	$39	$40	$41	$43	$45	$43	$39	$35	.68%	(9.3%)
Sports	$721	$707	$763	$807	$795	$810	$825	$815	$740	$660	12.78%	(10.8%)
Corp./Brand	$982	$963	$1040	$1060	$1081	$1086	$1090	$1060	$975	$880	17.04%	(9.8%)
Publishing	$44	$42	$45	$43	$41	$41	$41	$41	$37	$34	.66%	(8.1%)
Others	$35	$22	$10	$22	$15	$18	$12	$9	$6	$5	.10%	(16.7%)
Total	$5847	$5606	$5831	$5805	$5845	$5952	$6040	$5989	$5656	$5165	100%	(8.7%)

The chart below illustrates total licensing revenues by property type. Clearly, the licensing of entertainment and character properties dominates the industry, producing more than 46% (or $2.4 billion) of the total North American licensing revenues for 2009. The licensing of corporate or brand properties are second, generating about 17% (or about

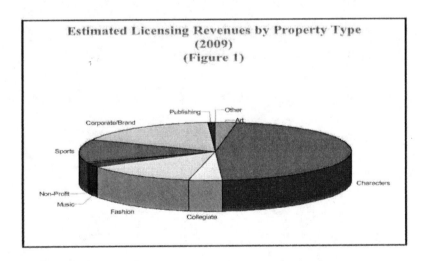

Estimated Licensing Revenues by Property Type (2009) (Figure 1)

$880 million) of the total licensing revenues for the year. The licensing of fashion properties was responsible for about 12.78% (or about $660 million) of total licensing revenues for the year. From this, the Harvard/Yale researchers projected retail sales of licensed products for each of these property types in 2009 as follows:

Art	$2.04 billion
Entertainment/Character	$36 billion
Collegiate	$3.0 billion
Fashion	$10.575 billion
Music	$1.5 billion
Non-Profit	$525 million
Sports	$9.9 billion
Corporate/Brand	$12 billion
Other	$75 million

The 2010 LIMA Survey reported that the licensing of apparel, toys & games and software & video games produced the greatest amount of licensing revenues. Yearly totals, broken down by each product category, were as follows:

Product Category	Estimated Licensing Revenue (in million dollars)										% of Total Rev.	% Change in Rev.
	2000	2001	2002	2003	2004	2005	2006	2007	2008	2009		
Accessories	$470.3	$450.03	$479.88	$479.1	$488.35	$504.3	$516.1	$519.2	$492.5	$433.7	8.6%	(11.9%)
Apparel	$937.8	$976.38	$1032.1	$1021.5	$998.87	$989.5	$1004.0	$962.1	$883.2	$793.5	15.7%	(10.1%)
Food/Bev.	$475.0	$418.27	$427.25	$440.51	$438.38	$444.4	$444.2	$434.3	$419.8	$403.2	8.0%	(3.9%)
Footwear	$176.1	$168.13	$173.03	$170.03	$169.47	$171.8	$165.6	$163.6	$154.3	$140.4	2.8%	(9%)
Home Decor	$291.6	$288.22	$299.74	$291.92	$311.61	$338.8	$377.2	$357.9	$325.0	$295.8	5.9%	(8.9%)
Gifts/Novel.	$512.7	$506.37	$492.48	$490.95	$491.94	$501.4	510.8	$512.7	$478.2	$440.6	8.7%	(7.8%)
Health/Beaut	$266.0	$241.62	$233.37	$242.83	$250.44	$258.8	$256.2	$251.2	$238.5	$217	4.3%	(9%)
Housewares	$146.0	$175.41	$202.53	$225.23	$264.3	$281.6	$287.7	$283.0	$264.5	$242.7	4.8%	(8.2%)
Music/Video	$62.5	$84.99	$88.70	$86.52	$88.58	$90.46	$92.9	$91.5	$89.4	$82.2	1.6%	(8.1%)
Infant Prod.	$97.1	$65.53	$58.48	$56.37	$56.77	$57.76	$58.7	$58.3	$54.8	$48.5	1.0%	(11.4%)
Promotions	$53.2	$38.98	$56.42	$41.16	$43.19	$44.18	$45.1	$45.1	$42.4	$38.6	0.8%	(8.9%)
Publishing	$183.6	$166.82	$170.66	$194.32	$196.53	$200.3	$203.9	$203.0	$190.6	$173.7	3.4%	(8.8%)
Sport. Goods	$63.9	$65.59	$86.06	$85.11	$85.55	$86.92	$88.2	$87.4	$85.7	$78.1	1.5%	(8.9%)
Paper/School Supplies	$156.9	$215.72	$202.96	$217.35	$220.26	$224.9	$229.3	$231.2	$217.7	$198.6	3.9%	(8.8%)
Toys/Games	$1000.1	$958.28	$1020.22	$975.12	$932.41	$908	$897.8	$881.2	$839.2	$785	15.5%	(6.4%)
Software/ Videogames	$632.8	$536.75	$569.42	$553.12	$547.68	$524.8	$541.2	$596.1	$589.1	$513.7	10.2%	(12.8%)
Other	$146.8	$109.91	$108.50	$98.89	$123.69	$178	$177.5	$177.2	$168.3	$164.9	3.3%	(2.0%)
Total	$5672	$5467	$5702'	$5670'	$5708'	$5806'	$5896'	$5855'	$5533'	$5050'	100%	

The LIMA Survey also addresses and considers which channels of distribution, e.g., specialty markets, mass merchandisers, department stores and direct sales, produce the most licensing revenues. The 2010 Survey found that licensed products bearing entertainment, corporate, fashion, sports and publishing properties were more likely to be sold through mass merchandisers while licensed products bearing art, collegiate and non-profit properties were more likely to be sold through specialty channels. Estimated licensing revenues by distribution channel were reported in the 2010 LIMA Survey as follows:

	Specialty	Mass Merchandisers	Department Stores	Direct
Art	50%	35%	10%	5%
Characters	19%	49%	30%	2%
Collegiate	60%	19%	14%	7%
Fashion	35%	35%	25%	5%
Non-Profit	50%	25%	15%	10%
Sports	25%	55%	15%	5%
Trademarks/Brands	25%	50%	20%	5%
Publishing	25%	55%	15%	5%

Mass Merchandisers: Includes mass merchandising, supermarket and drug stores
Select Outlets: Includes college stores and specialty chains
Department Stores: Includes premium and mid-tier stores
Direct: Includes websites, telephone and catalog marketing

3.2   International Scope of the Industry

While merchandising may have started out as an American phenomenon, it has since become truly international in scope. Properties are being developed and promoted in virtually every country in the world and products bearing those properties are similarly being sold worldwide. The global reach of merchandising is reflected in the makeup and structure of LIMA, which now has offices in the United Kingdom, Germany, China, Hong Kong and Tokyo as well as regional groups in Italy, Spain & Portugal, New Europe, India, Dubai, Brazil and Australia.

LIMA's membership is further reflective of the international scope of the industry, with approximately half of its membership coming from countries outside the United States. Most significantly, it is readily apparent to anyone working in this industry that future growth of licensing activity will occur primarily in emerging markets and on a global scale.

Chapter 4

Identifying & Clearing Licensed Properties

4.1 Evaluating Properties for Licensing

Now that you've gone through the fundamentals of licensing and seen some of the success stories, it's time to start applying these fundamentals to your own property to see whether it may be possible to duplicate the success of others.

What must be understood from the very start is that licensing is a financial venture. Therefore the opening task for the licensor is to determine why anyone would invest in licensing his particular property. Alternatively, from the licensee's point of view, the task is to determine whether or not a property is worth the investment. Both questions sound simple, but they are not always easy to answer. Regardless of which side of the license you are on—licensor or licensee—success in licensing requires the ability to judge accurately if a property has legitimate potential for licensing. At this stage, it is also very important to make sure that use of the property in question will not conflict with or infringe the rights of any other party. These are big hurdles, but they must be cleared before embarking on the development of any licensing program.

This first step in the process requires that the property owner remain strictly objective although, admittedly, this can be difficult. Nobody believes that their baby is ugly and, similarly, everybody thinks that their property is the best thing since sliced bread. The property owner needs to accurately assess its property, whether it's a cartoon character, a house brand or a piece of artwork, and realistically determine whether it is something that, if used by another party, could actually help that party sell its products or services and justify the payment of a royalty.

Since objectivity is important, it is frequently helpful to bring in an independent licensing consultant to provide conduct an evaluation. Simply because a house brand works for one's own product, or a comic strip character may be enjoyed by local readers, doesn't necessarily mean that it will have universal appeal on other types of products or in other regions. Thus, an independent evaluation of the licensing potential of the property is generally worthwhile.

In evaluating licensing properties, consultants will typically consider such factors as:

- How well known is the property?

- If the property is not well known, does it have the potential to generate licensees on the strength or appeal of its images, e.g., art properties?

- Is the property legally protected for at least the key product categories?

- Does the owner really "own" or at least "control" licensing rights for the property?

- Has the property been extensively promoted and, if not, can it be better promoted in the future?

- If it is used on a wider range of products, will it appeal to a broader class of consumers?

- What's the competition from other properties?

- If used by others, will it create legal problems?

Objectively evaluating a potential licensing property at the beginning will save everyone a great deal of time and expense in the long run.

4.2   How Well Known is the Property?

Potential licensees will want to know the answer to this question before they even consider taking a license. After all, the right to commercially exploit the recognition and popularity of the property is typically the main reason that a manufacturer is willing to take a license and pay a royalty for using it. Hence, the property owner will need to know just how popular and widely recognized its property is before proceeding with any licensing program, as it will need to convey this information to prospective licensees.

There are certain instances where licensees will take a license before a property actually becomes well known, e.g., a new motion picture. In those cases, the property owner will need to explain in detail what it intends to do in order to promote the property and make it a household word by the time the licensee's sales of licensed products actually commence.

The licensing of artwork is, of course, different, since in most cases promotion is not very important—licensees are usually only interested in the uniqueness or appeal of the artwork. In actuality, the prospective licensee might even prefer if the artwork was not extensively exposed, so as to avoid having a competitor see it and quickly develop its own version.

There are actually a number of objective ways to determine how well known a property has become. For starters, most licensing consultants will ask:

- How long has the property been used for its primary products or services?

- What were the sales and the breadth of distribution of products or services bearing this property?

- Have sales of these products or services been local, national or international and what was the breakout between these three areas?

- Has the property been regularly featured in advertising or promotions and, if so,

  o for how long;

  o where; and

  o how much was spent on media buys during the period?

- Has the property received media attention and, if so, how much and why?

- Has the property owner ever been approached about potentially licensing the property and, if so, what were the details?

It might also be helpful to research the property on the Internet using various search engines to see how often the property actually comes up and what people are saying about it. That is an easy and very inexpensive way to measure the public recognition of a potential licensing property. It is also quite helpful in determining whether there are other parties using the same or similar properties that could potentially pose problems for a licensing program.

For established characters and brands, there are services that will measure the extent of a property's public recognition and popularity and even compare it against like properties. One such service, the "Q Score" provided by Marketing Evaluations, Inc., is a measurement of the familiarity and appeal of a brand, company, celebrity or television show in the United States. A higher Q Scores means that the property is better regarded by the public. This service is used extensively by marketing, advertising and PR firms and, assuming that the resultant Q Score is sufficiently high, it might be an important point to make in the eventual "pitch" to a prospective licensee.

An interesting article appeared on CNBC.com about the Q Score for LeBron James after his decision to leave the Cleveland Cavaliers and join the Miami Heat in the summer of 2010. Prior to his decision, 24% of the general population viewed him in a positive light while 22% viewed him negatively. After he announced his decision on a prime time television special, only 14% of those polled viewed him positively (a 41% drop in popularity) while 39% viewed him in a negative light (a 77% increase). His new Q Score placed him among the six most disliked sports personalities, behind Michael Vick, Tiger Woods, Terrell Owens, Chad Ochocinco and Kobe Bryant. Whether that will discourage licensees from taking a license remains to be seen, but what it probably does mean is that fewer companies will be interested and their financial offers may be less attractive.

Licensing consultants might also want to run their own market studies or surveys to determine the merchandising potential of a property. These are done in much the same way that toy companies will play or market test a new toy product, using mockups of potential licensed products and gauging the reaction of consumers to such products. There are a number of independent market research and survey companies who will conduct such research and even run surveys to gauge consumer reaction to products that might bear a particular property.

These surveys can also be helpful in determining the best way to actually use a particular property on products. Such surveys may not only help the property owner with its subsequent licensing program but may even give the property owner some insight on how to best present the property on its own primary products. This type of data can be invaluable for future licensees and may actually help convince an otherwise reluctant licensee to take a license.

Any or all of these steps will help the property owner make that all important determination—is my property the type of property that, if licensed, will help a licensee sell its products or services? If, after such an evaluation, the answer to that question is in the affirmative, the property owner is ready to proceed to the next step in the process.

4.3   Ownership Considerations

Once it has been determined that the property has a potential value for use as a licensing property, the actual work begins. The property owner must confirm that it in fact owns the property to be licensed or, at the very least, controls the licensing rights to that property.

While these considerations may appear rather straight forward, this is not always the case and, if overlooked at an early stage, may have enormous consequences. One such example is the battle between MGA Entertainment and Mattel over the BRATZ property. Clearly, MGA Entertainment developed and extensively marketed the property but Mattel claimed that, since the original designer had been working for Mattel at the time of its creation, Mattel owned the underlying rights to the property. This dispute led to years of expensive litigation and, during the pendency of the dispute, cast a giant shadow over the viability of the property in the marketplace.

Confirming that the property owner does own or control the rights to the property being licensed is essential before proceeding further. In virtually every license agreement, the licensor is required to warrant to potential licensees that it owns or controls rights to the property and has the ability to grant the license. Should another party claim ownership in the property (even a related entity), the licensor may find itself in a breach situation that could potentially place the entire program in jeopardy. Under companion indemnity obligations in many license agreements, a licensor may be potentially liable for any damages that its licensee might suffer should it turn out that another party actually was the rightful owner of the property.

This inquiry is usually not necessary in connection with the licensing of a corporate brand that has been used for decades, if not centuries. For example, when the Coca-Cola Company decided to develop a licensing program for a trademark that it has owned and used for more than a hundred years, there may not have been the need to consider this issue beyond simply looking at the face of its federal trademark registration(s).

That said, the fact that a property owner may own a trademark for use on one category of products does not necessarily mean that it owns it for other categories. For reasons that will be described more fully in this chapter and the next, trademark rights are typically specific to particular product categories. The property owner must make certain that it not only has rights to use the trademark on its own products, but that it is or will be the owner of such rights on its licensee's products and services.

The question of international rights is another important consideration, particularly if a worldwide licensing program is contemplated. Trademark rights are territorial, i.e., you acquire rights only in those countries where you have actually used the trademark and/or registered it. If, for example, the property owner is a U.S. corporation that has never conducted business outside the United States or registered its brand in other countries, a good time to find that out is before signing on as an international licensee.

Particular care should be taken when the property is a corporate brand, since some companies actually set up trademark holding companies that own the corporate trademarks and then license them to the individual subsidiaries. This is typically done for tax reasons. In such a situation, the property owner must make certain that the entity that actually owns the trademarks is the entity that will conduct the licensing program or, if not, that there is a license agreement in place that gives that entity the right to conduct the program and grant licenses or sub-licenses.

It should be appreciated that these inquiries and considerations typically only relate to situations where the property is protected as a trademark. When a property is protected under the copyright laws, the considerations concerning product categories and countries are far less important since copyrights are not product specific and, under international conventions, they provide greater protection internationally.

The licensing of potentially copyrighted artwork does, however, present different problems, since the issues involving creation and ownership can be complex. Some of the questions that need to be asked in such situations are:

- If the creators of the property were not employees of the property owner, did they perform tasks under a "work for hire" agreement or did they otherwise validly assign their rights to the property owner?

- Were the creators of the property under any obligation or agreement with another party that might prevent them from validly conveying their rights to the property, e.g., BRATZ?

- Does the property include any components that were licensed (not assigned) to the property owner, and, if so, are these rights conveyable to licensees?

- If there are multiple layers in a corporate structure, does the entity that will be conducting the licensing program actually own or have a right to use the property?

- In the case of studio licensing, are there conflicting agreements with producers, directors, talent, etc. that might impact the studio's ability to conduct a licensing program, or provide rights to essential elements such as actors' likenesses?

- Are there any conflicting agreements involving the property that may limit what the property owner can do with the property, e.g., rights of first refusals, options or security agreements?

Of the above questions, the one that can be of greatest concern is where the property is created by an independent contractor rather than an employee. By law, if an employee creates such a copyrightable work, the employer is generally deemed the owner of that work by virtue of the employer/employee relationship. However, when the property is created by an independent contractor, the contractor may retain ownership of the copyright to the property if there was no written "work for hire" agreement in place with the property owner, or if the rights to it were not otherwise assigned.

The meaning of this is simple: if a company uses an independent contractor to develop artwork, etc., then it **MUST** have a written agreement with that contractor stating that such work was done on a "work for hire" basis or an agreement providing that the contractor assigns its copyright rights to the company, lest the contractor may be found to retain the copyright rights to the work.

Since many companies regularly use outside designers and independent contractors rather than employees to create new designs, this issue is a very important one and demands thorough consideration. There is no faster way to derail a licensing program than to discover that the licensor is not the owner of the property but, instead, it is actually owned by the outside designer who did the design work and retained the copyright rights.

As noted above, studio licensing presents some unique issues because the rights that they may wish to license are often multifaceted, with different elements derived from and potentially owned by different entities. Consider, for example, the STAR WARS property which consists of a number of different elements, including:

- STAR WARS logo;

- Character names, e.g., LUKE SKYWALKER;

- Representations of the actors playing the role of LUKE SKYWALKER;

- Images of the vehicles used in the motion picture;

- Images of weapons, used in the motion picture;

- The musical score played during the motion picture or voices of the actors; and

- Selected sets used in the motion picture.

In order to confirm ownership of each of these elements, it may be necessary to review literally dozens of agreements between all of the parties involved with the motion picture. Under normal circumstances, the studio owns the licensing rights but there are instances where a producer, writer, actor, vendor, supplier or even the creator of the property may have some residual rights that could potentially impact ownership of the licensed property and must be sorted out before a licensing program gets underway.

Similarly, when one is dealing with a television show that features a popular actor or actress, the line between what the studio may own versus what the actor playing the lead role may own can be blurry. For example, the television series "Everybody Loves Raymond" was based on the comedy of its star, Ray Romano. If, for example, a manufacturer wanted to produce a line of bobble head "Ray" dolls, would it need a license from the television studio or from the actor, or from both? Again, a careful review of all of the agreements is necessary to insure that the eventual licensor actually owns the rights being licensed.

A property owner needs to address and satisfactorily resolve all of these issues before embarking on a licensing program. Since virtually every issue is different, it is recommended that a property owner discuss its specific issues with their intellectual property counsel to avoid any surprises during the eventual licensing program.

4.4   Clearing Properties

The purpose of clearing a property for use in a licensing program is to make sure that when a licensee actually uses the property, such use will not infringe the rights of a third party. Licensees are typically not willing to take a license for a property that could potentially expose them to liability. As such, prudent property owners will want to first "clear" a property for all contemplated uses before proceeding further.

As noted before, trademark rights are category specific. Meaning, that when one adopts and acquires rights in a trademark for a particular category of good, its rights are typically limited to use of that property for that category (and, in some instances, to closely related categories) since unfettered use may potentially confuse consumers as to the source or origin of the related products.

It is not uncommon for two different owners to use the same mark for two different categories of goods. This happens quite often and is perfectly acceptable, provided that there is no "likelihood of confusion" between both uses. This is the reason why Paramount Pictures can own and use the mark PARAMOUNT for entertainment services while Paramount Chicken can own and use the identical PARAMOUNT mark for food products—the goods are sufficiently diverse that consumers would not be confused into believing that a Hollywood studio was producing chicken, or vice versa.

Similarly, Yale University is the owner of the YALE trademark for educational services but another company, Yale Security, has owned the same YALE mark for use on locks, keys and other related security products. Since educational services provided by an Ivy League university are sufficiently dissimilar from security locks and hardware, these parties have been able to operate side by side with no consumer confusion.

Before embarking on a licensing program, the property owner needs to be certain that no other party has adopted and started using its mark on products that it hopes to license in the future since, potentially,

67

these parties may have superior rights to the property owner. For example, because of the existence of Yale Security's use and registration of the YALE mark, Yale University would presumably not be able to grant licenses for goods that could arguably infringe the rights of Yale Security.

Again, trademarks are also territorial in nature. Simply because a party acquires rights for a trademark in the United States, doesn't necessarily mean that it has rights in other countries in the world unless it has taken appropriate steps to protect the mark in those countries.

How does one clear a trademark for use in a licensing program? The simple answer is to search, search, and then search some more. Generally speaking, trademark searches are conducted on a number of different levels. A good starting point for property owners is the website maintained by the United States Patent and Trademark Office ("PTO") at www.uspto.gov, which is available at no charge to the public and includes existing United States trademark registrations as well as pending applications. The PTO database is relatively current and is an excellent starting point for any search.

Additionally, it may be wise to run an Internet search using any of the major search engines to see if anyone is using the proposed property or mark for the same or similar types of products.

Unless a worldwide licensing program is absolutely ruled out, it is advisable to also search on the various international databases. The WIPO database is one place where international trademark searching can be done and is accessible at www.wipo.int/ipdl/en/madrid.

At the conclusion of this initial round of searching, the property owner should have an excellent idea whether there are other parties who may have acquired rights in the property that could potentially conflict with their licensee's use of the property.

A WORD OF WARNING—it is the rare trademark that is cleared for use in all classes in all countries. Some conflicts will almost always be found and it is, therefore, prudent for a property owner to consult with its intellectual property counsel to consider all of the references found and obtain an opinion that use of the property for the contemplated licensed products will not infringe the rights of a third party.

An intellectual property attorney may want to expand the search, using more extensive databases that include state trademark office records and, if warranted, expand the international portion of the search.

Similarly, it may well be advisable to request that an outside search firm conduct an extensive common law search to determine whether another party might be actually using the mark but never got around to registering it since use of a trademark is sufficient to create rights in the mark. One of the more prominent trademark search firms is CompuMark Thomson at www.compumark.thomson.com.

It should also be appreciated that the line between whether or not use of a particular mark on a certain product is likely to cause confusion with a slightly different mark on a different product is a complex one. If there is any doubt, the advice of the property owner's intellectual property counsel should be sought.

Clearing artwork or material that is otherwise covered by a copyright is much more difficult and time consuming. This is due, in large measure, to the vast number of copyrights that have been registered with the U.S. Copyright Office as well as the difficulty in being able to quickly and easily search them. For example, there may well be thousands of copyright registrations for "superhero characters" but without manually reviewing each of these images, it is difficult to determine whether a new superhero character is in fact substantially similar to a prior copyrighted one. As such, despite conducting a copyright search, one never truly knows whether they have found the most relevant references.

Another inherent problem with copyright searching stems from the fact that copyright owners do not always register their copyright claims immediately, if at all. They may choose to wait to file an application only if an infringement problem surfaces.

Actual copyright searching may not always be necessary, however, since the basis for any claim of copyright infringement is actual copying. If the creator of the property is *absolutely* certain that its work is original and was not copied from another's work, there may not be a need to perform any copyright search since, under such a scenario, there could be no copyright infringement. Reliance on the creator's assurance that the work was not copied, however, is very thin reed since memories fade and what one may consider inspiration for a new work, others might consider slavish copying.

The courts do recognize that proving actual copying is difficult, if not impossible and, as a result, permit a copyright owner to establish infringement by showing that the alleged infringer had access to the copyrighted work and that the two works are "substantially similar."

Finally, there is the issue of "public domain" material. Material that was never protected, or material whose protection expired, is in the public domain and can be freely adopted by all. Some properties, by their very nature, are in the public domain. One example of a public domain property that was successfully licensed is the Statute of Liberty in New York City. The fact that it was in the public domain did not, however, prevent the Statute of Liberty Foundation from developing and conducting a very lucrative licensing program to commemorate its 100th anniversary in 1976. The Foundation created an "official" artist's rendering of the famous structure, obtained appropriate trademark and copyright protection for the rendering, and then proceeded to license the rights to it. The program would go on to generate millions of dollars for the Foundation.

While non-licensed manufacturers could certainly produce their own representations of the famous lady based on their own designs, they could not use any of the IP that had been protected by the Foundation. As it turned out, the public flocked to the "official" products over the unlicensed imitations.

When considering public domain material, a property owner must be creative, attempt to develop some form of IP protection and use that IP protection as the basis of its program.

Chapter 5

Protecting Licensing Properties

5.1 Introduction

Once a property owner has identified the property to be licensed, determined that it is the true owner of that property and there are no potentially conflicting rights, and confirmed that a licensee's use will not infringe the rights of any other party, the next step is to take the necessary measures to protect it BEFORE actually commencing with the licensing program. The process of securing protection for the property at an early stage is vitally important, since most licensees will insist that the licensor have some form of intellectual property protection in place prior to signing a license agreement that will obligate them to pay the licensor for the right to use the property.

Even if the licensee is "trusting," it will still require that the licensor obtain some protection for the property as soon as practical. A licensee is not being unreasonable in asking the property owner to put such protection in place since, once the licensee actually starts to sell licensed products and pay a royalty for such right, it is going to want assurance from the licensor that its competitors cannot compete with it on a royalty-free basis, thereby undercutting the value of the license.

5.2 Developing a Protection Plan

While most property owners and licensees agree that licensed properties must be protected against unauthorized use, the specific form of protection applied will be dictated by the type of property, e.g., as a trademark, copyright or under the right of publicity or patent laws. The property owner should work with its intellectual property counsel to determine the most cost effective way to protect the property.

The three statutory forms of intellectual property protection include patents, copyrights, and trademarks. Additionally, many states in the United States (although few other countries) recognize the "right of publicity," which provides celebrities with a protectable right in their name, image and likeness. Utility patents are used to protect functional devices and inventions and are rarely used in protecting merchandising properties, although some features of a licensed product may be patented.

71

Design patents are used to protect the ornamental appearance of articles of manufacture and, like utility patents, are rarely used to protect merchandising properties.

Most licensing properties in the merchandising area are protected as trademarks and/or copyrights. A trademark may constitute any word, name, design, logo or shape that functions as an indicator of the source, origin or sponsorship of a product or service. Copyrights protect original works of authorship that are fixed in tangible mediums of expression and include, for example, literary works, pictorial or graphic designs, motion pictures and sound recordings.

To illustrate, the design or image of the MICKEY MOUSE character may be copyrighted as a graphic design. When that image is applied to a product such as, for example, a coffee mug, the same image functions in a trademark sense in that it serves as an indicator that the property owner, Disney, "sponsored" or "licensed" the mug.

It should be appreciated that trademarks and copyrights have specific advantages, as well as disadvantages. For example, copyright protection is immediate. Rights are created upon the creation of a work. Moreover, registration of a copyright is easy and inexpensive and the registration affords the owner some degree of international protection.

Trademark protection is similarly immediate; one acquires trademark rights when the mark is applied to a product and sold or offered for sale in commerce. The registration process is, however, more complicated, more expensive and ultimately will only protect the property owner in the country where registration is sought. In order to protect the trademark in other countries, additional registrations must be obtained.

Perhaps the most significant difference between the two is the length of protection that each offers. Copyright rights are valid for only a finite period of time while trademark rights may continue for so long as the mark is actually being used in commerce by either the property owner or its licensee. That is the reason why owners of some of the classic properties like MICKEY MOUSE and PETER RABBIT rely on both forms of statutory protection. That way, when the copyrights in the graphic designs expire, their property owners can still rely on trademark protection which will last for so long as the marks continue to be used.

Celebrity rights are protected under what's called a "right of publicity" and which is mostly governed by state law. The right of publicity protects a celebrity's name, image, signature, voice, etc., against commercial exploitation by another. In most cases, registration of the right is required. The right of publicity can also extend to deceased celebrities, although many states require that the right be exercised during the celebrity's lifetime for protection to extend after their death.

There is an obvious overlap between trademarks, copyrights and the right of publicity and celebrities typically rely on all three forms of protection to protect their rights. The trademark laws are used to protect their name when it is used on a product; the right of publicity is used to protect their name and image; and the copyright laws are used to protect a specific image or representation of the celebrity that may form the basis of a licensing program.

5.3   Trademark Protection

Trademark protection extends to any word, name, symbol, or device, or any combination, that is used to identify and distinguish an individual's goods from those of another and to indicate the source or origin of such goods.

Service marks are marks that are used in association with services rather than products. For example, when the mark McDONALD'S® appears on the outside of a McDonald's® restaurant, that mark is functioning as a service mark to identify the restaurant as one owned by the McDonald's Corp. When, however, it appears on a hamburger wrapper, it is being used as a trademark.

While trademark rights are acquired in the United States upon the first use of the mark, this is not the case in some other countries. Registration of the mark is always advisable and, in some countries, essential to obtaining protection. Registration of a mark in the United States provides certain procedural and substantive advantages for the owner, including a right to bring suit in federal court for trademark infringement and the establishment of constructive notice of the owner's claim in the mark. A trademark registration will also permit the owner to record the registration with the U.S. Customs Service to stop the importation of infringing and counterfeit products at the border.

Most licensees will demand that the licensor register the mark for the goods or services it will be selling under the license or, at the very least, have applied to register the mark since they want as much protection as the property owner can provide against unauthorized competition.

The requirements for obtaining a trademark registration in the United States are straightforward. In order to be registered, the mark must be distinctive, i.e., it must distinguish or be capable of distinguishing the owner's products or services over that of another.

That means that the mark cannot be merely descriptive of the goods or services for which registration is being sought, nor can it be a generic reference to the product or service. For example, WINNIE THE POOH is potentially registrable for a coffee mug since it is neither the name of the product nor does it describe the product. If, however, one sought to register the words BLUE MUG for a blue coffee mug, it would probably be refused registration because it would be considered descriptive of the product, i.e., a blue mug.

A trademark applicant must be the first party to have used that mark for the subject product or service and he cannot be aware of any other uses of the mark that might be confusingly similar to its mark and use. Thus, if XYZ Company applied to register WINNIE THE POOH for a plush bear based on very recent use, that application would undoubtedly be rejected on the grounds of Disney's earlier use and registration(s).

Trademark applications can be filed with the U.S. Patent & Trademark Office ("USPTO") in one of two ways, as: (1) a use-based application, relying on the applicant's actual use of the mark in interstate commerce; or (2) an intent-to-use application, based on the applicant's *bona fide* intention to use the mark in interstate commerce. Acceptable use of a trademark can be established either by the owner or its licensee.

For a use-based application, the applicant must state the date that the mark was first used on the goods, in both intrastate and interstate commerce, and provide specimens showing how the mark was actually applied to the goods or used in conjunction with the services for which registration is sought.

In each type of application, the applicant must identify the mark to be registered and the goods or services on which the mark has or will be used. The USPTO divides all types of goods and services into 45 different classes and an applicant must select one or more of them for which registration is being sought.

Trademark applications can be filed either by a paper filing or an electronic filing. The USPTO filing fee for a paper trademark application is (as of 2010) $375 per class, or $325 per class if filed electronically. Both types of applications are prosecuted by the PTO in the same manner.

Typically, the property owner will determine what classes to include in the application after consultation with its licensing director and will include those classes where licensing activity is expected.

Most trademark applications for merchandising properties are filed on an intent-to-use basis since they are often filed well in advance of the commencement of the licensing program and, thus, before any use has occurred. The mark must ultimately be used on actual products before any registration can issue, although the property owner may have as much as four years to commence use.

A **WORD OF CAUTION**: the mere filing of an intent-to-use application alone doesn't give the owner any enforceable rights in the trademark until use actually starts. At that time, the property owner receives the benefit of the filing date of the original application, assuming that the application is still pending at the time. That means that the owner cannot sue an infringer for trademark infringement until it (or its licensee) actually commences use of the mark on the products.

As noted, there are 45 different classes of goods and services in which one can seek to register a mark. For licensing purposes, the most common classes in which registrations are typically sought are:

Class 9—Electrical and Scientific Apparatus (DVD's and video)

Class 14—Jewelry

Class 16—Paper Goods and Printed Matter

Class 18—Leather Goods

Class 20—Furniture and Articles Not Otherwise Classified

Class 21—Housewares and Glass

Class 25—Clothing

Class 28—Toys and Sporting Goods

Assuming that the trademark application meets the necessary requirements, it receives a filing date and serial number and is assigned to a Trademark Examining Attorney who will review the material and conduct a search to see if it is confusingly similar to any other mark.

The application will eventually be either allowed or finally rejected. Rejections can be appealed to an appeals board within the PTO. If it is allowed, the mark will be published for opposition and anyone can oppose registration if they believe that they have a basis for doing so.

Assuming that no one opposes the registration of the mark, the procedure differs between use-based applications and those filed on an intent-to-use basis. Unopposed use-based applications proceed directly to registration. Intent-to-use applications, however, will not be registered until use commences and the owner submits a Statement of Use.

Trademark registrations are granted for a term of ten years from the date of registration and may be renewed for an unlimited number of additional ten year terms upon a showing of continued use. Between the fifth and sixth year of the initial term, the owner must file a declaration demonstrating that the mark is still in use. Failure to file such a declaration will result in the cancellation of the registration.

Once a registration is cancelled (and assuming that the original registrant has ceased use of the mark), anyone may adopt the cancelled mark and commence their own use of the mark.

A WORD OF CAUTION: the fact that a trademark registration was cancelled doesn't necessarily mean that the original registrant lost its rights in that mark. Some registrations are inadvertently cancelled although use of the mark continues. In that situation, the owner still maintains its underlying rights in the mark and can simply apply to re-register that mark with the same date of first use in the original registration.

The ™ designation is used to identify a property that is considered a trademark by the owner but is not federally registered. Similarly, the designation ˢᴹ indicates that the word, symbol, or logo is considered by its owner to be a service mark. There is no particular legal necessity for inclusion of either designation other than to indicate to the public at large that the user considers it to be its trademark or service mark.

The ® symbol is used to designate a federally registered trademark. Some trademark owners prefer to use the designations "Registered in the U.S. Patent and Trademark Office" or "Reg. U.S. Pat.

& TM Off." This is a matter of choice, although the ® symbol is often preferable, simply because it's easier to place.

This is probably a good time to discuss good "trademark practice" for both the property owner and its licensees. The following simple guidelines should always be followed:

- Always use the trademark as an <u>adjective to describe the</u> <u>product</u> for which it is being used, e.g., a STAR WARS toy;

- Always capitalize <u>the trademark relative to the type of</u> <u>product</u> for which it is being used, e.g., a HARRY POTTER book;

- Never use the trademark as a noun or a verb or in the plural form, e.g., "I want to xerox the drawing"; and

- Always follow each usage of the property with an appropriate trademark notice, e.g., BATMAN^{TM} costume.

5.4   Copyright Protection

Copyright protection covers any original works of authorship fixed in a tangible medium of expression and typically includes the following:

- Literary works;

- Musical works, including any accompanying words;

- Dramatic works, including any accompanying music, pantomimes and choreographic works;

- Pictorial, graphic, and sculptural works;

- Motion pictures and other audiovisual works; and

- Sound recordings.

The actual term of a copyright varies, depending upon the type of work, when it was created and whether it was published or not. In most instances, the term is the life of the author plus 70 years. For works of corporate authorship, the term is typically 95 years from publication or 120 years from creation, whichever first occurs. It should be appreciated that these terms were recently extended.

As stated, copyright rights to a potentially copyrightable work arise upon the creation of the original work. Under prior law, it was necessary to apply a copyright notice to the work in order to obtain such right, but that requirement was eliminated in 1989 when the United States became a signatory to the Berne Convention.

While the application of a copyright notice is no longer required in order to create rights in the work, the application of such a notice and the registration of the copyright with the Copyright Office is good practice as it gives notice to potential infringers and offers certain procedural and substantive advantages.

The three elements of the copyright notice are:

- The symbol ©, the word "Copyright," or the abbreviation "Copr.";

- The year of first publication of the work; and

- The name of the owner of the copyright (e.g., a complete copyright notice might be: © LIMA 2010).

If the copyrighted goods are sound recordings, a circled P is used rather than the ©. The legend "All Rights Reserved" should follow the standard copyright notice when distribution is contemplated in South America in order to conform to the requirements of the Buenos Aires Copyright Convention.

The copyright notice should be affixed to the copies in such a manner and location as to give reasonable notice of the claim of copyright. It should also be permanently legible to an ordinary user of the work under normal conditions of use.

It is advisable to file a copyright application to register the copyright claim with the Copyright Office, since copyright registrations provide the owner with a number of advantages, including the right to bring an action for copyright infringement and, if successful, to obtain statutory damages and an award of attorneys' fees against an infringer.

To be eligible for copyright protection, the material must be the original work of the author and it must fall within one or more of the protectable categories listed above. While the actual amount of originality required for copyright protection is unclear, it is generally acknowledged that the standard of originality is less than the novelty requirement for patent protection.

Registering a copyright with the Copyright Office is relatively simple and inexpensive. The process requires only the submission of the application for copyright registration (obtainable at www.copyright.gov); deposit of the work for which copyright protection is claimed and the payment of the statutory fee of $35 for an on-line application, or $50 for a paper application (as of 2010).

Copyright registration affords the property owner the exclusive right to:

(1) Reproduce the copyrighted work in copies or phonorecords;

(2) Prepare derivative works based on the copyrighted work;

(3) Distribute copies or phonorecords of the copyrighted work through sale or other transfer of ownership, or by rental, lease, or lending;

(4) Publicly perform or display the copyrighted work, including the individual images of a motion picture or other audiovisual work; and

(6) Publicly perform the copyrighted work by means of digital audio transmission sound recordings.

One may seek copyright protection as a "derivative work", i.e., deriving from an earlier copyrighted work. The scope of rights that an owner may have in a derivative work is dependent on the amount of creativity that it added to the original work.

A significant limitation on copyright protection is the "fair use" doctrine, which permits one to use a copyrighted work without the owner's consent for certain specific purposes, e.g., criticism, comment, news reporting, teaching, scholarship, or research. Fair use is more liberally applied when the copyrighted work is primarily factual and informational in nature, e.g., a news story rather than a work of mass market fiction. Similarly, the doctrine is also liberally applied when the use of verbatim quotations is required for accurate reporting.

Unfortunately, the standards for the application of the fair use doctrine are anything but clear. There is no judicial definition of what constitutes "fair use," although the Copyright Act does set forth the following factors to consider as to whether the use made of a work in any particular case is fair use:

(1)   The purpose and character of the use, including whether such use is of a commercial nature or is for nonprofit, educational purposes;

(2)   The nature of the copyrighted work;

(3)   The amount and substantiality of the portion used in relation to the copyrighted work as a whole; and

(4)   The effect of the use upon the potential market for or value of the copyrighted work.

In order to prove infringement, a copyright holder must establish ownership of a valid copyright and that the alleged infringer had actually copied the copyrighted work.

Since trying to prove that someone actually copied a work can be difficult, if not impossible, courts will permit a copyright owner to establish copying by circumstantial evidence, i.e., demonstrating that the alleged infringer had access to the copyrighted work and that the allegedly infringing work was "substantially similar" to the copyrighted work.

Attempting to prove copying by circumstantial evidence only establishes a presumption of copying which the alleged infringer may rebut by establishing that it independently created the work in question. It should be appreciated that while independent creation is a valid defense, when the two works are so similar that they are virtually identical, there is an inference that one was copied from the other.

Chapter 6

The Licensor—Licensee Relationship[1]

6.1 Introduction

Licensing is a process that is fundamentally based on two separate parties cooperating together to generate a product, service or promotion. The property owner/licensor and the licensee, who will manufacture or produce the licensed products, enter into a licensing agreement that will define the terms of their business relationship. The respective roles and obligations of each party are the focus of this chapter.

The age-old question, "Which came first, the chicken or the egg?" applies when assessing the roles that each party plays in licensing, as well as their relative importance. Fact is, it really doesn't matter which is more important or influential, since both the egg and the chicken perform a vital function in this relationship. Similarly, the willing participation and cooperation of both parties to a licensing agreement are also necessary if the collaboration is to succeed. Like the Chicken vs. Egg question, there is little purpose to assigning greater significance to one party over the other, as each plays a distinctive and integral role.

6.2 The License Agreement

In licensing, an intellectual property owner grants the right to use the property to a licensee in exchange for the payment of some form of financial consideration. Both parties must invest something up-front in order to profit from the relationship. The licensor has already made an investment, by virtue of developing and securing the necessary legal protection for a property that the licensee believes has value. The licensee, upon obtaining the license, is obligated to develop a desirable product, design attractive packaging, and manage the responsibilities associated with manufacturing, marketing, selling and delivering the licensed goods to the retailer and/or consumer. The premise upon which licensing operates is that each party receives something of value. The licensee obtains the right to use another party's intellectual property in

---

[1] Written by Danny Simon, a past LIMA Chairman and President, The Licensing Group, 6363 Wilshire Blvd., Ste. 305, Los Angeles, CA 90048

conjunction with its product or service, which should make it more attractive to consumers. The licensor, likewise, is compensated for the use of the property. Today, faced with rising expenses, a more difficult retail climate, and greater uncertainty as to which licenses will achieve sell-through success, licensees are commonly less willing to pay high advances and guarantees as the standard cost of doing business. With bidding wars over licensing rights that can push advances and guarantees into the stratosphere, and "sure-thing" licenses failing to deliver promised financial returns, many licensees feel warranted in refusing to make a significant up-front financial commitment to licensors on top of the investment that they will have to make to design, manufacture and market the licensed product.

The prevailing attitude among licensees today is that royalties must be earned through actual product sales, rather than on the basis of ambitious sales forecasts compiled before the licensed products are ever introduced at retail. With that said, however, advances and guarantees do serve a purpose and are very significant aspects of any licensing relationship.

6.3   Establishing Payment Terms

Naturally, in the course of negotiating any license agreement, the parties tend to focus most on the terms of the deal that relate to compensation. Licensing compensation typically includes three principle components: the guarantee, the advance, and the royalty rate. Despite what one may hear to the contrary, each figure is negotiable.

6.3.1   The Guarantee

The guarantee is an essential part of the formula for financial compensation contained in most license agreements. Although the licensor is entitled to earn a royalty on each licensed product sold, the rationale for including a guarantee is based on the fact that there is no assurance the product will succeed in the retail market *or* that the licensee will maximize the opportunity to use the licensed property during the term of the agreement. Therefore, the guarantee assures that, regardless of whether or not the licensee is able to successfully or fully exploit the licensing rights held, the licensor will receive a certain minimum amount of money for the rights that it has licensed.

The real question is, as it has always been, how do the parties establish a fair guarantee for those rights that the licensee is acquiring?

Be assured, a reasonable advance or guarantee is not some budget number that the licensor needs to achieve for his quarterly or yearly balance sheet, or some "ideal" dollar amount that would satisfy a producer or superior. Advances and guarantees must reflect realistic sales projections which, in some measure, are representative of the popularity of the property, the sales appeal of the product in question and, certainly, the current economic conditions of the marketplace.

If you are negotiating for the right to license a popular property, but in a product category that has only limited appeal, the financial terms should reflect both factors. The same is true if the general economic conditions of the market are soft and overall retail sales are down. These considerations must be taken into account in order to arrive at a financial compensation package that is both equitable and realistic for both parties to the agreement. To proceed otherwise, creates a lopsided deal that will prove difficult to enforce, is likely to be re-negotiated down the road or, worse, may strain future relations between the licensor and licensee.

Too often, license agreements are negotiated in the *heat of the moment*, with little thought given to the fact that there will be other properties and opportunities to consider in the future. It is this same mentality that can lead licensors to push for unreasonable and excessively high advances and guarantees; terms that might meet their own current budgetary demands, but which are otherwise impractical in the context of realistic sales projections or current market trends.

Likewise, throngs of unwitting licensees frequently overlook, or plainly ignore, glaring pitfalls when driven by impulse. Too many simply lock onto an attractive, potentially lucrative licensing opportunity in spite of the fact that the up-front obligations involved may be unwarranted.

6.3.2 The Advance

In order for any property to attract interest from licensees, it must exhibit a certain level of originality and appeal to convince them that, if used on licensed products, it can generate significant consumer sales.

When negotiating the terms of a license, it is reasonable to assume that the property owner has already made a considerable investment of time and money to create the property. This is the licensor's contribution to the licensing process. It cannot be overlooked and, as such, any fair licensing transaction should include some form of advance payment made up-front by the interested licensee for the right to use the property. Typically, the advance is payable upon signing of the license agreement. As its name implies, the advance (usually) represents a pre-payment of royalties that the licensee can credit towards future royalties due the licensor. The amount of the advance is frequently a percentage of the negotiated guarantee. Whether the advance is payable as a single payment upon signing the license agreement or made as a series of payments within a certain time frame, is always negotiable.

6.3.3   The Royalty Rate

In licensing, the main financial payoff for the licensor is the royalty payments. Royalties are generally based on a percentage of the licensee's wholesale sales of the licensed products. Like any other cost associated with the creation of the licensed item, it is factored into the retail selling price as a cost that is passed on to the consumer.

For almost every type of product imaginable, there is a pre-existing average royalty range. Whether the royalty agreed upon by the parties is within, above or below the average royalty is often a reflection of consumer demand. Greater demand entitles the licensor to a higher royalty, while less popular licenses may command royalties that are at or below the average royalty rate.

However, consideration should always been given to the fact that the royalty rate will affect the retail price. Thus, charging too high a royalty can actually have an adverse effect if it inflates the retail price of a licensed product above what the consumer is willing pay for such product.

The ideal financial terms are those that provide the licensor a reasonable (advance) and (guarantee) as well as a royalty rate that falls within the traditional range of royalties charged for that product category. Under such terms, the parties should anticipate that earned royalty payments will ultimately exceed the negotiated advance and/or guarantee.

6.4   Product Development

Once a license agreement is in place between the licensor and licensee, focus shifts to developing the licensed product. This phase requires close collaboration between the parties and specific performances by each in order to create an appealing, marketable and quality product that consumers will want to buy.

6.4.1   Style Guide

A primary responsibility of the licensor is to furnish the necessary guidelines that the licensee will use in developing the licensed products. This material is usually provided in the form of a style guide. The scope and detail of the materials required is totally dependent on the type of property in question but, at a minimum, it must contain enough information for a licensee to be able to create the product and ancillary materials in accordance with the terms of the license agreement.

The best way to build a strong and readily identifiable product image is through the uniform and consistent use of trademarks, images and color palettes as set forth in the style guide. This consistency is important to developing everything from products and packaging, to advertising and press releases. The style guide should provide the licensee with all the information needed to create a consistent look and feel for the products developed under the licensing program. The essential elements of a style guide are discussed in greater detail in Chapter 11.

6.4.2   Legal Notices

As all merchandising licenses are based on the use of properties protected by copyright and/or trademarks, licensees are required to include such information on products and packaging. Instructions concerning the content, form and placement of such legal notices must be clearly communicated by the licensor.

6.4.3   Forms

Most licensors have various standard forms that the licensee is required to use when submitting materials for approval, as well as royalty payments. Therefore, a licensor should provide the licensee with samples of all required forms at the commencement of the license.

6.4.4   Samples

Sometime prior to, or shortly after, introducing a licensed product, the licensee will need to deliver samples of each licensed product to the licensor for approval. The actual number of samples required by any given licensor varies and is generally negotiable. One factor in determining the number of required samples is the price of the product, i.e., licensors may consent to the submission of fewer samples for higher priced goods.

6.5   Approval Process

Virtually every license agreement requires that the licensee obtain approval from the licensor for all products, packaging, promotional and advertising materials associated with the licensing program. While the process of submitting samples for approval is always spelled out in the license agreement, it is good practice to also include this information in the style guide to ensure compliance and, therefore, expedite the turnaround time. Failure by the licensee to obtain such approvals is considered a material breach of the license agreement, and provides the licensor with the right to terminate the licensing agreement.

As the licensor may request changes to products and packaging, licensees will be well advised to make such submissions as early as possible in the product development process so as to avoid having to make costly changes or incurring significant time delays. Regarding approval-related questions, a good rule of thumb for any licensee is: *when in doubt, ask.*

For their part, licensors have an obligation to treat product and packaging approvals as a significant priority. Licensors need to appreciate that licensees frequently operate under time sensitive production schedules when it comes to developing products and packaging designs. Since approvals must be obtained before production can commence, delayed responses from a licensor during the approvals process can adversely affect a licensee's ability to remain on schedule and lead to costly delays in products reaching the retail shelf.

6.6   Royalty Payments and Statements

Once the licensed product has been approved, manufactured and delivered to the retail shelf, the licensee is faced with its continuing obligation of providing the licensor with timely payment of any royalties due, accompanied by a detailed royalty statement. Typically, royalties are calculated and payable on a quarterly basis, with payment and statements due 30 to 45 days after the end of the quarter.

The question of how the licensee is to calculate the royalties due from sales of the licensed products is always defined in the license agreement. The standard practice in the licensing industry is to base royalty payments on the licensee's gross sales of the licensed product, less certain agreed upon credits and deductions. This calculation represents the licensee's "Net Sales," which is the sum used as the basis upon which royalties are determined. Close attention must be paid as to what constitutes allowable deductions, since failure to clarify this can easily result in an under or over payment of royalties. For more detailed discussion on net sales and permissible deductions, see Chapters 7 and 8.

Typically, licensees are also required to submit a royalty report along with the payment of the royalty. Often the licensor will supply a form that the licensee must use when submitting these reports. Like the question of allowable deductions, there is no "industry standard" royalty report form. Generally speaking, however, the license agreement will detail what type of information the royalty report must include and in what format it is to be submitted.

As licensees are often obligated to supply the licensor with sales information on each licensed item sold, the licensee is well advised to understand exactly what level of detail is required, prior to commencing sale of the licensed products. In doing so, the licensee can more easily provide the required information due along with the royalty payment.

6.7   Product Liability Insurance

In our litigious society, product liability insurance naming the licensor as an insured party on the policy is a must. Though most manufacturers will have such insurance, undoubtedly the license agreement will specify the minimum level of product liability insurance the licensee must carry, coupled with the demand that the licensee add the licensor (and licensing agent if there is one involved in negotiating the license agreement) as insured party(s). The licensee will be required to provide a certificate of liability insurance to the licensor, which must be furnished prior to the distribution of any licensed merchandise.

Like other elements of the license agreement, the amount of minimum liability insurance coverage is negotiable. The average minimum level of coverage, however, is about three million dollars.

6.8   Terms and Extensions

If the licensee has the right to renew the license agreement for one or more extension terms (licensing term(s) that follow the original term), frequently the licensee is compelled to deliver notice to the licensor of the intent to renew the license agreement, sometime before the renewal date. The required time period as to when the licensee must provide such notice will be addressed in the original license agreement. The average time frame for delivery of such notice is usually 30 to 90 days prior to the end date of the license agreement.

The licensee's right to renew the license agreement is (usually) subject to the licensee meeting some pre-determined financial threshold, which is often expressed as a minimum amount of royalty income paid during the term of the license agreement. Like so many other points in the licensing agreement, the terms that a licensee must meet in order to have the right to renew the agreement are subject to negotiation. If the license agreement provides for the right to renew, licensees are well advised to calendar the date that notice to the licensor is due. Failure to provide such notice may provide the licensor with the right to disallow the grant of an extended term.

Chapter 7

Royalty Rates

7.1 Introduction

While there are a host of different ways to "value" a license, most merchandising license agreements require that the licensee pay a royalty to the licensor for the right to use the licensed property. A royalty is a percentage of the licensee's net sales of licensed products paid to the licensor. *gross sales ≠ Net Income*

The reason why the royalty model is so commonly used is that it permits the licensor to be able to share in the licensee's success in selling its licensed products. As the licensee's sales (and attendant revenues) increase, the amount of royalties paid to the licensor increase proportionately. Thus, the licensor is able to share in the licensee's "upside."

The licensor's "downside" is protected by the requirement that a licensee pay a guaranteed minimum royalty, or simply a "minimum guarantee." That way, the licensor is assured of receiving a certain minimum amount in the event that the licensee's sales (and corresponding royalty payments) prove to be less than robust.

7.2 Setting Royalty Rates

In the overall licensing world, there are four different methodologies used by economists to establish or set an appropriate royalty rate for a particular transaction:

- Cost Approach
- 25% Rule
- Income Approach
- Market Approach

The first three valuation techniques are primarily used for setting royalty rates in transactions that involve patent and/or technology transfer licensing. In these areas, there can be a vast difference between the types of properties being licensed, e.g., software, computer hardware, biotech, chemical processing methods, etc., as well as the manner in which the licensee actually uses the licensed property. As such, there are aspects of virtually every technology licensing transaction that make comparing them almost impractical.

The "cost approach" measures how much the licensee would have to invest if it were to develop the property itself. It then arrives at a royalty rate that would compensate the licensor for the approximate amount of such a hypothetical investment. This is clearly the least relevant method for arriving at a reasonable royalty for the licensing of any type of intellectual property, particularly a merchandising property, since it ignores the market value of the property or its income potential.

The "25% rule" assumes that the royalty rate should equal approximately 25% of the licensee's gross profits from the sale of licensed products on a pre-tax basis. This method ignores the fact that every licensed property is different and that there are marketing costs associated with the sale of such products and an inherent risk. The 25% rule also fails to consider what the impact of a 25% royalty rate would be on the retail price of the licensed item.

The "income approach" measures how much the property can generate over its lifetime, considering such factors as: (i) the amount of income that can be generated by the property; (ii) the duration of the projected income stream; and (iii) the risk associated with the use of the property. It is, perhaps, the fairest means of establishing royalty rates.

Finally, there is the "market approach" which is the approach frequently used in the merchandising area for setting royalty rates, particularly for "average" properties that are being licensed for commodity type products, e.g., T-shirts, board games, etc. This approach is, by far, the easiest to understand and to calculate. The "market approach" considers the rates charged in the market for similar types of properties and then compares the particular property to the overall market. It requires both an active public market, and an abundance of comparable properties. When considering average properties and commodity products for merchandising, both factors are widely present and the resulting royalty charged will most likely allow the licensed item to be marketed at an attractive price point.

The "market approach" is used every day by real estate brokers in attempting to arrive at an asking price for a piece of real estate, i.e., by comparing the property in question to comparable properties in the neighborhood during the relevant period. The method is also commonly used for determining the value of franchises, computer hardware, vehicles, and the like. This is not meant to imply that a licensing property is the same as a house, but the analogy is being made simply as an example of how the valuation process typically works.

Economists who rely on the market approach frequently build databases of royalty rates charged for comparable licensing transactions in related areas. From that, they can develop a matrix for arriving at an appropriate royalty rate for a particular property when it is being licensed for a particular product.

The challenge, of course, is to find truly comparable properties to compare or, for that matter, comparable products. For example, both STAR WARS and MEN IN BLACK are properties based on popular motion pictures, yet one commanded royalty rates significantly higher than the other. The reasons for this difference are attributable to a number of factors, including:

- The strength of the property in the particular industry;
- Whether the property is dominant in its industry;
- The existence of an identifiable customer base;
- The demographics of the audience;
- The strength of the licensees that were brought onboard; and
- The commercial history of the property.

So, how does one actually arrive at the "right" royalty rate for a property when licensing it for a specific product?

For the experienced licensor with a long track record, the inquiry typically starts with looking at the last deal the property owner did for a comparable property and a similar product. In most cases, the licensor then will "adjust" that rate depending upon a number of factors unique to the specific deal, e.g., the licensee's anticipated profit margin, the extent of the competition, the popularity of the particular property, the manner in which it is going to be sold, whether there are significant development costs in creating the products, whether the licensee will need to invest significant sums in advertising and promoting the product, whether the property is protectable, etc. In some instances the desired retail price point may also be a factor in establishing the royalty rate.

Licensors need to be fully conscious of the potential problems that its licensees will face in the marketplace and the economics of their particular industry. If a licensor insists on charging a very high royalty for a low margin item, the licensee runs the risk of having to set the price too high relative to its competition, thereby potentially pricing the product above a competitive price point.

The food industry is a prime example of one that typically commands lower rates, since most food producers operate on very small margins. Most licensors charge substantially lower royalty rates for these types of products, e.g., perhaps half of the royalty rate charged for a higher margin item such as apparel. This differentiation is also one reason why some of the larger licensing departments organize their sales staff by industry. By enabling each group to develop an understanding of the particular dynamics at play in a given industry, they are better positioned to work intelligently with their licensees on arriving at a compensation package that makes financial sense for everyone.

Setting a royalty rate for a new property that is controlled by an unproven owner can, however, be more challenging and especially so if the licensed product being considered is unique. It would be advisable for a new property owner to consult with agents and other licensors in its category and to review industry surveys and reference materials.[2]

Royalty rate negotiations are ultimately the same; the licensor will seek the highest rate possible while the licensee will want to pay a much lower rate. In most negotiations, the parties tend to meet somewhere in the middle and arrive at a compromise rate. That said, a licensee needs to provide the licensor with justified reasons for lowering the rate—something more than simply, "I can't pay that much." Reasonable licensors will usually listen to such arguments and, if valid, may well adjust the rate accordingly.

Negotiations for hot properties can be the most difficult, particularly where there is competition for a particular license, or a licensee needs to appease the licensor in order to achieve a particular goal and maintain its relationship. In such a situation, a licensor may be less willing to compromise on the royalty rate.

There are different theories concerning how to open royalty rate negotiations with licensees. Some licensors prefer to avoid setting a figure directly and ask that the licensee simply "make them an offer."

---

[2] Such references include the annual series published by Aspen Publishers, *Licensing Royalty Rates* by Battersby and Grimes; EPM's *The Licensing Letter's Royalty Trends Report*; ABA Press' *Fundamentals of Intellectual Property Valuation* by Anson; and Wiley's *Royalty Rates for Licensing Intellectual Property* by Parr.

The number of problems with this approach could fill up a book of its own, since it implies that the property owner is truly receptive to considering "offers," which is rarely the case…unless, of course, the offer is higher than what they had originally contemplated. Such an approach creates an "auction" environment, which might well work on eBay, but is generally not preferable for the rest of the world.

Most licensors follow a more traditional approach, in which they advise a licensee of what their average royalty rate is for the property and see where that takes them. Such an approach certainly places each prospective licensee on an equal footing and avoids surprises for both parties. Even those licensors, however, are typically prepared to negotiate lower royalty rates for products that command lower margins.

Whichever approach a property owner takes, the most important thing is that it needs to carefully consider its property, including its strengths and weaknesses, fully investigate the market, take the licensee's perspective into consideration and, ultimately, agree to a royalty rate that will make the license workable for all parties. The property owner needs to remain flexible with regard to the establishment of the actual royalty charged since, at the end of the day, it is the licensee who will determine the "right" royalty rate for a particular deal.

For example, a licensor may truly believe that its property is the next WINNIE THE POOH and establish a royalty rate of 14% because that is what he thinks Disney gets for POOH. When the licensing program gets launched, however, and the licensor finds no licensees interested in paying that rate, the licensor will need to "rethink" its strategy if it is truly interested in actually having a licensing program.

Reality is the name of the game. Many a licensing program has failed simply because the property owner arbitrarily sets a standard royalty rate that was simply not appropriate for the particularly property.

7.3   Types of Royalty Rates

The licensing industry has changed dramatically over the past twenty years and, in response to these changes, most licensors actually have different average royalty rates to accommodate the various ways that licensed products are sold in the marketplace. These specific rates include:

- Domestic Royalty Rate
- FOB Royalty Rate

93

- Royalty Rate on Direct Sales
- Royalty Rate for Services
- Sublicensing Royalty Rate
- Split Royalty Rate

7.3.1 Royalty Rates on Domestic Sales

When a licensor refers to its average royalty rate, it is usually referring to the royalty rate that is applied to licensed products sold on a domestic, landed basis through normal or conventional channels of distribution, i.e., typically from domestic warehouses to a distributor or directly to a retailer. This is also the royalty rate typically reported in most of the studies on royalty rates and other types are normally adjusted off of this rate.

It should be appreciated that in the domestic market, royalty rates are rarely, if ever, applied to the retail selling price of a licensed product. There are, of course, exceptions, e.g., publishing, video games, etc., but, as a rule, it is the licensee's wholesale selling price that will typically serve as a starting point for determining the royalty base.

The domestic, landed royalty rate can apply to virtually all types of licensed products, irrespective of where they are manufactured, provided that they are actually sold to the retailer (or wholesaler) on a domestic landed basis with the manufacturer bearing the cost of shipping the product from its point of manufacture.

The price to the retailer or distributor is a "loaded" price and typically includes the licensee's cost of manufacturing the product, advertising or promotional costs, shipping expenses from the point of manufacture, insurance, possibly an agent's or sales representative's commission, taxes, and a profit. The combination of all these costs and expenses is what determines the manufacturer's wholesale price.

7.3.2 Royalty Rates on F.O.B. Sales

With many licensed products being manufactured off-shore, it has become common for retailers to take delivery of these products on an "F.O.B." (free-on-board) basis at their point of manufacture, which is typically in the Far East. The retailer then assumes the responsibility and cost for the transportation of these products to their eventual point of sale.

By taking possession at the point of manufacture and bearing the transportation costs, the retailer is frequently able to negotiate a significant reduction in the selling price of the product, often by as much as 30-40% from the domestic landed price. Retailers have found that they may be able to obtain lower shipping costs than a licensee, because they are often able to consolidate products from a number of manufacturers and may also avail themselves of larger volume discounts that might be unavailable to a manufacturer.

From the licensor's perspective, this practice can have a dramatic impact on the royalty revenue that it actually receives from a licensee. If the licensor applied the same royalty rate used for domestic sales to F.O.B. sales (which can be sold for as much as 40% below the domestic landed price), the licensor would receive significantly lower royalty revenue due to the product's reduced sales price.

For example, if a 10% royalty rate was applied to a $10 product sold on a landed basis, the licensor would receive $1 in actual royalty revenue for every item sold on a landed basis. If that same $10 product was sold on an F.O.B. basis to the retailer at $6, the licensor would only receive $0.60 in royalty revenue for every item sold on a FOB basis. Thus, maintaining the same royalty rate for both types of sales could effectively reduce the licensor's actual earned royalty income by as much as 40%.

As a result, most licensors will provide for an "F.O.B. Royalty Rate" on goods sold in such manner. Frequently, the differential is at least one percentage point and, more commonly, between 2 and 4 percentage points higher than the standard royalty. Thus, if the royalty rate for products sold on a domestic or landed basis is 10%, the F.O.B. royalty rate is typically set at between 12% and 14%.

7.3.3   Royalty Rates on Direct Sales

Many licensees not only sell their licensed products to retailers and wholesalers, but also sell the licensed products direct to consumers through their own mail order catalogs, factory stores and on their websites. Since the retail selling price for such direct sales is typically higher than the wholesale price, a royalty rate adjustment may also be necessary. For example, if the same royalty rate that was used for these wholesale sales was applied to its direct sales, the licensee could be paying a significantly higher royalty amount to the licensor. Thus, for example, if a toy company sold a plush product to a retailer for $10, it would pay the licensor $1 in royalties at a 10% royalty rate. If, however, the same product was sold direct to consumers on its website at $20, i.e., the price at which its retailers would be selling the product, its actual royalty to the licensor would be $2 assuming that the same royalty rate applied.

It should be appreciated that most licensees who engage in direct sales are reluctant to sell their licensed product on a direct basis at a price much lower than that being charged by their retailers, lest they undercut their retailers' sales and possibly damage their relationship.

To compensate for the growing popularity of direct sales, a licensor may want to negotiate a different (and probably lower) royalty rate for such direct sales where the royalty is applied to retail and not the wholesale price. This will allow both parties to benefit from the increased profits generated through such sales.

7.3.4 Royalty Rates for Services

A number of licensed properties, particularly characters and celebrities, are used by licensees for advertising and promotional purposes. For example, SNOOPY has become the corporate "spokesdog" for Metropolitan Life Insurance Company and GARFIELD has been used to promote Embassy Suites.

Calculating a royalty rate for using a property in conjunction with the sale of such services can be difficult and there is hardly a standard method or model used by all licensors. One method that has been used is to negotiate an appropriate royalty rate and then apply it to the amount of advertising media purchased by the licensee. Setting the royalty rate at a point between 2% and 15% of the actual media buy has been done in a number of instances with the understanding, of course, that more popular properties would command higher rates.

That said, the value of having SNOOPY appear on the Met Life blimp that flies over dozens of NFL and college football games a year is incalculable using this formula. In such situations, another commonly used and perhaps more equitable approach is to simply charge an annual fee for the licensee's right to the use the property, that reflects how extensively the property will be used in its media buys and promotional activities.

7.3.5 Sublicensing Royalties

While most licensors will not permit their licensees to sub-license their rights to a third party, in those rare instances where sub-licensing is allowed, the question always arises as to how the licensor should be compensated.

There are a number of different methods for allocating sublicensing income, which include applying the licensee's own royalty obligation to the sale of sub-licensed products. Another commonly used method is to simply divide up the sub-licensing revenues between the licensee and the licensor pursuant to some equitable formula. A 50-50 split between the two is not uncommon, although circumstances and will dictate whether the licensor's share is higher or lower.

In any event, one factor to consider is the cost associated with locating and administering the sub-licensee, e.g., where the licensee is acting in more of an agent capacity. Such costs are frequently borne by the licensee out of its share of the sub-licensing revenue.

7.3.6   Split Royalty Rates

As the popularity of licensing has grown, so have the number of situations where a licensee takes multiple licenses for combined use on the same licensed products, e.g., a MICKEY MOUSE and UNIVERSITY OF MICHIGAN branded baseball cap; or where multiple sports licenses are taken, e.g., a license from MLB Properties to use a team name in combination with the name and image of one or more players. It is also quite common for a manufacturer to add licensed music and/or graphics to the product and, in other cases, may have to pay a designer or inventor for the right to use licensed technology or patents.

As one can readily appreciate, a licensee that finds itself in the unenviable position of having to pay royalties to two, three or even four different property owners for the same product may conclude that it simply cannot afford to absorb multiple royalty obligations and still offer competitively priced product.

In such instances, it is not uncommon for one or more of the licensors to agree to a reduced royalty rate in order to permit the product to remain economically viable in the marketplace. The question, of course, becomes which of the property owners will agree to reduce their otherwise "standard" royalty rate to allow the deal to occur. The answer is simple: the one with the least leverage.

7.4   Average Royalty Rates

The following average merchandising royalty rates by property type were reported in a 2009 study by Aspen Publishers:

- Art   3-8%
- Celebrity   6-10%
- Entertainment   7-10%
- Collegiate   6-9%
- Corporate   6-9%
- Designer/Fashion   3-7%
- Events   9-14%
- Sports   8-11%

It should be appreciated that these rates are the average royalty rates charged for domestic, landed "net sales" of licensing properties and are in the mid-range for each property type, i.e., in the 25-75% percentile. Thus, blockbuster properties will command higher rates while lesser known or non-promoted properties will fall below the range. Obviously, the actual royalty rate chosen will vary as a function of the property and, more importantly, the type or category of product on which the property is used.

Literally, whole books are written on what merchandising royalties are appropriate for different properties used in combination with various types of licensed products. One such reference, Battersby & Grimes', *Licensing Royalty Rates*, is published by Aspen Publishers and revised annually. The work features an extensive chart that provides detailed information covering eight different categories of licensing properties and their corresponding royalty ranges for more than 1500 types of licensed products. Further information about this book is available at www.aspenpublishers.com.

7.5   Net Sales, Advances and Guarantees

While the actual royalty rate that a licensor charges a licensee for the right to use its property is important, it is but one of a number of compensation issues on which the parties must come to agreement. As one can imagine, there is a tremendous degree of interplay between each of these different negotiation points.

In some cases, particularly with respect to new, emerging properties that have little or no track record, a licensee may be prepared to pay a higher royalty rate in exchange for a reduction in the advance and/or guarantee sought by the licensor. Understandably, if the licensee does not have total confidence that the licensed products will sell through, it will want to avoid facing a high guarantee obligation at the end of the license for products that ultimately did not perform well. An increased royalty rate could be more palatable though, on the rationale that if the licensed products are a success then the licensee can afford to pay the higher royalty. Alternatively, if the licensor insists on requiring the licensee to commit to a high guarantee, it may have to make a concession on the royalty rate charged.

Similarly, it should be appreciated that the royalty rate is usually applied to a licensee's net sales of the licensed products, which is represented by the gross sales figure less certain defined discounts, allowances, deductions and credits. Licensees will usually want to take as many deductions and allowances as possible in order to reduce the ultimate net sales figure, while a licensor will want to limit them as much as possible since the greater the number of deductions permitted, the lower the royalty income will be that it receives. One of the most closely scrutinized details in any royalty investigation is always the discounts and allowances that a licensee actually takes, versus what it is allowed to take under the license agreement.

With this in mind, some licensors have actually begun requiring that royalties be calculated on a licensee's gross sales, with no credits extended for any discounts, allowances or deductions, so as to avoid any argument over whether a particular deduction was permissible or not. In such a situation, it might be necessary to account for this by lowering the royalty rate because the gross sales number will always be higher than any net sales number. For further information on how "Net Sales," "Advances" and "Minimum Guarantees" are defined and calculated, reference should be made to the discussion of these topics in Chapters 8 and 13.

7.6   Marketing Contributions

Depending upon the category of licensed property, many licensors will require a contribution from most, if not all, of its licensees to a pooled marketing fund. The amount of such contribution is typically based on a percentage of the licensee's net sales of licensed products, often with a minimum payment required every quarter and/or year. Many view it simply as an additional royalty obligation. The range for these marketing contributions or fees varies greatly, although most fall between 1-2% and, depending on how successfully a licensed product sells, can become substantial.

Always an issue is exactly what the licensor is required to do with the revenue that it receives from these marketing contributions.

Typically, the fund is used to purchase media and advertising space for the collective benefit of all licensees involved with the program. While the licensor's actual obligation may be stated in the license agreement, it is generally assumed that the funds will not be used to underwrite the licensor's operating costs.

Chapter 8

The License Agreement

8.1 Introduction

The cornerstone of any licensing program is the license agreement that is entered into between the licensor and a licensee, as it will govern the eventual relationship between the parties. A good license agreement can make the program run smoothly, while a bad one can cause more problems than either party needs. It is often the case that once the licensing agreement is signed the parties never find need to refer back to the document again, but should the need arise its contents and structure become crucial.

License agreements can take many shapes and forms and it is the rare case that one licensor will use the same form agreement as another licensor. Moreover, while the property owner/licensor typically starts off with a "standard" agreement, negotiations between the parties will ultimately result in a number of changes. Consequently, the final signed agreements may vary significantly from one licensee to another. In an ideal situation, however, the core provisions of the licensor's standard agreement will remain consistent.

8.2 Negotiating the Terms of a License

The negotiations leading up to the drafting of a license agreement are typically handled by the relevant business executives charged with responsibility for negotiating the license. While there are occasions where one or both parties may be accompanied by their attorneys during these negotiations, the presence of counsel is usually reserved for larger or more complex transactions. Where the licensing executives are experienced and the issues are relatively straightforward, there is no need to involve counsel at this point. The purpose of these negotiations is to arrive at some consensus relative to the business terms of the agreement and there is normally sufficient time later in the process for the attorneys to get involved and conclude the agreement.

The negotiation of a license agreement is like most other business negotiations, i.e., typically, one party is in a stronger bargaining position than the other. Similarly, one party may have a stronger incentive to enter into the license than the other, which can shift the bargaining leverage to the other party.

In negotiating license agreements, leverage is not always about size and power but, more commonly, about a party's need to enter into the agreement, which can be the result of a variety of different circumstances. For example, one party might have a desire to enter a particular market and the license is their means of accomplishing it, while another party might desperately need to include a licensed property on its products to stay competitive. Whatever the motivations, it is rare that both parties have equal leverage in licensing negotiations.

Prior to entering actual licensing negotiations, the parties should have each fully investigated the other party to insure that they are compatible and can work together in the future. For example, the owner of a famous trademark, such as TIFFANY, should understandably be hesitant to license its famous mark to a manufacturer who has a reputation for producing low-price, low-quality impulse items.

The only sure way to conclude that the eventual relationship will be a good fit is for the property owner to fully investigate the potential licensee. Many licensors require that a potential licensee fill out a "License Application Form" which requires the prospective licensee to provide its full and complete financial information, as well as information concerning other licenses that it may hold or has held in the past. This is a good practice that should be followed by all licensors.

When the licensor actually obtains the completed application it should do more than simply read and file it. If the prospective licensee looks good "on paper," the licensor should use it as a starting point. The licensor would be well advised to fully check the references provided and speak directly with other licensors to learn how the licensee performed for them. While past performance is no guarantee of future success, past failures may well be an indicator of future failure.

After vetting the prospective licensee, the parties are then ready to begin the negotiation process. While it is the rare negotiation that covers all of the points that will ultimately be included in the final license agreement, most negotiators will start with the essential elements of the business transaction. If the parties cannot reach agreement on the fundamental business terms, it may not be worthwhile to proceed any further. The following items will typically be discussed in the course of most licensing negotiations:

- What licensed properties will be included in the agreement, i.e., the licensed property?

- Are there any elements of the property that will not be included in the license, e.g., the likeness of an actor.

- What are the specific products or services that will be included in the license, i.e., the licensed product(s)?

- In which territory will the licensee be able to sell licensed products, i.e., the licensed territory?

- In what retail channels will the licensee be permitted to sell the licensed products, i.e., the channels of distribution?

- How long will the licensee be able to produce and sell licensed products, i.e., the term?

- Can the licensor grant similar licensing rights to other parties, i.e., exclusive or non-exclusive rights?

- When does the licensee have to begin marketing and selling licensed products, i.e., the product introduction and distribution dates?

- How much does the licensee have to pay for the right to sell licensed products, i.e., the royalty, advance and guarantee?

It should be appreciated that these are only some of the points included in a typical negotiation and they will certainly vary from one to the next. Nevertheless, they will serve as a good starting point for most scenarios.

In this regard, it is important that the parties discuss and agree upon the specific licensed property that will be included in the license agreement as well as the licensed products for which the property is being licensed. In defining the property, it's important to define it specifically, e.g., does the licensed property include simply the PEANUTS name, or does it include the right to use the characters CHARLIE BROWN and SNOOPY?

When defining the licensed products, it is similarly important to be as specific as possible and they should be limited to only those products that the licensee is actually capable of manufacturing and selling. Broad definitions should be avoided wherever possible.

103

For example, if the licensee intends to use the licensed property on T-shirts, the licensor would be well advised to define the licensed products more specifically, e.g., "100% cotton men's T-shirts without a collar from sizes S-XL."

This, of course, leads us to the question of exclusivity. Will the license be exclusive to the licensee, exclusive to the licensee with the licensor reserving the right to produce the licensed products itself, or simply non-exclusive? In recent years, the trend has been toward non-exclusive licenses since they pose far fewer problems if the licensee does not perform as expected or, worse yet, goes into bankruptcy. Additionally, some entities, such as state-funded universities, have a policy of only granting non-exclusive licenses.

The parties need to discuss and agree upon the length or "term" of the agreement and the "territory" in which the licensed products can be sold. The term of the agreement is always a difficult negotiation since the licensee will want the agreement to extend for as long as possible, while the licensor will want to limit it to a relatively short period of time. The licensee's position is that it will be investing substantial sums in developing and marketing the licensed products and will therefore require time to recoup its initial investment. Conversely, the licensor is concerned that it will be tying up its valuable property right for a prolonged period of time with no guarantee that the licensee will actually exploit the property.

The typical compromise is to set the term for a reasonable period of time, e.g., two to three years, with the licensee having the option to renew for additional periods upon meeting certain performance criteria. For example, the term might be for two years with two separately exercisable options to renew the agreement for additional extended terms of two years each. There are notable exceptions where longer terms of, perhaps, five to seven and maybe even ten years are the accepted standard. Use of such longer terms, however, are usually reserved for product categories that require the licensee to make a sizeable investment in the development of the product, and/or when the product requires a more extensive development period, e.g., video games.

Similarly, there is a basic difference between what the licensor and licensee each wants with respect to the licensed territory. Most licensors prefer to limit the territory to only those countries where the licensee can demonstrate its ability to distribute licensed products. Most licensees, on the other hand, will want to extend the territory as broadly as possible, usually on the chance that they may expand into those countries in the future. Caution should be exercised when granting broad territorial rights to a licensee, without reasonable assurances at the start of the agreement that it is capable of achieving distribution in each of the desired markets.

Where a licensee requests the rights to a broad territory, but the licensor is uncertain that it can fully exploit them, one possible compromise is to consent to the proposed licensed territory for a limited period of time and impose specific performance requirements on the licensee. For example, if the licensee does not commence the sale of licensed products in Australia within 18 months from the date of execution of the agreement or generate at least US $100,000 in royalties from sales in Australia within 24 months from such date of execution, the licensor shall have the right to delete Australia from the licensed territory.

The negotiation of product introduction dates and first sale or retail distribution dates are also important to insure that the licensee will actually work the license. If such dates are not met, the licensor would have the right to terminate the agreement. Some licensors may tend to minimize this requirement with licensees who commit to paying a sizeable advance and a large guarantee, but that should never be a reason to totally ignore these performance requirements.

The issue of compensation has been left to last in this discussion because to a majority of licensing executives it is the most important provision and, theoretically, consumes the most negotiating time. In actuality, however, the financial terms of many license agreements typically generate the least amount of negotiation. Many licensors have fixed in their minds what they are looking for in terms of financial requirements, taking the normal variances between product categories into consideration. For example, if someone wanted to take a license for a Disney character, the royalty rate will almost never be negotiated—it will probably be the same as in the other 150 license agreements that Disney has granted for that property.

There may, however, be some give and take on the advances and minimum guarantees, particularly in tougher economic times. Still, these numbers are heavily based on the licensee's sales projections. For example, if the agreed upon royalty rate was 12% and the licensee has projected a million dollars in total net sales for the licensed product, the licensor will typically apply that royalty rate to the projected sales figure and arrive at an appropriate guarantee and advance based on such projections. Some licensors will require that the licensee guarantee at least half of the projected royalties for a royalty period and then pay half of the guarantee as an advance.

It should be appreciated, however, that these percentages are simply a starting point for negotiation and licensees will (and should) always seek to negotiate a lower percentage for the guarantee, e.g., 25-40% and the corresponding advance. Since the licensor is relying on the licensee's own projections, a licensee would be well advised to be conservative in its sales projections so as to provide a "comfort zone" in negotiating the guarantee and advance.

Where there often is significant room to negotiate the compensation package is when there is little or no history for that property type and/or product and, as such, no established royalty exists. In these situations, the parties may spend significant amounts of time negotiating the royalty rate and any advances or guarantees. The standards used to determine an appropriate compensation package will be discussed in much greater detail later in this book.

There are many strategies used in conducting licensing negotiations. Regardless of the strategy, however, there is no substitute for preparation. In virtually all negotiations, preparation will result in a better deal for the party. For example, if an issue develops concerning the establishment of an F.O.B. rate, the parties should understand and be prepared to discuss: 1) how the licensed products will actually be shipped and sold; 2) the purpose of an F.O.B. rate; 3) the cost of the item on a domestic vs. F.O.B. basis; 4) the impact of the royalty rate on these two forms of costing; and 5) what the other side has historically done on the question and what is the standard in the industry. Armed with such knowledge, the parties will be in a significantly better position to negotiate a rate that will work for everyone.

A technique employed by some negotiators is the "Take it or Leave it" approach, typically when there is a larger disparity in the bargaining leverage between the parties and one side is assuming a more aloof position—some may call it condescending. Many an attorney or executive has heard the dreaded statement, "This issue is non-negotiable. If your client won't accept it, we're done." Translated, that means "Take it or leave it."

A licensee or licensor should NEVER be intimidated by such a threat since it could simply be a negotiating ploy. Unfortunately, there is no accurate way to know for sure what is in the mind of the other negotiator and whether he is serious or simply bluffing. One needs to follow their own instincts and determine whether they have really reached the end of the negotiations or whether there is more room, while at the same time giving consideration as to how important it is to conclude the deal. The best way to test a take it or leave it response is to simply make an offer and see how it is received.

8.3   Term Sheets/Deal Memos

One of the most effective ways to insure that these oral negotiations between a licensor and a prospective licensee ultimately result in a formal license agreement is through the use of a basic term sheet or deal memo, which is entered into between the parties at the conclusion of their negotiations. The term sheet is normally a one or two page document outlining the salient business provisions that were negotiated, but usually leaves out most of the legal points. When the term sheet is initially prepared, specific business terms, such as the royalty rate, advance, territory, etc., are usually left blank and it serves as a checklist for the negotiations between the parties. At the conclusion of the negotiations, the parties can then insert the appropriate numbers agreed upon during the negotiations.

The term sheet is intended to serve as a preliminary document that memorializes what the parties have negotiated, subject to entering into a formal agreement within a stated period of time. The term sheet should state that the failure to conclude a formal agreement by a predetermined date will result in its expiration. This insures that the term sheet does not become a binding agreement in the event that the parties fail to conclude a formal license agreement.

Term sheets are particularly useful when the initial negotiations are conducted by the licensing executives with the understanding that the matter will then be turned over to their respective attorneys for finalization of the formal agreement. Absent a term sheet, it is often difficult to "conclude" negotiations, as there is no formal documentation of the terms that have been agreed to by the parties.

Despite the existence of a completed term sheet, one party may occasionally decide to reopen the negotiations. The existence of a signed term sheet, however, makes it more difficult for one side to try to renegotiate points that have been previously agreed-upon.

Ideally, the term sheet should address the following essential elements of the arrangement:

- Nature of the grant (exclusive versus non-exclusive);
- Clear and specific identification of the property and product(s) to be covered by the license;

- Licensed territory;

- Term or period of the agreement, usually including specific dates for both;

- Renewal options, including any requirements that must be met;

- Royalty rate, advances and guaranteed minimum royalties, and any specific dates by which such payments must be made;

- Dates when marketing and distribution will commence;

- Amount of product liability insurance required; and

- Time period within which a definitive formal agreement will be worked out.

A sample term sheet/deal memo is included here as Appendix-4.

8.4   The License Agreement

When the parties conclude their negotiations, regardless of whether or not a term sheet or deal memo is signed, it is time to memorialize their agreement into a formal, written license agreement. The first question that immediately comes to mind is which party should prepare the agreement?

The answer may depend on whether the license agreement is part of a larger licensing program conducted by the licensor or is a one-shot agreement. It is usually incumbent on the licensor to prepare the first draft of the agreement, since it owns the intellectual property rights and has a vested interest in preserving those property rights. This is particularly true if the transaction is part of a larger licensing program. The licensor will want to have a certain degree of uniformity among all of its licensees since it will not typically want to have different licensees operating under very different license agreements. Indeed, maintaining some degree of uniformity for a licensing program is important.

8.4.1   Definitions

The terminology used in most license agreements varies often and is almost always a reflection of the attorney drafting the agreement. For a better understanding of the terms most frequently used, Chapter 1 offers a useful reference point.

Different licensors call different things by different names. At the end of the day, however, it doesn't matter what something is called, it only matters what it means. What is important is that the parties expressly define what the key terms mean and these definitions are typically contained in the first part of every license agreement.

8.4.2 Grant of Rights

The one essential provision in any license agreement is the "Grant of Rights" provision, since this is where the licensor formally grants to the licensee the right to use its intellectual property. It typically identifies the specific elements of the property that are being licensed and for what purpose(s). If the property includes multiple components or elements of artwork, it may be advisable to physically attach the artwork or define the components separately in an attached schedule or exhibit. In some cases, this provision may also identify any specific elements that are not being licensed since the inclusion of both helps to avoid future misunderstandings.

Also expressed in the grant of rights is the type of license being granted, e.g., exclusive versus non-exclusive. To review, an exclusive license agreement is one in which the licensee is the only party that can use the licensed property on the licensed products in the licensed territory for sale in a particular channel of distribution. Note that the grant is restricted by these four parameters: the licensed property; the licensed product; the licensed territory and the channel(s) of distribution. This means that the licensor can grant other exclusive (or non-exclusive) agreements to third parties for items other than the licensed property, or for products other than the licensed product, or for sale outside the licensed territory or in different channels of distribution.

In a non-exclusive grant, the licensee may be one of potentially a number of licensees permitted to use the licensed property for the licensed product in the licensed territory and within the channels of distribution. As noted previously, the trend in licensing is toward non-exclusive licenses, which are far less risky for licensors.

The license agreement should also recite whether the licensee has the right to grant sub-licenses to third parties. In the event that the licensee is permitted to grant a sub-license, it is advisable for the licensor reserve the right of pre-approval, be a named party in the sub-licensing agreement or, at the very least, be notified of such grant. If sub-licensing is allowed, the agreement needs to clearly establish how the sub-licensing revenues will be handled.

Finally, the agreement should provide that the licensee will operate within the licensed territory and not knowingly ship the licensed products to entities outside the licensed territory or sell the licensed products to parties that it knows will ship the licensed products outside the licensed territory. Obviously, this provision is intended to address the issue of gray market goods where goods authorized for distribution in one country are shipped into another country that has not been authorized by the licensor.

The licensor may attempt to specifically reserve rights to certain future technologies. This has been a hotly contested issue over the years, particularly involving entertainment and motion picture rights and whether film grants included videocassette and eventually digital rights. As such, many licensors now specifically reserve all non-granted rights including, rights in any future developed technologies that incorporate the licensed property.

There may be cases where the licensee has pre-existing materials that it owns and wants to continue to own after conclusion of the license agreement, e.g., video game engines, etc. The agreement should specifically identify such materials and provide that they will remain the property of the licensee after termination or expiration of the agreement although all elements of the licensed property must be removed.

Care needs to be taken when attempting to impose control over where the licensee may sell the licensed products or the manner in which they may sell and distribute such items, since certain restrictions could conflict with relevant antitrust laws. It is preferable to simply identify those territories or channels where the licensee can sell and distribute licensed products rather than identify those territories or channels where they cannot sell or distribute. As previously noted, sometimes, inclusion of the official language(s) that can be used when referencing the licensed product will tend to limit the markets in which the product can be distributed. Specification of language rights is often provided for in publishing agreements.

8.4.3   Term of the Agreement

The term of any license agreement will define the relevant time period during which the license agreement shall remain in effect. The term may vary depending upon the licensor's pre-established criteria, or the product category. Many licensors will only grant licenses for a term of two or three years although, as mentioned, licenses for certain product categories, e.g., video games, are commonly granted for longer terms due to the time and/or cost required to develop such products. The terms of agreements that relate to copyrighted materials, e.g., in publishing agreements, are typically tied to the length of copyright protection afforded such properties.

In those instances where the term is established for a fixed period of time, a licensee will frequently request one or more options to renew the license agreement for extended terms. Options are intended to protect a successful licensee from a licensor who wishes to leverage the licensee's success and seek out a new licensee on better terms after expiration of the initial agreement. An option gives the licensee some contractual assurance that, if it has been successful, it will be able to continue the license.

The exercise of an option, however, is generally dependent upon the licensee meeting certain threshold performance-related criteria. For example, a licensor may grant a license for a fixed term of two years with the option to renew the agreement for an "extended" or "renewal" term of an additional two years *provided* that the licensee has submitted $[X] in royalty payments, was not in breach of any material provision of the agreement and notified the licensor in writing of its intention to renew the agreement at least 30 days prior to the expiration of the term then in effect.

8.4.4   Compensation Provisions

The manner in which the licensor is compensated for the use of the licensed property by the licensee and any sub-licensees can vary widely. Possible options include:

- A one-time lump sum payment to the licensor;

- Ongoing royalty payments to the licensor, based solely on sales of licensed products by the licensee, with no advance or guaranteed minimum payment;

- Either of the above, except that the licensor is paid an advance and/or a guaranteed minimum royalty payment, which is usually recoupable against future royalty earnings.

As explained in Chapters 7 and 6, the most common form of compensation is a royalty calculated as a percentage of the licensee's net sales of the licensed products. To reiterate, "Net Sales" is almost always a term specifically defined in every license agreement. Though the actual definition varies, it will always be based off of the licensee's gross sales of licensed products less certain enumerated deductions. These details of will change from agreement to agreement. For the reasons explored previously in Chapter 7, a licensee should pay very particular attention to how net sales is defined as this can have an enormous impact on its royalty obligation.

Again, it should also be appreciated that various types of royalties are frequently charged. Each is a function of how the licensed products are actually distributed, such as when the licensed products are manufactured offshore, or in such cases where the licensee may also sell the licensed products directly to consumers. F.O.B. (sometimes called an L.C. or Letter of Credit) rates are typically between two and four percentage points higher than domestic rates due, principally, to the fact that F.O.B. sales are made at a lower price point. In those instances where the licensee has both the right and the ability to sell the licensed products directly to the consumer, the royalty rate may also fluctuate. Direct sales, as this is usually referred to, provides the manufacturer the ability to sell products at the retail price. Therefore, many licensors will require that the royalty be paid on the higher retail price rather than on the wholesale price.

Most licensors require licensees to pay an advance against royalties upon execution of the license agreement, as well as some form of minimum royalty obligation. The advance against royalties is just that—an advance against the licensee's actual earned royalty obligations. It is therefore creditable against the licensee's future earned royalty payments due the licensor. In most instances, it is treated as non-refundable.

The need for an advance is quite important in the licensing industry, as it accelerates the licensor's cash flow. In most instances, the licensee will not commence the sale of licensed products for months, if not years, after entering into the agreement. Without an advance, some licensors could go more than eighteen months before they begin to see any actual royalties from a licensee. The other reason for an advance is that it serves as a further incentive to insure that the licensee will not simply take a license and then sit idle with the property. By paying an advance, the licensee has made a definitive financial commitment to the program.

There may be some instances where a licensor requires the licensee to pay a non-refundable, non-creditable licensee fee at the time the license agreement is executed for the right to actually take the license. This is not very common but does occur in some categories.

Many license agreements also include a minimum royalty provision that can be either guaranteed or non-guaranteed. A guaranteed minimum royalty, as the name implies, means that the licensee is committed to paying a certain minimum amount in royalties to the licensor over either the term of the license or for a specific period. That way, if the licensed products are a failure, the licensor knows it will receive at least some minimum amount in royalties. In certain categories, e.g., art licensing, licensees will not agree to any minimum guarantee, although they may be willing to agree to a "non-guaranteed" minimum royalty which, if not met, will give the licensor the right to terminate the agreement.

8.4.5 Sub-Licensing

Few, if any, merchandising licensors allow their licensees to engage in sub-licensing since they want to control the ultimate use of their properties. While there are certainly ways to control how and what a sub-licensee does with the property, in practice, controlling a sub-licensee is inherently more difficult for a property owner than controlling a licensee.

It should be noted that—*as a matter of law*—a licensee has the right to sub-license its rights in the absence of a specific prohibition in the agreement, which is why most merchandising license agreements expressly prohibit sub-licensing.

There are, however, instances in which sub-licensing is permitted, typically with respect to international rights where sub-licensing can be a valuable substitute for a distribution arrangement. In those instances, the terms of any sub-license grant should be addressed. An alternative to sub-licensing international distributors is a sub-distribution agreement. Under this type of agreement, the licensee would continue to remain obligated to pay the licensor a royalty on product sales on the same royalty basis as for all other sales.

Where sub-licensing is permitted, the license agreement should further address how the licensor will be paid for sales made by the sub-licensee. In many cases, the licensor and licensee simply agree to share the sub-licensing revenues on some mutually agreeable basis. Again, a 50-50 split between the licensor and the licensee of net sub-licensing income (gross sub-licensing income less the cost of conducting the program, or an agent's commission if an outside agent is used) is quite common. Such a formula gives the licensee the ability to deduct its operational costs against such income prior to an equitable sharing of the profits with the licensor.

Another approach to allocating sub-licensing revenue is where the licensor receives the same royalty on the sub-licensee's sale of products as it would from the original licensee for its own sales. In such a situation, the licensee may elect to charge the sub-licensee a higher royalty than it is paying to the licensor and retain the difference.

8.4.6   Accounting Provisions

As mentioned above, one of the most important considerations in any license agreement is the definition of net sales, since this is the basis for calculating the licensee's royalty obligation to the licensor. In most any license agreement, "Net Sales" refers to the licensee's gross sales of the licensed products less whatever deductions the parties agree to permit, e.g., shipping costs, taxes, credits and discounts, and returns. It should be appreciated that the actual definition of net sales will vary from licensor to licensor and, for some, even from one product category to another.

A licensee should make certain that it has the right to deduct non-recoupable "government fees" from its gross sales. Similarly, licensors should not permit a licensee to deduct the cost of manufacturing and/or promoting the licensed product, or the cost of the royalty paid to the licensor.

A common practice in structuring licenses for publishing properties and in certain other industries where unsold goods are returnable is that the licensee will have the right to deduct a "Reserve for Returns" from the royalties due on a per quarter basis. A fixed percentage of royalties, often 20% to 30%, is deducted from the total royalty payment to compensate for the return of the product. Most agreements will require that any reserve deducted must be accounted for in next royalty report. Therefore, if the licensee deducts a reserve of 20% in the preceding quarter when actual returns equal only 10% of the reserve deducted, the remaining 10% that is outstanding will be added to the current royalties due.

Some companies prefer to negotiate a flat percentage for all deductions rather than attempt to individually itemize each one. Such percentages normally range from between 5 % and 10% of gross sales. The inclusion of returns in this flat fee deduction can, however, cause problems for some licensees, particularly in industries where returns are commonplace. Similarly, many licensors actually impose a cap on the amount of such deductions.

Royalty accounting for most licensees is typically provided on a quarterly calendar basis with statements and payments due within 30 (sometimes 45) days after the conclusion of the previous quarter. Thus, licensees will normally report and pay royalties by January 30th, April

30th, July 30th and October 30th of each year. In certain industries, such as publishing, royalty accounting is provided less frequently, e.g., semi-annually or annually. Alternatively, in situations where a licensed property is particularly hot or when the reliability of the licensee comes into question, royalty accounting may be required on a monthly basis.

The agreement should clearly spell out what form the licensee's royalty statement should take and the degree of specificity required in the accounting. Many licensors require electronic reporting, in addition to hard copy. A good practice is to actually append a copy of a sample royalty statement to the agreement. Many licensors also require that the royalty statement be certified by an officer of the licensee to underscore the need for accurate and truthful reporting.

Questions frequently arise as to when a royalty obligation accrues, e.g., upon the sale or payment of the item. Many license agreements specifically address this question and typically require that the royalty obligation will accrue at the earliest date possible, e.g., when an order is placed rather than when payment is received.

Another question frequently presented involves the issue of inter-company sales at a discount. Most agreements provide that in such a situation, the transfer will be deemed a sale and the price can be no lower than the typical selling price for the licensed product to a third party. The failure to provide language dealing with this issue can allow the licensee to be able to distribute the licensed products at a lower effective royalty cost. There have been occasions where licensees established a bogus entity to purchases the licensed products, which then became the paper entity that distributed them to retail.

The payment question is always an issue, particularly if the licensee is located in a different country. Most licensors require that all payments be made in the licensor's national currency, typically by check or wire transfer drawn on a bank in the licensor's country. This is done to avoid incurring bank collection fees. Currency fluctuations could, however, be a reason for requiring that royalties are paid in the licensee's currency.

A "blocked currency" provision is frequently requested by a licensee, particularly when it is selling product in countries where it might be difficult to get currency out of that country. Many licensors refuse to agree to such a provision, particularly if the licensee knowingly sells into a market where there is the possibility that currency will be blocked.

The agreement should also provide that the licensee will pay interest on any late payments made to the licensor. It is a good idea to establish how interest will be calculated, e.g., 0.5% per month from the date the payment was originally due. Some licensors fix the interest rate at the current cost of money, e.g., prime interest rate, or cite a specific interest index as the basis used to calculate interest due. If underpayments of royalties have occurred over a prolonged period of time, computing interest charges can be complicated due to the fact that interest rates tend to fluctuate.

Many licensors include an acceleration provision in the agreement which provides that, upon termination of the agreement for cause, all outstanding guaranteed monies will become immediately due and payable. This avoids the unpleasant situation of having to wait (or worse yet, chase) a terminated licensee for outstanding monies.

The licensor should have the right to audit the licensee's books and verify the accuracy of the licensee's accounting. Reasonable notice is normally required and the inspection should be at the licensee's place of business during reasonable business hours. The licensor should have the right to make copies of what it is shown during the course of the audit, and the licensee should be required to cooperate with the audit. It might be wise to specify that the audit provision survives termination of the license agreement to avoid conflicts where a licensor elects to audit a terminated licensee.

The license agreement should further provide that in the event the audit reveals an underpayment above a threshold amount, the licensee will not only be required to pay the underpayment with interest, but will also have to pay the licensor's audit costs and any attorneys' fees required to collect same. The actual threshold amount will vary from license to license, but it is common to set it as a percentage of the amount actually paid for the period, e.g., 3% to 5%. Some agreements provide that if the underpayment reaches a second, but higher, threshold amount, e.g., 25%, the licensor may also terminate the agreement.

The agreement should further include a provision that requires the licensee to maintain all of its books and records for inspection over a period of time and at a location where they can be easily inspected. A typical time period for retaining records is three years from the date to which they pertain. See Chapter 13 for a more thorough treatment of accounting issues.

8.4.7   Quality Control Provisions

Every merchandising agreement gives the licensor the right to exert some degree of quality control over the licensed products produced by the licensee. There are many reasons for such a provision, although the most important one is that the licensing of a trademark without monitoring the quality of the licensed products is considered "naked licensing" and can result in a loss of the property owner's underlying trademark rights.

Most licensors prefer to monitor the quality of the licensed products even if the property being licensed is not a trademark. They will frequently require the licensee to submit samples of the licensed products for review and approval at various stages of the development and manufacturing process. Such submissions are for the purpose of reviewing the actual licensed products to insure that they meet certain minimal quality levels, as well as to confirm that the licensed property is being properly used and that all appropriate legal notices are included.

In the merchandising area, at a minimum, licensors will typically require a licensee to submit samples of the licensed products at the following stages:

- Preliminary artwork depicting the licensed property;

- Final artwork depicting the licensed property;

- Initial prototypes of the licensed products;

- Final prototypes of the licensed products; and

- Production run samples of the licensed products.

While the above may appear to be "overkill," it is important to ensure that the licensee is on the right track to manufacturing licensed products of a type and style that will be eventually approved by the licensor. Such a policy is actually beneficial for the licensee, since it helps identify any potential problems at an early stage and allows the licensee to make the necessary changes and corrections before starting its production run. Making changes at the earliest stages of product development will very often save the licensee both money and time.

A WORD OF CAUTION: most licensees are more than capable of producing the products without any help from the licensor. Ideally, the professional licensor is supportive of the licensee and does not use the approval process to assert artistic control over the licensed product. Reviewing products for quality and to ensure that they comply with trademark and marking requirements is far different from using the

117

process to insist that a certain color is of the proper hue, for instance; unless, of course, such details are necessary to comply with the property's style-guide.

In addition to the licensed products, most licensors will require the right to approve a licensee's proposed packaging as well as the placement of any intended advertising. This measure helps to assure that the selected media outlets are of a type and style consistent with the image that the licensor wants to portray, that they properly depict the licensed property and that they contain all appropriate legal notices.

One primary concern of every licensee is that the licensor will unreasonably delay consideration of its sample product submissions. As noted earlier in Chapter 6, most licensees are working on very tight production schedules, usually dictated by a retailer. If a licensor fails to act promptly in the review and approval process, it can have a significant negative impact on the success of the licensed product.

Professional licensors are rarely, if ever, dilatory in their review of sample submissions, although the actual process does take time. One way to approach this issue in the agreement is to establish a set timeframe for conducting the review and a provision for what happens if the licensor does not respond within such a timeframe. Most licensees want a failure to respond within the set period to constitute approval, while most licensors will insist that such a failure to respond be deemed disapproval. This, of course, is a matter of negotiation and compromise is always possible.

8.4.8   Representations and Warranties

Every licensor will be asked to make certain representations and warranties to the licensee, including:

- Licensor has the right to enter into the subject agreement and there are no other agreements in place that conflict with it;

- Licensor is the sole and exclusive owner of the property; and

- Property does not infringe upon the rights of any third party.

The first two warranties are relatively straightforward. The last one, however, can be problematic. This warranty is tantamount to a guarantee that the licensee's use of the property will not infringe upon anyone else's intellectual property rights. That is a very serious warranty and one that most licensors do not take lightly—particularly with respect to relatively new properties. Such a warranty requires the licensor to conduct extensive trademark and copyright searches to ensure that the use by the licensee of the licensed property will not result in the infringement of the rights of another party. For a more in depth discussion of this issue, see Chapter 4.

Most licensors require a licensee to warrant that it will use its best efforts or, at least, reasonable commercial efforts, in advertising, promoting, and marketing the product. It is also not uncommon for a licensor to require that the licensee commence actual distribution of the licensed product by a specific date in order to maintain its rights under the agreement. For example, a toy licensee may be required to introduce the licensed product by New York Toy Fair 2012 (the "Product Introduction Date") and actually commence shipment of licensed products by another certain date, e.g., April 30, 2012 (the "Initial Shipment Date" or "Distribution Date"). The licensee's failure to meet either of these dates would give the licensor the right to terminate the agreement.

If the agreement is a worldwide agreement, consideration must be given to the distribution of the licensed product outside the United States. Frequently, the licensee is given one year from the introduction in the United States to introduce and begin selling the product abroad. Consideration may also be given to approaching this on a country-by-country basis. For example, if the licensee has not begun selling product in a particular country by a particular date, the licensor has the right to delete (or "recapture") that country from the license grant.

8.4.9 Indemnification and Insurance

Indemnification means that in the event a third party should make a claim against or sue one party to the license based on the actions (or inactions) of the other, the other party will be responsible for defending such claim and paying any costs or judgments arising from a lawsuit.

In most license agreements, the following cross indemnities are typically provided:

- Licensor will indemnify the licensee against claims based on any breach of the licensor's warranties, including claims for infringement; and

- Licensee will indemnify the licensor against claims based on any breach of licensee's warranties, including claims for product liability.

The first is fairly simple: if the licensee gets sued because its use of the licensor's property infringes the rights of another party, the licensor is responsible and should defend and bear all costs associated with any subsequent lawsuit. This is one of the reasons why it is so important to first clear a property before commencing a licensing program, since the licensor will typically be responsible for any such claim. As stated earlier, there is no faster way to derail a licensing program than to find out that the property being licensed infringes the rights of an outside third party. The cost of even defending an infringement lawsuit can easily run into the millions of dollars and the potential liability is even larger.

The second situation is also very straight forward. If the licensee's products are defective or cause injury or death to a third party, it is the licensee's responsibility and it should be prepared to defend and indemnify the licensor as a result of any such claims.

Most licensors require that a licensee carry product liability insurance to fund its indemnity obligation and, further, that the licensor and its licensing agent be added as a named insured to the insurance policy. In this manner, both parties are clearly covered. There is typically no cost or fee for adding an additional party to such a policy. By extension, most licensors will require that they be notified should the licensee fail to maintain such coverage or, alternatively, change the limits of their coverage. In many agreements failure to maintain the required product liability coverage gives the licensor the right to terminate the agreement.

The licensor should take special care in reviewing these policies, paying particular attention to the licensee's selection of the carrier as well as the limits of product liability insurance. The minimum product liability limits will vary according to the type of licensed product. Obviously, any licensed product that can be considered reasonably dangerous, including knives or lighters or any products that can be ingested, including food products, candy, and drinks, should justify a higher limit of insurance than the standard level of $2 to $5 million per occurrence.

8.4.10 Termination Provision

The termination provision is, perhaps, the most important provision in any license agreement, since it will be the first provision reviewed should a problem develop between the parties. If the relationship between the parties proceeds in the manner both expected at the time they entered into the agreement, there may never be an occasion to review the written document in any significant detail. However, in the event that a problem develops in the underlying relationship between the parties and one party wants to end the relationship, the termination provision will become critically important.

A well-drafted termination provision should give the licensor the right to terminate the agreement upon the occurrence of certain events, including:

- Licensee's failure to obtain the licensor's product approvals prior to the distribution of the licensed goods.

- Licensee's failure to introduce product prior to the product introduction date;

- Licensee's failure to meet the initial shipment date;

- Licensee's failure to maintain product liability insurance;

- Licensee's failure to make the minimum royalty payments;

- Licensee's failure to continuously sell or market products;

- Recall of the product by the Consumer Product Safety Commission;

- Licensee's protracted inability to conduct business; or

- Licensee's repeated failure to pay royalties when they come due.

In addition to the above, both parties should have the right to terminate the agreement on notice (normally thirty days) in the event of a breach of a material provision of the agreement by the other party and the party's failure to cure that breach within the notice period.

It may also be advisable for the licensor to have the option to terminate a portion of the license agreement and reclaim some of the rights being granted without terminating the entire agreement. For example, a licensor might want to reclaim a country where sales did not commence by the distribution date or even a particular type of licensed product that was simply not introduced or sold.

The termination provision should similarly address the issue of what the licensee can (and cannot) do after termination or expiration of the agreement. In most cases, the licensee will be required to cease all manufacture of the licensed products, return all of the licensor's materials and provide the licensor with an accounting of all inventory on hand. Most terminated licensees will be permitted to dispose of any existing inventory for a limited "sell-off" period, provided that the termination was not the result of inferior quality products or improper use of the property. The length of such a sell-off period will vary from agreement to agreement.

8.4.11 Boilerplate Provisions

The use of the term "boilerplate" can be misleading because it implies that these provisions are blindly included in every agreement without thought or consideration. Nothing could be further from the truth. These provisions are very much intended to govern the conduct of the parties and to control how certain events will be treated. That alone makes them practically as important as the provisions discussed above.

Some of the more important "boilerplate" provisions establish:

- Who is responsible for obtaining and maintaining intellectual property protection, both domestically and internationally;

- Who is responsible for pursuing infringers and how any recovered assets are to be divided;

- Manner in which notices are to be given under the agreement;

- Manner in which disputes are to be resolved and what law will control;

- Conditions under which the parties may assign the agreement along with its rights and obligations; and

- Integration of the agreement and amendments.

[A]   Intellectual Property Protection

It is typically the licensor's responsibility to obtain and maintain intellectual property protection for the property. This is understandable since it is the actual owner of such property rights and the licensee is paying for the right to use the property. A property owner should think seriously before allowing another party, particularly a licensee, to assume responsibility for protecting its intellectual property.

The question of who should pay for international trademark protection is not always as clear-cut, however, principally because of the expense associated with obtaining and maintaining such protection. As explained earlier, international trademark protection must be acquired on a country-by-country basis and, as such, can get very costly. Some property owners (particularly smaller ones) are simply not in a financial position to undertake an international filing program without some assistance from its licensees. In such instances, it is not uncommon for the licensee to advance the costs associated with an international filing program with the understanding that it will be able to take a credit against its royalty obligations in the amount of such expenses. Clearly, this approach benefits both parties.

In this regard, the agreement should specifically address how much cooperation between the parties is expected and obligate the licensee to cooperate with and assist the licensor in refining the intellectual property rights protection. This will, of course, help to avoid subsequent disputes involving a refusal by the licensee to execute any necessary documents to perfect such rights.

A "licensee estoppel" provision is frequently contained in license agreements that do not involve patents. This provision prevents the licensee from challenging the validity of the licensor's underlying intellectual property rights. While courts have consistently held that licensee estoppel provisions relating to patent rights violate the antitrust laws, they are allowed in trademark and merchandising agreements.

[B]   Third Party Infringements

The right to sue infringers typically rests with the licensor. While most intellectual property statutes provide that actions can only be brought by the owner of the intellectual property rights, some courts have held that an exclusive licensee can bring an action for infringement. To address this, many license agreements expressly provide that the licensor is the only party that can initiate an action against an infringer. Some licensors do allow a licensee to bring an action of its own, however, either with the licensor's consent or if the licensor does not act in a timely manner.

In any event, the agreement should not require the licensor to pursue any and all infringements. Enforcement litigation is extremely expensive and there is always a law of diminishing returns. That is not meant to imply that property owners should not take reasonable steps to stop the infringement of its intellectual property rights, but the rule of reason needs to apply. It might simply not be worth spending $100,000 in legal fees to shut down a company that is selling $350 worth of infringing product. This issue is explored in fuller detail in Chapter 14.

[C]   Notices

Every license agreement needs to specifically provide how notices are to be given under the agreement and how payments are to be made, including notices for breach. There are instances where a party might want to include its counsel and its licensing agent in the notice provision to insure that an actual copy of the notice is immediately received and acted upon.

[D]   Disputes and Forum

Most agreements address the question of disputes, specifically, what law is to apply and how and where disputes are to be handled. In domestic licensing situations, the governing law is of lesser importance since federal law will typically apply, although questions of contract interpretation can vary significantly from state to state. What is important for a licensor, however, is to make sure that all of its license agreements consistently provide for interpretation under the same state law in order to avoid a situation where a court sitting in one state interprets a particular provision differently than a court sitting in another state. In international licensing, the choice of law provision becomes particularly important and requires thorough review by qualified legal counsel.

How and where disputes will be resolved is also an important consideration. The choice is typically between litigation versus arbitration and where any such proceeding will be held. Mediation is a very effective tool for dispute resolution and a number of licensors regularly require mediation as an initial step in the dispute resolution process.

[E]   Assignability and Transfer

Courts typically consider license agreements to be personal and, as such, they may not be assigned as a matter of law without the consent of the other party. Most licensors re-affirm this in the body of their agreement.

An issue that has been of particular prominence in recent years involves the "transfer" of a license agreement, where it moves along with a corporation that was acquired by another corporation. In such event, no assignment of the agreement is typically required. To avoid this outcome (or at least assert some authority over it), many licensors expressly prohibit the "transfer" of the license agreement in the event that control of the licensee changes hands. Some even impose the payment of a "transfer fee" as a condition for their approval.

[F]   Force Majeure

"Force Majeure" is a doctrine intended to protect the licensee in the event of excusable non-performance caused by an act of God, the government, war, terrorism, fire, flood, or labor troubles. Such a provision will typically excuse such non-performance during the period of trouble and then for a fixed period thereafter.

[G]   No Joint Venture

While many licensors commonly refer to their licensees as "partners," they are not so as a matter of law. In fact, most licensing agreements expressly state that the parties are not partners or joint venturers.

[H]   Integration

Every agreement typically includes and should end with an integration clause, which provides that the license agreement is the final and entire understanding between the parties, incorporates all prior written or oral agreements between the parties and may not be changed or modified except by written agreement signed by all parties. This provision is intended to restrict a party's ability to rely on any statements not contained in the agreement and effectively "integrates" everything into the final license agreement.

Chapter 9

Best Practices in
Licensing Administration[3]

9.1 Introduction

Once all the preliminary steps have been completed, it's time to start the process of developing a licensing group or department. While the procedures outlined in this chapter are aimed primarily at property owners who are seeking to establish their own licensing departments, many of the steps and procedures have equal applicability to licensing agents who are managing licensing programs for their clients.

The first step in the development of any licensing department is the appointment of a leader to oversee and direct its operations. This individual is typically called a "licensing director" although other titles, such as "licensing manager" or "licensing administrator" are frequently used. Obviously, it is important for the licensing director to have some experience in licensing, preferably on a managerial level. While the actual running of such a department is something that an otherwise sound business manager should be able to easily handle, having experience in the industry will certainly accelerate the learning process and will reduce the chance of errors along the way.

If the person selected to run the licensing department lacks actual licensing experience, it might be a good idea for the property owner to bring in a licensing consultant for a period of time to assist with establishing the procedures that will be required to actually run the program. In the licensing industry, experience is important and there really is no substitute for it.

9.2 The Licensing Department

In order to begin making the critical decisions concerning the structuring and staffing of the department, the property owner should revisit the reasons why it decided to go into licensing in the first place and what its

---

[3] Based on a CLS presentation on *The Fundamentals of Creating and Administering a Licensing Program* by Peter Van Raalte of THE VAN RAALTE CO.,INC., 229 Midland Avenue Montclair, NJ 07042

original objectives were. The three most common reasons for embarking on a licensing program are:

- Increasing brand awareness through extensions into other product categories and through the associated PR and advertising;

- Strengthening the property owner's trademark and copyright protection through use of the property on ancillary products; and

- Generating additional revenue through royalty payments.

Not surprisingly, most licensing departments are structured in such a way that they address each of these objectives.

While there are many ways to organize and staff a licensing department, perhaps the most effective way is to divide the group by responsibility with everyone reporting to the licensing director. Typically, this would include the following groups:

- Marketing Group, with responsibility for handling marketing, advertising and public relations;

- Sales Group, with responsibility for soliciting and developing licensees;

- Legal & Contract Administration Group, with responsibility for overseeing legal matters, reviewing and administering all license agreements and supporting the other groups;

- Finance Group, with responsibility for tracking and collecting royalties, overseeing independent audits and providing reports to the licensing director; and

- Creative Group, with responsibility for developing brand identity, translating brands into images and handling product approvals.

This does not mean that every licensing department requires a minimum of five groups or, for that matter, even requires five different individuals to accomplish these objectives. Many excellent licensing departments are composed of only one or two individuals, each wearing various different hats and sharing these different responsibilities. At the same time, other larger departments have more than a hundred people (and possibly more) broken down by groups and sub-groups.

9.2.1 The Marketing Group

The marketing group is responsible for pulling together the marketing material that the sales group will use in seeking out licensees as well as overseeing all marketing, advertising and public relations activities.

Licensing is all about lead times. If a licensor wants to accomplish something in 18 months, steps must be taken today to set the wheels in motion. As such, the marketing group must work with the licensing director to initially develop a merchandising or marketing plan that will serve as a roadmap for the entire licensing program.

Perhaps the easiest way to create such a merchandising plan is by developing a time line schedule using, for example, the Gantt chart features that are included in such Microsoft Office products as Excel, Visio or Project. Such a schedule should be broken down by product category and, for each category, should identify when: (a) presentations need be made to potential licensees; (b) license agreements must be entered into with licensees; (c) presentations should be made to potential retail partners; (d) products must actually be introduced by licensees; and (e) sales of licensed products should commence. The timeline should also note the dates of all relevant industry trade shows.

In developing the plan, the property owner needs to consider the appropriate lead times that its licensees will need to manufacture, ship and introduce the licensed products, taking into consideration potential delays caused by local customs and holidays, e.g., Chinese New Year, etc. It should also identify where and when new products in a particular category are typically introduced.

The marketing group also has responsibility for planning and overseeing the group's attendance and participation at various licensing trade shows, e.g., the licensing shows in Las Vegas, London, Tokyo, Germany, Shanghai and Hong Kong as well as category-specific trade shows such as Toy Fair, MAGIC and the Bologna Book Fair. Since attendance at such trade shows is an essential part of the marketing process and occurs throughout the year at various locales around the world, this can be a time consuming task, if done thoroughly.

Attending tradeshows is one of the best ways to learn about a specific industry and become knowledgeable about the current trends, styles and new developments in that industry. It is also a good place make or renew contacts with potential licensees and agents. As such, property owners will always want to attend and, ideally, exhibit at these shows.

When attending a trade show, it is important to have a plan. Most trade shows are large, but are frequently organized into various sections by category. A great deal of time can be lost by not using the trade show directory to see what sections of the show are worth visiting. Trade show directories are also a valuable resource for use after a show, as they often provide excellent information about those companies who exhibited at the show.

Finally, the plan should include other relevant milestones for the program, including the commencement of any advertising programs and where and when such advertisements would be placed. It should further include planned PR programs, as well as consumer and retail promotions. Also, it is important to time trade advertising and PR programs to coordinate with the applicable trade shows that its licensees will attend.

Is advertising worthwhile? It can be expensive and should only be undertaken if the property owner can afford it. More importantly, placement is critical. A great ad in the wrong place will not produce results. The message delivered must be clear, compelling, and provide enough information to connect with the desired audience. Selection of the right advertising vehicles is equally important. If the intent is to reach companies and decision makers in a particular industry, then ads promoting the availability of the property need to appear in the specific trade publications most often read by these individuals.

The best places to advertise for a property owner launching a new licensing program are the leading licensing trade magazines. These magazines are read by a wide variety of manufactures and retailers, and provide the best exposure to the market that is looking to buy licenses.

The PR program is also an important element of a property owner's marketing effort since it can create a "buzz" without the expenditure of a tremendous amount of money. It is a particularly good way to build brand awareness. Industry magazines and newsletters (both print and e-mail) thrive on industry news and the marketing group should plan to release a steady stream of communications in order to stay out in front of potential customers.

If the property lends itself to promotional activities, e.g., parties, branded product giveaways at trade shows, etc., these activities should be planned and built into the merchandising strategy as well.

The marketing group is also typically tasked with responsibility for working with both the sales group and the creative group to produce a sales kit that will be used by the sales group in soliciting and closing deals with licenses. A good sales kit will typically include the following components:

- Description of the property to be licensed;

- Style guide illustrating how the property should be used as well as all of the available artwork for the property;

- Overall merchandising plan to allow a prospective licensee to see how their products fit in with the broader program;

- Demographics of potential purchasers of licensed products and the target audience;

- Broadcast partners and initiatives, identifying air dates, frequency, etc., including the partners' marketing and support plans;

- Comprehensive retail plans identifying potential retail partners and product rollout schedules;

- Licensor's independent advertising and marketing plans to show how the licensing program interacts with the overall business development agenda;

- Advertising and publicity plan identifying planned trade advertising, public relations, mall tours, costume character program, etc.;

- Sizzle video plus PowerPoint sales presentations; and

- Boards and sample product concepts illustrating how the property will potentially look when applied to products.

Finally, the Internet cannot be forgotten. We live in an on-line world and virtually all property owners will create a website featuring its property and licensing program, or use a social network such as Facebook to promote the availability of the property. Most go live early in the process and responsibility for the development and maintenance of the site typically falls under the marketing group.

9.2.2 The Sales Group

The Sales Group is tasked with the responsibility of implementing the merchandising plan by identifying a list of all potential licensed products, a list of possible licensees for each product, and then actually "selling" a license to potential licensees using the sales kit discussed above.

The sales groups of larger licensing departments are typically broken down by property, market segment and then by product category, e.g., MICKEY MOUSE licensed merchandise toy products. The theory behind this is that the relevant sales executive becomes an expert in a particular industry, capable of not just understanding its key players and dynamics, but of actually working with the licensee to help develop better product. Selling a license for merchandise sales can be quite different than selling one for promotional sales or directly to retailers.

Finally, the group will include support personnel to assist in making and scheduling appointments and closing deals.

The first order of business for the sales group is to identify those product categories where licensing would be most appropriate and then to develop a list of possible licensed products within those categories. Once done, the group needs to assemble a list of potential licensees for each of these possible licensed products.

This is typically done by researching the particular category and identifying those manufacturers who would be in the best position to manufacture product of the type and quality required by the licensor, but who also have the resources and distribution channels to maximize sales. While every category typically includes a host of choices, many experienced licensing salesmen find themselves going back to the same manufacturers who they have worked with in the past and did a good job.

This is one area where manufacturer's representatives play a major role because they will approach the sales group on behalf of their clients and actually sell their clients to the property owner.

Potential licensees can also be identified using the LIMA database of licensees at www.licensing.org. The database is broken down by product categories and types of products within each category. There are also a number of industry directories published by the various trade publications. Finally, potential licensees can also be identified by simply walking the various industry specific trade shows, where virtually all manufacturers in a potential category are present, irrespective of whether they carry or have ever carried licensed products. Each of these trade show producers publish a directory which can also be a good source for locating potential new licensees.

Once the sales group creates a list of potential licensees, it must then contact and potentially meet with the most promising manufacturers to discuss licensing opportunities. This is where the sales group must "sell" the license to a potential manufacturer, stressing the benefits that taking a license for the property can offer the licensee. The dynamics of such meetings will largely depend on the property, i.e., whether it's a "hot" property or one that has never been licensed before. Obviously, selling a license for a hot property takes far less effort than trying to convince an otherwise reluctant manufacturer to take a chance with a new, untried property. It's no different than a car salesman trying to sell *Road & Track*'s Car of the Year, versus one that has just recently been introduced.

The basic tools of selling a license[4] are fairly straight forward:

- **Know Your Property.** Do your homework and know all that you can about the property. To the prospective licensee, you *are* the expert on the property you are selling.

- **Know Something About The Category You Are Trying to License.** You cannot successfully sell a manufacturer without knowing some basic information about the product category.

- **Familiarize Yourself With The Potential Licensee.** The more you know about the company you are trying to sell to, the better your chances of success.

- **Know Your Competition.** Be prepared to respond to questions concerning competitive properties.

- **Build Your Case.** Know the strengths and weaknesses of your property—no property is perfect, so acknowledge its shortcomings while accentuating the positives. It's important to have the facts and figures relating to your property at your finger tips. Know what you are trying to accomplish *before* you start your presentation and remember, you are leading the meeting, so know where you are heading!

- **Good Presentation Tools are Essential.** In today's techno-marketplace, good presentation tools are expected and essential. The better the visual, the easier it is for the prospective licensee to picture the application of your property to his product. Your marketing and sales materials need to be both informative *and* attractive.

- **Believe in and Get Excited About Your Property.** Enthusiasm is infectious. The more excited you are about the property you

---

[4] Based on a CLS presentation *How to Sell a License* by Danny Simon, President of The Licensing Group, Ltd. 6363 Wilshire Blvd., Los Angeles, CA 90048.

are selling, the better it will be received. Of course, enthusiasm will not replace or cover up a lack of knowledge about the property, product category or your ability to sell a license!

The salesman should also emphasize the benefits that may be derived from taking a license, including increased sales, the ability to sell other products in their line, building exposure and awareness of the manufacturer's own brand and product line and opening up distribution into different channels.

Once the list is narrowed down and there is an expression of interest by one or more potential licensees, they are typically asked to fill out and submit a "Licensee Application" in which the prospective licensee provides important information about its company, financial strength, licensing history and manufacturing and distribution capabilities. A sample Licensee Application is included at Appendix-3.

The Sales group then reviews and evaluates all of these completed licensee applications and ultimately selects the one that appears the best fit for the property. The evaluation process varies from licensor to licensor, but some of the more important elements considered by most include:

- What type of products they are proposing and whether they will be a good fit for the property;

- What is their quality history, e.g., have they manufactured high quality products in the past;

- Size and structure of the company, e.g., is it a major player in the field or a start-up business;

- Strength of design and manufacturing capabilities, e.g., who will actually design the products and where and by whom will they be manufactured;

- Capitalization and financial strength, e.g., are they sufficiently capitalized to meet the financial conditions of the license and to put resources behind the license, or are they on the verge of bankruptcy;

- Distribution capabilities, e.g., how and in what markets will they distribute the product;

- How the license will fit in the manufacturer's product mix;

- Sales history, e.g., what are their sales revenues and what percentage of their total revenues will the licensed products represent;

- Licensing history, e.g., have they had prior licenses and how have they done with them; and

- What financial terms are they offering.

It should be noted that financial terms were specifically identified as the last consideration because, for a license to be successful, it needs to be more than just about who is willing to pay the highest royalty rate or the largest advance or guarantee. If the licensee is not capable of manufacturing quality product or does not have sufficient market penetration, the selection of such a licensee can cause serious problems for the entire program.

Most licensors do not simply rely on the potential licensee's answers in the Licensee Application but will do their own due diligence to confirm various facts. It is quite common for licensors to run Dun & Bradstreet reports to confirm a potential licensee's financial information and whether they are paying their obligations when they become due. Similarly, licensors will also ask for and check the licensee's references, including bank and credit references, as well as their experience with other licensors.

Once a potential licensee has been vetted and is selected, the final step for the sales group is to "close the deal" on the best terms possible for the licensor. Typically, this process starts with the preparation of a term sheet or deal memo which identifies the relevant terms of the transaction. A sample term sheet or deal memo is included here at Appendix-4.

It is important to keep the entire licensing group aware of how these discussions progress as well as the terms being discussed. In many instances, it might even be necessary for other sections of the property owner's organization be involved or, at the very least, kept advised. The use of a sign-off sheet is a good idea to insure that the sales group doesn't offer terms or conditions that the property owner is simply unable or unwilling to offer. Getting as many people involved in this process as necessary is important to avoiding an embarrassing situation or, worse yet, one that must be unwound. Frequently, the sales group will work with the contract administration and legal group in this regard.

9.2.3   The Contract Administration and Legal Group

The contract administration and legal functions are typically intertwined as they cover both the legal protection that is required to support a licensing program, as well as the contract administration function. Frequently the same individual or individuals handle both functions.

[A]   Trademark Clearance and Protection

The necessity for clearing and protecting a licensing property is covered at length in Chapter 4. Trademark clearance is typically the responsibility of the property owner, even if an agent is used.

Prior to actually launching the licensing program, global trademark searches should be conducted to insure that the use of the property by potential licensees will not infringe the rights of anyone else. In performing such searches, special attention should be given to third party uses in those classes with the most licensing activity, i.e., apparel, publishing, toys and video games.

Assuming that the property is cleared for these classes, appropriate trademark applications should be filed to commence the protection process. For a more thorough discussion of this process, see Chapter 5.

[B]   Licensing Forms

Creating a set of standard forms that will be used for the licensing program is very important and should be done at the very outset to insure uniformity throughout the program. Some of the forms that need to be developed are:

- Licensee application form
- Term sheet or Deal Memo
- Standard license agreement
- Approval forms
- Royalty Report form

Of all of these forms, perhaps the most important is the "standard" license agreement that the property owner will use during the licensing program. Special care should be taken in the development of this standard agreement because it will serve as the operative document that will ultimately define the relationship between the parties. Chapter 8 details what should be contained in a license agreement and a form License Agreement is also included as Appendix-5.

It should be appreciated that license agreements are "evolving" documents, meaning that as issues develop and lessons are learned from both good and bad experiences, most licensors will adapt their standard license agreements for future deals to address such issues. Unfortunately, it is usually not possible to change an agreement that has already been signed with a licensee, so if the form is properly prepared in the first place, fewer changes will be required going forward.

This is not to suggest or imply that every licensee will accept the property owner's standard form—most will want some changes and that is to be expected. The goal, however, is to keep the changes to a minimum so that there is a degree of uniformity from agreement to agreement within a program.

[C]   Contract Administration

As the name would imply, the group's primary function is to insure that all licensees comply with their obligations under the respective license agreements. The group will have day to day management responsibility for the licensing program and, in this regard, will frequently work in combination with the finance and creative groups.

It is advisable to establish strong, workable internal systems from the very beginning to make sure that the program proceeds smoothly and without any problems. The group should control the paper flow of the licensing process, typically commencing when the initial licensee proposal is accepted, through termination of the licensee. In most cases, the group is responsible for the following activities:

- **Preparation and Completion of the Deal Memo.** It is important that the deal memo be routed through the appropriate groups for review and approval.

- **Licensee Review and Evaluation.** This entails conducting financial and risk management reviews for all potential licensees and ultimately selecting the final licensee. An important consideration is recognizing any potential product liability issues.

- **License Agreement.** This includes the preparation, negotiation and execution of the license agreement and any amendments. It is good practice for summaries of the license agreements to be prepared and circulated to the various departments and kept readily accessible.

- **Licensee Administration.** This requires the development of a docketing system and "punch list" of all relevant due dates by licensees which should be circulated to other relevant departments, e.g., product approval dates to creative, royalties due for finance, etc. Additionally, and perhaps most importantly, it facilitates constant communication with licensees to insure compliance with the terms of the license agreement.

Established licensing programs may quickly find themselves in a position where they have to track literally hundreds of licensees on a worldwide basis for multiple licensed properties and licensed products. While some have and continue to do this manually, the better practice is to computerize the operation using a comprehensive contract administration software package that also features a royalty tracking/accounting module. Selecting and implementing the right package at the beginning of the program will avoid having to change procedures and systems in mid-stream, which only complicates the issue since it necessitates data conversion, etc. An effective contract administration software package should be able to:

- Assemble license agreements by the selection of individual clauses;

- Generate summaries of the license agreements and sort these by property, licensee, territory, term and product(s);

- Generate form letters or e-mails to licensees for reminders and failures to comply with due dates;

- Track all licensees, licensed products, submission dates and approval dates;

- Generate monthly reports, invoices and reminders;

- Monitor licensees' royalty and guarantee payment status;

- Manage all other aspects of the licensees' financial requirements and obligations;

- Track third party participation revenues for disbursements; and

- Produce management, sales, marketing and product approval reports as well as other relevant information anytime, anywhere.

While some property owners prefer to develop their own, proprietary, contract administration systems, there are a number of excellent third party packages available that will meet the needs of most licensors. Most of these packages are designed to run on PC's and

Macintosh platforms and are surprisingly reasonable in price, compared to the cost of actually developing one's own program. A few of the more commonly used packages as of this writing include the System 7 Universal Rights Management system by Jaguar Consulting; Dependable Rights Manager (DRM) by Dependable Solutions; and the Pelican ProFiles suite by Counterpoint Systems, Inc.

Companies that market off-the-shelf licensing packages can be found in the "support services" section on LIMA's licensing database at www.licensing.org. Most of the companies listed in this section will provide potential customers with evaluation copies of their products as well as detailed sample reports that the program can generate.

9.2.4 The Finance Group

The Finance Group typically gets involved once the license agreement is actually signed and licensing revenue starts flowing, i.e., when the advance gets paid. This group is tasked with the responsibility of tracking payments due from both licensees as well as sub-agents in various countries. It will work closely with the contract administration group, utilizing their software to track all payments due and revenues received from licensees. This group also compiles the reports that will enable the property owner to quickly and easily evaluate the success of the overall licensing program, including the status of individual licensed properties, the licensees and the licensed products.

9.2.5 The Retail Group

In the early days of licensing, licensors would sit back and rely on their licensees to interact with the retail community. Times have changed. Successful property owners now understand the key role that the retailers play in the success or failure of a licensing program and actively seek to engage them during the entire process to help licensees maximize the market presence of their licensed products. Consolidation at retail has given major retailers enormous power and the penetration into one or two of the major chains can be the difference between boom or bust for a program.

Many licensors begin presenting their licensed properties and licensing programs to retailers more than a year before licensed products are actually scheduled to reach the retail shelves, in order to generate excitement for their properties and pave the way for its licensee's products. Retail presentations should clearly convey:

- Property uniqueness, including identification of writers, production quality and possible storylines;

- Identification of broadcast partners and broadcast plans;

- Identification of key licensing partners, including master toy, apparel, publishing and video game licensees, since retailers want to know who has signed on to the licensing program as a critical part of their evaluation;

- Identification of promotional partners, the amount of advertising support for the property and planned in-store cross promotions;

- Property owner's plan to leverage its own assets and any relationship(s) it may have that could help promote the property, e.g., in-theater and DVD trailers, etc.; and

- Advertising and publicity plans for the property to help create consumer awareness.

Some tips for making retail presentations[5] include:

- **Don't Be Vague.** Make sure your presentation has direction and a point of view specifically tailored for the retailer you are presenting to.

- **Allow the Retailer to Take It In.** Once you make your case, allow the retailer to absorb and interpret it for themselves. They understand their venues best and may know details of which you are unaware.

- **Identify Only Your Actual Licensees.** If you are giving out a licensee list, make sure that the licensees are on board since the retailer may call them.

- **Don't Mention Other Retailers Who Have Passed.** If other retailers have passed on the property, keep it to yourself.

- **Think Out of the Box.** Don't limit yourself to the tried and true. Explore the host of new channels of distribution currently available. They may not be the biggest, but they could ultimately become the most successful and lead to bigger opportunities down the road.

- **Be concise.** Time is precious, so make sure to convey your message in an efficient and concise manner.

---

[5] Based on the LIMA webinar entitled *Presenting to Retail: The Good, The Bad and the Ugly*, by David Niggli, former Chief Marketing Officer for FAO Schwartz.

- **Be passionate!** Your approach should not be, "I wanted to see what you thought of this property", but rather "I have a new property that is right for you and let me tell you why."

In recent years, many retailers have not been content to simply sell licensed products that were manufactured by conventional licensees but, instead, have gone directly to the property owner and taken "direct to retail" licenses for products, which they then have manufactured in their own factories or by another third party. By eliminating the conventional licensee and their profit from the equation, the retailers are conceivably able to offer the licensed products to the consumer at lower prices. See Chapter 12, for a more thorough discussion of the retailer's role in licensing.

9.2.6   The Creative Group

The creative group is tasked with the responsibility of controlling how the property appears and will actually be used on the licensed products. It is also responsible for the review and approval of all licensee submissions to ensure that the quality standards are being met and the licensee is using the property correctly on its products.

Most property owners provide their licensees with a "style guide" that illustrates how the property should be depicted and used, as detailed in Chapter 6. It is a "road map" for the licensing property and should be closely followed by all licensees. Today, most style guides are delivered in digital format rather than in hard copy and many are maintained on-line for ease of reference by a licensee.

Again, the primary purpose of a style guide is to inform a licensee as to how it may present the property on the licensed products and thereby enable them to create the best licensed products possible. It will also assure that there is uniformity between all licensees regarding how they will each present the property on their products as well as on packaging and in advertising.

A typical style guide will include:

- How the property is to be depicted and displayed, what characters or brands are included, etc.;

- Rules for use of the property, e.g. "Character X should never..."

- If a character is included, what poses can (and cannot) be used;

- Vehicles and environment art guidelines;

141

- Size ratios of characters, backgrounds, color charts, quotations, and logos as well as a color palette;

- Packaging and hangtags;

- Product concepts;

- Product approval requirements that outline when and how a product must be submitted to the licensor for approval; and

- Legal Notices.

Many property owners prepare their own style guides while others outsource the project to companies that specialize in their preparation. There are a number of such entities and they can be found in the "support services" section on LIMA's licensing database at www.licensing.org.

As licensees are brought on board, the creative group monitors how the property is incorporated with the licensed products. As spelled out in their license agreements, licensees will be required to submit proposed product, packaging and advertising to the licensor for approval at various stages of the production cycle and it is the responsibility of the creative group to review and approve such submissions. Also, as noted earlier, licensees are typically not permitted to proceed to the next step of any process unless they first obtain written approval of their submissions and, in many instances, the failure of a licensor to expressly approve a submission will be deemed disapproval of the submission.

Many licensors involve the creative group in the licensing process as early as possible so that both parties are on the same page when it comes to product development. By reviewing early renderings of product and packaging, potentially devastating problems can be avoided, e.g., where the licensee has produced and shipped 500,000 products only to find that they are not acceptable to the licensor. When the creative group is involved at an early stage, small problems can often be corrected before they become large and expensive ones.

Keeping track of licensee submissions, let alone the approval and disapproval of such submission, can be a job in itself, particularly as the licensing program expands. As such, it is advisable for the creative group to work with the contract administration group and its computer systems to docket when such submissions are due and when responses are required. A program with 50 licensees, for example, may have to track more than 5,000 required submissions every year—no easy feat to do manually.

9.3   International Licensing

Licensing is a global business and one cannot simply focus on the country where the property is created and initially merchandised. This is particularly true for entertainment licensing.

If the property is represented by a licensing agent, the agent should prepare an international licensing plan and submit it to the property owner before the commencement of any international sales effort. Such a plan should, ideally, include the countries and the products that the agent believes would be appropriate for the property, recommendations for the choice of a sub-agent in a particular country or region and any further steps that might be necessary to protect the property in these countries.

As is the case with most licensing matters, successful licensors work backwards from the date when they expect licensed products to first hit their respective markets. The following steps should be taken in the development of an international program:

- Immediately after the decision is made to proceed with an international licensing program, seek trademark protection in each country where licensing is contemplated as well as those countries where licensed products will likely be manufactured, e.g., China, Thailand, Vietnam, Malaysia, etc.;

- Immediately after a broadcast commitment has been obtained:

    – Set up a network of agents in countries where licensing is contemplated;

    – Develop territory-specific tools, e.g., dubbed sizzle reels, translated one-sheet brochures with relevant territory information, broadcast information, global key category partners, etc.; and

    – Identify territory-specific opportunities and work with the appropriate agent(s) to secure them.

- At least one year before the projected launch of licensed products in a particular country:

    – Create sub-agent representation agreements with those sub-agents who will represent the property in their market;

- Manage the sub-agents through systems that reinforce deal execution, product development, retail commitments and product roll-out schedules; and

- Provide support to toy licensee(s) at international toy fairs in Hong Kong, London and Nuremburg including the creation of sizzle video, posters, costume characters, handouts, etc.

9.4   Ethics in Licensing

Some cynics who refer to licensing as the "last bastion of hucksterism" may think that the phrase "ethics in licensing" is an oxymoron. It's not, and as the industry has grown from its modest beginnings into a well regarded and profitable marketing machine, professionalism within the industry remains important and that means that licensing professionals need to deal with each other on an ethical basis.

Webster defines "ethics" as, the "principles of conduct governing an individual or a group." In the context of any professional group, "ethics" is typically considered to be:

• Honesty and candor, instead of gamesmanship and overreaching;

• Seeking enforceable, yet workable, business arrangements; and

• Protecting and enhancing the profession's reputation.

The International Licensing Industry Merchandisers' Association (LIMA) has adopted a Statement of Ethical Principles, addressing the manner in which licensing should be practiced. It states the following:

LIMA supports and encourages its members to conduct themselves in an ethical manner in the course of their business dealing involving licensing properties and licensed products.

A member of LIMA should respect the rights of others and should comply with all applicable local, national and international laws and regulations governing his or her business dealings.

A member should make fair representations as to the nature, quality and extent of the property being offered for license or of the capabilities of the company seeking a license. Any statement not supported by fact should be identified as opinion. A member should not engage in any misleading advertising or solicitation

144

that could lead to false or exaggerated expectations as to the member's skill, experience or ability.

A member should not represent conflicting interests in the same transaction without the knowledge and consent of all parties involved.

A member should hold inviolate all confidences, whether written or implied.

In addition to LIMA'S Statement of Ethical Principles, the American Bar Association observes a code called the Model Rules of Professional Conduct. While obviously many of these model rules have no applicability whatsoever to licensing, there are some that do, particularly Model Rule 4.1 which states:

> In the course of representing a client, a lawyer shall not knowingly:
> (a) Make a false statement of material fact or law to a third person; or
> (b) Fail to disclose a material fact to a third person when disclosure is necessary to avoid assisting a criminal or fraudulent act by a client, unless disclosure is prohibited by Rule 1.6.

In the commentary to Rule 4.1, the committee drafting the rule stated that "[u]nder generally accepted conventions in negotiation, certain types of statements ordinarily are not taken as statements of material fact. Estimates of price or value placed on the subject of a transaction and a party's intentions as to an acceptable settlement of a claim are in this category."

What does that mean in a licensing context where everyone postures and puffs? Puffing is a statement of inference or intention while lying is a misstatement of an objectively, verifiable fact. Puffing in negotiations is not unethical but lying can be. While there may be a fine line between the two, care should be taken not to cross it.

For example, if a negotiator made the statement that his client "would not accept less than 4% royalty," that would generally be considering puffing, even if he knew that he was authorized to accept a royalty rate as low as 2%. If, however, he provides a specific reason as to why he cannot accept lower than a 4% royalty, e.g., "our agreement with the producer prevents us from accepting any royalty lower than 4%," and that reason is untrue, the line between puffing and lying has been crossed.

Under Rule 4.1(b), it is also not ethical to remain silent in a negotiation on a material issue of fact when one knows that its opponent could be misled by such silence. The line between ethical and unethical conduct is, again, a fine one.

For example, if a licensor was asked by a licensee whether its property is valid and whether anyone has ever challenged such validity, the licensor is obligated to answer truthfully. If, however, the licensee does not ask such a question, are they obligated to address the issue? The answer is, probably no. Yet, if the licensee has told them that the issue of trademark validity was very important and the property owner knew of the existence of at least two claims by third parties charging that their trademark was invalid, silence might be considered unethical even if the licensee failed to ask that specific question.

The ABA Model Rules concerning potential conflicts of interest, while interesting and potentially instructive, are generally not relevant in many licensing situations. Because of the potential that lawyers may have access to a client's confidential or privileged information, they are generally held to a higher standard than most licensing professionals, for whom the possibility of disclosing privileged information does not typically arise.

That said, conflicts of interest in licensing can prove particularly problematic because the industry is relatively small and individuals frequently find themselves at different times on different sides of the same negotiating table. It is difficult, if not impossible, to address every particular situation that might arise, but one rule of thumb almost always applies. In the event that a licensing executive enters a potential conflict of interest scenario, e.g., where they are representing a licensee who is looking to take a license from their former employer, or worse yet, they are an agent who is representing both the licensor and potential licensee, if they elect to remain involved in the transaction they would be well advised to disclose this information to all relevant parties at the earliest possible occasion. Virtually all conflicts of interest can be waived by full disclosure to both parties and with their consent, preferably in writing. If the parties do not agree to a waiver, they would be wise to withdraw from the negotiations.

9.5   Ensuring Social Compliance[6]

Social compliance is a relatively recent concern for many licensors due, in large measure, to negative media attention focused on working conditions in factories that produce licensed products, most notably in China. The problem received national attention in the United States in 1996 as a result of a controversy involving Kathie Lee Gifford.

The news media and social activist groups around the world exposed the fact that some factories were applying sub-standard working conditions and were employing prison and child labor to produce the products. This put pressure on the private sector to play a role in trying to improve such conditions.

Make no mistake about it, there is a serious problem in this industry. Some factories blatantly violate their local laws, falsify their records and even bribe inspectors. This is a way of life in some countries and to think otherwise is to simply ignore the problem.

The private sector's reaction was the development of codes of conduct for these factories to abide by if they wanted to continue to work with a particular property owner. The first code of conduct was actually adopted by Levi Strauss in 1991. In 1998, the Fair Labor Association was created with White House support and developed its own code.

Over the past decade, many licensors, retailers and trade associations have adopted social compliance standards which they require their partners and suppliers to follow. The purpose of these codes is to raise the standards of working conditions in factories that actually manufacture licensed products and promote social responsibility.

While there are slight differences between many of these codes, in one form or another they all address the following issues:

- Maximum working hours for employees;

- Compensation of employees; and

- Social insurance that an employer must carry for its employees.

LIMA has its own Code of Business Practices, which may be found at http://www.licensing.org/about/business-practices.php.

---

[6] Based on a 2009 LIMA webinar presentation entitled *Social Compliance: Introduction and Overview* by Ian Spalding, President, InFact Global Partners, 16A, Dotcom House, 128 Wellington Street Central Hong Kong.

Establishing standards is one thing—enforcing them is quite another. Very few licensors simply ignore the issue altogether and, at the very least, most require their licensees to conform to some standard. While they may not aggressively enforce such a requirement, they will reserve the right to terminate the licensee should it be determined that the licensee was non-compliant. This is the minimum that any licensor should do in this regard.

Most licensors actually go further and, do, in fact, actively look to enforce these standards, typically by auditing the factories of their licensees. This is done by either their internal auditors or by third parties who specialize in such audits. While some simply audit on a superficial basis and tend to look the other way when violations are found, there is an increasing number of licensors that require a non-conforming licensee to either correct the problems or face termination of their license agreement.

Some licensors will actually go the extra mile and work with licensees to make sure that their factories are in compliance with these standards. They have shifted focus from mere monitoring to actively promoting continuous improvement, even to the point where they are willing to share in the associated cost of reaching compliance. They have begun to emphasize education and capacity building, as opposed to simply conducting more audits. Longer-term corrective action plans are necessary and ultimately reinforce better business practices. Appropriately, a growing number of licensors today recognize the implications of non-compliance, which can seriously tarnish not only the attractiveness of its primary and licensed products but of its moral image and reputation as well.

Chapter 10

Licensing Agents & Consultants

10.1 Introduction

Every new licensor asks the same question when it faces the task of actually conducting a licensing program—should I do this myself or should I retain an independent licensing agent and let them run the program?

Licensing programs succeed because of the efforts of quality, hard working people with experience in the area. Thus, the answer is simple: if the property owner is satisfied that it possesses such personnel with sufficient expertise, it should proceed on its own. If not, the property owner should consider retaining a licensing agent and letting them assume responsibility for the entire program.

There are a number of licensing agents and consultants readily available to assist the property owner in guiding them through the licensing maze. Most are former in-house licensing professionals from the studios, sports leagues and corporations who have formed their own firms or joined existing agencies. As such, they typically bring with them contacts and relationships with other licensors and licensees. While their clients include a number of first time licensors, many well-known and established licensors simply prefer to outsource their entire licensing programs to such professionals and are content to sit back and let them work their magic.

It should be appreciated that while these individuals are called "licensing agents," they are not "agents" *per se* in a legal sense, since they typically do not have the power to bind or sign agreements on behalf of the property owner. Instead, their role is to simply seek out and find the best potential licensees for a property owner and bring those licensees to the property owner for consideration, approval and, eventually, signature. They also have the responsibility for administering the subsequent program.

Irrespective of the type of property that they handle, almost all licensing agents are compensated in the same way, i.e., they receive a commission or percentage of the licensing revenue that they generate for the property owner. Some may also receive a monthly fee or retainer on top of their commission which may (or may not) be creditable against the commission.

Typical commissions for a licensing agent range anywhere from 25% to 40% of the royalty income paid by licensees and most commissions are in the 30% to 35% range.

When some property owners look at these percentages, they frequently ask whether the agent is worth it. Most property owners realize that it's often necessary to spend money to make money and an incentivized agent will typically work harder for the property owner and maximize licensing revenues. Many understand that receiving 65% of a larger pie is far better than keeping 100% of a smaller pie or, worse yet, no pie. Moreover, it must be appreciated that the licensing agent will typically bear many of the costs and expenses associated with running the program, thus saving the property owner significant sums in the process.

Licensing agents bring with them credibility in their field and an ability to open doors that the property owner may not otherwise be able to enter. Also, based on their experience in the industry, they are frequently able to negotiate the best deal possible for the property owner. Thus, over the long run, most good agents earn their commission.

There is also a middle ground, where some property owners bring licensing consultants on board to help jump-start the program which they will eventually administer themselves. There are a number of available licensing professionals who will work on a consulting basis. Rather than assume responsibility for conducting the entire licensing program, these individuals will consult with and assist the property owner in creating and running their own licensing department. Licensing consultants are typically paid on a fee or retainer basis although, in some situations, they may also receive a small commission or bonus based on the licenses that they help create or develop.

Licensing consultants are particularly effective at conducting an independent review or audit of a licensing program, or when a licensor wants to expand its program into different types of licensed products. For example, a property owner who might want to add an apparel line to its licensing program may seek out someone with specific experience in that area to find the right licensees for the property.

10.2   The Role & Compensation of a Licensing Agent

The reasons why a property owner elects to retain a licensing agent vary. Some decide to engage an agent because they lack the requisite expertise, while others bring an agent on board because they don't have the time or resources. Still others decide to use an agent because they believe the agent will help them penetrate markets at a much faster rate than if they tried to do it themselves.

Whatever the reason, the first step is to find the right licensing agent for both the property owner and the property, which begins by identifying possible agents who specialize in a particular type of property. This can be done by asking friends and colleagues for recommendations or by thoroughly researching all potential agents and making an independent selection.

The LIMA database at www.licensing.org is an excellent way to initiate this process. One of the search fields is labeled "licensing agents" and they are further indexed by property type. Thus, it is relatively easy to identify all of the licensing agents that specialize in a particular property category, e.g., corporate brands. Their listings typically will also include the specific properties that each represents.

Selecting a licensing agent is very different from buying a house where brokers repeatedly advise that it's all about, "location, location, location." While the location of the agent and their proximity to the property owner is a factor to be considered, it should not be the determining factor. With telecommunications and overnight package delivery services, it is relatively easy to keep in touch with an agent across the country. If the agent is the best qualified to represent the property, they should not be eliminated simply because of distance. Most property owners will quickly learn that if the right agent is selected, there will not be many times when face to face meetings are required and that most issues, even serious ones, can be resolved by telephone.

After identifying potential agents or brokers, it is important to meet with each of them and discuss the possibility of their representing the property. The agent will obviously want to see the property before agreeing to represent it and a property owner should not be reluctant to show it to them. Some property owners may want the prospective agent to sign a confidential disclosure agreement, although such an agreement is probably unnecessary except in cases where truly confidential information is to be shared with the agent, e.g., business plans, marketing information, etc.

The property owner should ask the agent for a description of its background and capabilities as well as a list of references, particularly similar properties that it has represented in the category. We live in an age of specialization and most agents specialize in representing particular types of properties, e.g., corporate, art, entertainment, etc. Simply because an agent has successfully represented a property in one category, e.g., a sports property, does not mean that the same agent will be equally successful with a different type of property, e.g., an art property.

Licensing is a relationships business. The agent's role is to deal with and develop relationships with potential licensees. At the same time, manufacturers are similarly specialized. As such, an agent who works primarily with manufacturers that have only taken sports licenses in the past may not have sufficient contacts or relationships with manufacturers who specialize in licensing art properties. The game is for the property owner to take full advantage of the agent's relationships and the best way for that to happen is to retain an agent with strong contacts among the best potential licensees for that category of property.

During these meetings and interviews, the question of compensation should be discussed. This is an essential element of the relationship and should not be avoided. As stated above, most agents are paid on a commission basis, i.e., they receive a percentage of the gross revenues generated by any licensees that use the property. Gross revenues include *all* monies, paid by both licensees and sub-licensees, as well as any entertainment revenues. Commission rates vary widely and are typically negotiable, although they tend to range between 25% and 40% with most in the 30%-35% range.

Some agents will seek an ongoing fee or retainer in addition to the commission. This may be paid on a monthly or quarterly basis and is frequently paid only during the first year or so of the relationship. Agreeing to pay a retainer may result in the agent agreeing to lower its commission rate. For example, an agent who typically charges a 35% commission may agree to work for a 25% commission if the property owner also paid a $10,000 per month retainer.

When a retainer is paid, the parties need to agree on whether that retainer will be treated as a non-creditable fee or whether it is creditable against any commission due the licensing agent, in much the same way as an advance against royalties by a licensee is handled. Both are acceptable and common although this should be discussed and established upon up front so that there are no surprises. In almost all instances, retainers are non-refundable, except in the event of a material breach of the agreement by the agent.

Similarly, the parties need to agree who will be responsible for the costs and expenses that the agent will incur in connection with its duties. Normally, the agent is responsible for all of its own operating costs and expenses. Property owners are, however, typically required to bear the costs associated with protecting the property; any required legal or auditing support; artwork; marketing materials; developing a style guide and sales materials; any materials necessary to commence product development and exhibition costs at the various licensing shows and other trade shows.

In selecting an agent, the property owner should make sure that there is the right "chemistry" with the agent. The agent will not only be representing the property but the property owner as well. It is, therefore, important that the agent fit the right mold. Much of what an agent will be required to do is based on trust. Therefore, the property owner should have a good feeling that the agent not only can, but will, represent the property owner's best interests.

As a matter of basic due diligence, the property owner should ask for and check the agent's references, including speaking with other property owners that they represent. Ask them how it worked out and whether they were satisfied with the agent's performance. While the agent will probably only provide the names of satisfied clients, what these satisfied clients have to say (or not say) can be revealing.

Perhaps the most important question to ask each of their clients is, "did the agent actually do everything that they said they would do for you before you retained them?" If the answer is yes, the property owner has probably found the right agent. If the answer is no, don't simply dismiss the agent—dig further. The fact that an agent may not have been able to develop a successful licensing program for a property does not mean that the agent didn't do a good job; some properties are simply not merchandisable no matter how hard the agent may have tried.

Most agents will only work on an exclusive basis, which means that the property owner will be contractually tied to that agent for the term of the agent agreement. During that period, any licenses that are entered into within the agent's territory, whether developed by the agent or others, will be subject to the payment of a commission to the agent.

The reason for this is that the agent does not want the property owner working behind its back and potentially negotiating for the same rights with a different potential licensee. If this should happen, it can damage the credibility of the property and even expose the property owner to potential liability. If nothing else, it can and often will lead to confusion in the marketplace as to who actually has the rights to represent the licensor. Potential licensees want to know that they are dealing with *the* entity that has the rights to represent the property.

Similarly, agents will often want to have representation rights that extend as for long as possible—typically for a minimum of two years and, frequently, longer if the selling cycle is abnormally long.

10.3 Licensing Agent Agreement

It is imperative that the agent agreement be in writing so as to avoid any possible misunderstandings. Nothing should be left to chance. While some agent agreements may take the form of a letter agreement, a formal written agreement is preferable. For reference, a sample Licensing Agent agreement is included at Appendix-1.

Many agents have what they may call a "standard" agreement. The property owner should recognize that an agent's "standard" agreement is typically anything but that—it is probably one of a number of "standard" agreements that they have and use to fit a particular circumstance. Moreover, the property owner must appreciate that this "standard" agreement was undoubtedly drafted by the agent's attorney and will resolve most, if not all, issues in the agent's favor.

Thus, the property owner should be prepared to carefully review and negotiate the agent's proposed agreement. If in doubt, it should ask its intellectual property counsel to review the agreement and provide appropriate suggestions or revisions.

At the very least, a well-drafted agent agreement should address the following issues:

- Whether the agent is to represent *all* of the property owner's properties for all markets, or merely a particular property for a particular market;
- Whether the relationship is exclusive or non-exclusive;
- The territory, or territories, where the agent will operate;
- The term (length) of the relationship, and whether the agent has the right to renew the agreement for additional terms;
- The specific duties and responsibilities of the agent;
- Who will be responsible for reviewing licensee submissions and making approvals;
- Who will receive revenues from the licensees and how the revenue will be disbursed;
- How the agent will be compensated for its services;

154

- How and when the agreement may be terminated; and

- Whether the agent will continue to receive a commission after termination of the agreement and, if so, for how long and what the commission will be.

The scope of the agent's representation should be clearly defined to avoid future problems. Will the agent be representing all of the property owner's properties or just one? If the agent is representing all of the properties, does that include just the properties currently in existence or will it include future developed properties? Whatever the parties decide, it should be clearly defined in the agreement.

If the agent is being engaged to only handle a specific property, the agreement should make that clear. In such a case, the property owner would be free to use another agent to license its other properties or, alternatively, directly license them on its own.

There are situations where an agent is retained solely for the purpose of developing a specific licensee. For example, an agent may have a special relationship with a particular company, e.g., an animation house. The property owner might be willing to engage the agent solely for the purpose of working out a licensee with that entity while reserving all other rights for itself.

As noted earlier, agents can be appointed on either an exclusive or non-exclusive basis, although most licensing agents in the merchandising field work on an exclusive basis. An exclusive arrangement means that the agent will be the *only* person or firm that can represent the property owner during the term of the agreement. In a non-exclusive relationship, the property owner is free to employ other agents or represent the property itself. The agreement needs to clearly define this.

The agent agreement should also define the geographical territory in which the agent may act on behalf of the property owner. The territory of the agent grant is similar to the licensed territory of the eventual license agreement—United States, North America, Japan, worldwide, etc. Before granting worldwide representation rights, however, the property owner should satisfy itself that the agent has adequate contacts in all countries in the territory.

The term of the agent relationship also needs to be defined, i.e., the period during which the agent will be representing the property or the property owner. Most property owners prefer to keep the agent's term relatively short, e.g., between six months and a year, which may not be sufficient time for the agent to establish a viable licensing program. Agents usually prefer significantly longer terms, e.g. three or four years. While the "standard" term of representation will depend on the property involved, what the agreed upon goals are, the type of licensed product(s) the agent is attempting to license and the agent's reputation, the typical term is most often at least two years. The reason for this is simply that licensing programs take time to get established. If the agent is responsible for assisting the property owner in the initial preparation of all requisite materials, this task alone may consume the first six months of the term. If the term was only a year, there would be precious little time for the agent to actually work the licensing program.

Irrespective of the length of the actual term, the property owner should build into the agreement some mechanism to be able to terminate a non-performing agent, particularly if the agreement is exclusive. This is generally accomplished by including performance milestones that must be met by the agent in order for it to continue to retain the right to represent the property. Typical milestones include a requirement that the agent generate a certain minimum amount of licensing revenues or conclude a minimum number of license agreements during a particular period. These milestones are negotiable and will depend on the type of property and the territory involved.

Performance is the name of the game in any relationship with an agent. If the agent is performing and meeting its milestones, the agent should be able to retain the rights for a longer period. If, however, the agent is not doing the job and is falling short of reaching these milestones, the property owner should be able to terminate the relationship.

An alternative approach is to provide for a shorter term and build in a series of options for the agent to automatically renew the agreement upon reaching the same or similar milestones. Both approaches are commonly used and equally effective.

As noted above, most licensing agents are not "agents" in the classic sense, since they generally lack the ability to bind the property owner to a license agreement. In actuality, they are more like a sales representative for the property owner.

There are, however, rare situations in which an agent has the power to bind the property owner and may even be a named party to the license agreement. Such a situation should be avoided, if possible, since the resultant relationship can create potential problems, particularly if the property owner ever decides to terminate the agent. Untangling and removing the agent from a host of license agreements can be difficult and is almost always contentious. Thus, the agent should never be given the authority to enter into a license agreement on the property owner's behalf unless absolutely necessary.

Agent agreements should clearly spell out the agent's duties and responsibilities in connection with the licensing program. Unfortunately, however, they rarely do—perhaps because many such agreements are drafted by agents. During the discussions leading up to the finalization of the agent agreement, an agent will typically identify, in great detail, what it intends to do on behalf of the property owner. This is an excellent road map by which to measure the agent's future performance and the property owner should insist that this list be incorporated into the agent agreement.

The following is a list of certain duties that are commonly expected of the agent:

- Assist the property owner in refining and developing the property into a licensable property;

- Provide assistance in determining which product categories the property owner must file in for trademark protection;

- Developing marketing and presentation materials for use in presenting the property to prospective licensees;

- Identifying prospective licensees likely to be interested in taking a license for the property;

- Presenting the property to those prospective licensees most likely to be interested in the property;

- Negotiating the terms of all agreements between the property owner and the licensees;

- Administering the licensing program, including periodically reviewing all licensee submissions of licensed products and associated advertising, packaging and promotional materials to insure that the quality control provisions of the agreement are met;

- Wherever necessary, personally inspecting the licensee's manufacturing facilities to insure that the quality control provisions are being complied with; and

- Collecting all advances, guaranteed minimum royalty payments and actual royalty payments from licensees.

In short, the licensing agent should be tasked with doing everything that a vigilant property owner would do if it was running its own licensing program.

The mechanics of how the licensing agent actually gets paid, and by whom, always leads to interesting discussions. Most agents will want to directly receive the revenues from the licensees, have the ability to deduct its commissions and any approved expenses, and then remit the balance (within a specified period of time) to the property owner. This is quite typical since the agent normally has the best understanding of what a licensee's expected royalties should be from quarter to quarter. Since this is the agent's principal means of income, they are frequently more diligent than a property owner in ensuring that royalties are promptly paid.

Permitting a well-established licensing agent to collect royalty income directly from a licensee, deduct what it is owed, and then distribute the balance to the property owner, should not pose a problem for most property owners. In fact, that puts the onus on the agent to do the necessary accounting. If such an approach is followed, a property owner may request that the agent allocate these licensee revenues into a dedicated account so as to not co-mingle it with the agent's other assets.

Some property owners may further require that their agent maintain a special bank account in the name of the property owner for receipt and deposit of such royalty payments. The agent would be given access to such special account during the term of the agreement and may deduct its commission and remit the balance to the property owner.

A property owner may not, however, have the same comfort level with an agent that is relatively new to the business. In such instances, the property owner might prefer that licensees remit their royalty payments directly to the property owner who will then assume responsibility for accounting and compensating the agent.

If there is an impasse over this point, one possible compromise is to have the licensees pay their royalties, etc. into an escrow account maintained by a third party escrow agent, e.g., a bank, an accounting firm, etc. The escrow agent would be empowered to collect such revenues and distribute them to both the agent and property owner in accordance with the terms of an escrow agreement. It should be noted, however, that use of an escrow account usually creates additional expenses that will reduce the amount of income the licensing program will generate.

The "post-termination compensation" provision is, undoubtedly, the most hotly negotiated provision in any agent agreement. This provision governs what, if anything, the agent will receive after expiration or termination of the agent agreement and for how long.

It should be appreciated that since most agents work on a commission basis, their income is back-ended, i.e., they get paid in the future for the work that they do today. Accordingly, agents want to protect themselves from a situation in which they may have worked tirelessly to develop a successful licensing program for their client, only to be terminated before the future royalty stream actually commences. Accordingly, most agents will want to continue to receive their commissions after termination or expiration of their agent agreement based on royalty revenues paid by those licenses that they had developed while operating under the agreement.

Property owners are, of course, reluctant, to agree to such an open-ended, post-termination commission stream and will attempt to limit the scope and time of such commission payments. Their concern is that once the agent is terminated, they will have to assume responsibility for managing the program themselves or have to pay another agent to assume such responsibility. In either event, they will incur administration costs and the prospect of having to pay a double commission is not terribly attractive to many property owners.

This is a very real issue that undoubtedly generates more disputes than any other provision in an agent agreement. As such, this issue needs to be resolved at the outset of the relationship, NOT after the fact. There are a number of possible compromises, including:

- The agent will continue to receive its full commission on all revenues paid under all license agreements that were in place as of the date that the agent agreement expired or was terminated for the balance of the term of such license agreements, plus any renewals, modifications, substitutions, or extensions of such license agreements;

- The agent will continue to receive its full commission on all revenues paid under all license agreements that were in place as of the date that the agent agreement expired or was terminated but only through the original term of such license agreements;

159

- The agent will continue to receive its full commissions on all revenues paid under all license agreements that were in place as of the date that the agent agreement expired or was terminated but only for a fixed period of time, e.g., three years;

- The agent will receive a reduced commission on all revenues paid under all license agreements that were in place as of the date that the agent agreement expired or was terminated for a fixed period on a declining scale, e.g., 100% commission in year one, 50% in year two, 25% in year three, etc.; or

- any combination of the above.

It should also be noted that if the agent is to continue to receive compensation for licenses the agent generated during the term of representation, the agent may be required to continue the administration of those licenses. In such cases, the owner may want to replace the expired representation agreement with an agreement under which the agent is obligated to perform only administrative duties for those specific licensing agreements.

Another issue that needs to be addressed when negotiating post-termination compensation for the agent is how to handle those agreements that the agent may have been negotiating as of the date the agent agreement expired or terminated. This is a very common situation because of the amount of time that normally passes between when an agent finds and makes a sales presentation to a potential licensee and the time that the final license agreement is actually executed. If an agent finds and secures a potential licensee during the term of the agent agreement but the property owner doesn't actually finalize and sign the license agreement until after the agent agreement terminates or expires, the agent will want to be compensated for its work in finding and securing that licensee.

In order to protect themselves in such a situation, agents will typically seek to include what is called a "tail" provision in the agent agreement. This usually states that the agent will be entitled to receive its commissions for all license agreements that the property owner entered into during the term of the agent agreement, as well as any agreement that the property owner entered into within six (6) months after termination or expiration of the agent agreement that was based on a presentation made by the agent during the term of the agent agreement. Such a "tail" protects the agent from a property owner who may decide to delay execution of the agreement with the thought that by doing so they could avoid having to pay the agent its commission.

Another provision that some agents require in their agreements with property owners is a representation and warranty that the property owner actually owns or controls rights to the property and has the right to license the property to third parties. By extension, agents will also typically require that the property owner indemnify them against any claims made by third parties in connection with such warranties. Furthermore, as mentioned in Chapter 8, agents are also likely to insist that the agent and the agency be named as insured parties by the licensee in the product liability policy that the licensee is required to provide during the term of the license. These provisions are fundamental and generally non-negotiable from the agent's perspective.

10.4   Sub-Agents & International Licensing Agents

While location should not be a major consideration in choosing a licensing agent, there are exceptions when it comes to international licensing. A property owner located in California may easily be able to work with a New York based licensing agent for most matters, but it is an entirely different matter when it comes to working with agents in different countries, in different time zones, speaking different languages.

As a consequence, many licensing agents that oversee worldwide licensing programs (and even property owners running their own licensing programs) regularly employ international agents, in other regions or countries. These international agents may work directly for a property owner that is conducting its own licensing program as an "international agent" or, alternatively, as a "sub-agent" when working for the licensing agent. Irrespective of what they are called, they are responsible for developing the licensing program in a particular country or region.

The advantages of working with international agents are numerous, including more direct contact with local licensees, assistance with administration of the program in such countries, interpretation of local languages and customs, and even transfer of royalties from those countries where there may be currency restrictions, e.g., China, Brazil or India. It should be noted that typically international agents will be the party to whom the royalties are paid, deducting their fees and remitting the balance to the party (agent or owner) who engaged their services.

International sub-agents are generally paid in the same way that a licensing agent is paid, i.e., they receive a commission based on the revenue generated by licensees they secure within their country or region. If they are retained directly by the licensing agent, a sub-agent may share the licensing agent's commissions on that portion of licensing revenues from their country or region. For example, if the licensing agent had negotiated an overall 35% commission with the property owner, the licensing agent and sub-agent might agree that the sub-agent would receive 25% of the total licensing revenues from that country or region while the original licensing agent would receive 10% of the licensing revenues.

In many cases, a licensing agent will actually negotiate a higher commission rate with the property owner in regions where it is anticipated that sub-agents may be employed to allow for greater flexibility in negotiating such splits, e.g., the licensing agent would receive a 35% commission where no sub-agent was necessary and a 45% commission where a sub-agent was employed.

If the property owner directly retains the international agent, the property owner would be responsible for payment of the international agent's commission in much the same way that it pays the licensing agent.

How does one find the right international agent? There are licensing agents in virtually all countries throughout the world and most, if not all, are listed in the LIMA database at www.licensing.org which can be searched by country. When a property owner is working with a licensing agent, the selection of the sub-agent is often best left to the licensing agent.

As is the case with most domestic licensing agents, international agents typically have a particular specialty, e.g., entertainment, sports or celebrity properties. Most have their own individual "styles" and the property owner or licensing agent must be assured that such style meshes with their own.

It should be noted that the formation of the European Union has created its own share of issues with respect to licensing and it can impact the way licensing agents operate within the Union. Economically, the European Union is essentially one nation with individual states. Under European Union regulations, if a licensee acquires a license for one country within the Union, e.g., France, it has the ability to sell its products in other countries within the Union irrespective of what the license agreement may provide or restrict. The EU has strictly enforced this requirement and will impose substantial fines if a party attempts to limit such territorial freedom. There are reports of manufacturers being fined as much as €1 million for violating these regulations.

There are, of course, ways to mitigate the impact of these restrictions. For example, publishing licensors may simply grant licenses for language-specific rights, e.g., an English language version, rather than countries *per se*. This may help to limit the sales of products into non-English speaking countries. That said, this regulation has had an enormous impact on licensing and, more particularly, the work of agents and sub-agents within the various EU countries.

Another issue facing many of the international licensing agents is the problem created by gray market or parallel imports, i.e., where a licensee in a certain territory, for example, the United Kingdom, improperly exports otherwise genuine products into another country, e.g., the United States, such that the U.S. licensee is now faced with competition from an unexpected source.

Gray market sales have been an on-going problem in many industries, most notably the photography market in the United States, where New York City camera retailers regularly import and sell genuine products that had been manufactured for sale in other territories. Licensees and licensing agents in a particular territory face this problem on a regular basis because it can result in reduced sales and, accordingly, lower commissions.

Some highly successful property owners and licensors believe that international agents should be required to pay them for the right to represent their property in a particular country or territory or, alternatively, should guarantee that they will receive a minimum amount of royalties as a result of the agent's efforts. While that may occasionally happen, most international agents are reluctant to pay for such a right or consent to performance guarantees. International agents may, however, agree that if they have not generated a minimum amount of royalty revenues during a certain period, the property owner may terminate their services. A sample sub-agent agreement is included as Appendix-2.

10.5 Manufacturer's Representatives

While licensing agents typically work for the property owner or licensor, "manufacturer's representatives" work for the licensee to assist them in selecting the right property or properties for their client. They also assist in making introductions to various licensors and licensing agents, and in consulting with the manufacturer during the program on the marketing side of the business in order to maximize the sale of the licensed products. As is often the case with licensing agents, most of these manufacturer's representatives are seasoned licensing professionals with decades of licensing experience.

While licensing agents typically hone their expertise by working with major property owners and licensing companies, manufacturer's representatives frequently come from the licensee community, working for some of the major licensees where they would have been able to establish contacts with the major property owners and licensing agents.

Manufacturer's representatives are particularly helpful for manufacturers who are new to licensing and can help initiate them to the process. Many of the most successful licensees recognize the value that these manufacturer's representatives bring and continue their relationships well beyond the early stages.

Initially, they will study the manufacturer's operations and help them determine whether licensing would be profitable for their business and, if so, what category of licensed properties should be considered. They will then make recommendations to the manufacturer on specific properties that may best fit with their product line and how they could be incorporated into their product mix.

Working with the manufacturer, the manufacturer's representative will then reach out to the various property owners and licensing agents to explore whether there is any interest on their part in granting licenses to their clients and, if so, under what terms. If there is interest on the part of both the property owner and their client, the manufacturer's representative will then work on behalf of the manufacturer to negotiate the terms of a license agreement for the property.

Since manufacturer's representatives are intimately familiar with the licensing industry, they understand the norms and standards of licensing deals in these and other categories. As such, they are able to regularly counsel and advise their clients on the state of the industry, what their competitors are doing, and whether one deal is better than another.

Good manufacturer's representatives will not stop there—they will continue to work with their clients during the licensing program, collaborating with them on product development, marketing strategies and potentially seeking other properties that would fit into their product mix.

Much like a licensing agent, the manufacturer's representative is typically compensated on a commission basis relative to the amount of royalty income that their client pays to the property owner under license agreements for which they are responsible for bringing in. While the range of compensation for a manufacturer's representative depends upon the role they are expected to fill, it is quite common for them to receive about 2% of their client's net sales of licensed products. For example, if their client paid the licensor a 10% royalty on its net sales of licensed products, the client would pay the manufacturer's representative an additional 2% of its net sales as compensation.

It is not uncommon for a manufacturer to pay its manufacturer's representative a monthly retainer for its services which may (or may not) be creditable against the commission. Like most things in licensing, that is the subject of negotiation between the parties. Similarly, there are instances where a manufacturer will simply pay the manufacturer's representative a consulting fee with no commission.

The issue of exclusivity is always an issue with respect to manufacturer representatives since it may dictate when a commission is owed. In the case of an exclusive relationship, the manufacturer's representative is typically paid its commission irrespective of whether they were responsible for acquiring the license or not. In non-exclusive arrangements, however, the manufacturer is only paid a commission on licenses which they were responsible for acquiring. A sample manufacturer's representative agreement is included at Appendix-6.

10.6 Making the Relationship Work

The secret of working with any outside professional is the same—communication, communication, communication. The more that the property owner or the licensee communicates with its agent or representative, the more helpful these professionals can be.

When working with outside licensing professionals, it is advisable to refrain from adopting the "mushroom theory of management", i.e., the best way to motivate someone is to: (a) keep them in the dark and (b) feed them manure. While this admonition holds true with respect to virtually any outside professional, it is particularly true when working with a licensing professional.

While a licensing professional may possess substantial expertise in the licensing industry and even the category in which they may be working, they probably do not understand all the intricacies of their client's particular business and rarely know the personalities of its management.

It is advisable to think of the agent as an extension of the entity it is representing. With this in mind, the more information that a property owner or licensee can provide the agent, the more they will likely accomplish. That, alone, should be sufficient incentive to both parties.

Chapter 11

MARKETING & PROMOTING LICENSED PROPERTIES

11.1   Introduction

The name of the game in licensing is marketing and promotion—for both property owners and licensees alike, albeit for different reasons. Licensors are typically more concerned with promoting the property for use on their primary product or service, e.g., their television show or book, etc. While potentially important if they intend to develop a licensing program, the idea of promoting the property *per se*, i.e., independent of their primary product or service, is more of an afterthought for many.

Similarly, licensees typically have a singular purpose when they look at promotion in that they usually are only interested in promoting their line of licensed products so as to increase sales thereof.

While licensors and licensees may seem to be approaching the issue of promotion from opposite ends of the spectrum, when a licensing program actually gets up and running, their interests converge. The more popular and well known a property becomes, the greater its value—for the licensor in terms of increased licensing revenues and for the licensee in terms of increased sales of licensed products.

This is what has led many licensors to create marketing funds to help raise the visibility of their properties. These marketing funds are underwritten collectively by the licensees, usually by having them pay an additional royalty or marketing fee. These marketing fees typically run between 1% and 3% of the licensee's net sales and are pooled together to fund a common promotional program on behalf of the property which covers advertising, promotions and public relations. Presumably, such a program should save the individual licensees from having to conduct their own programs or, at the very least, reduce the amount of money that they may otherwise need to spend for such programs.

11.2   Advertising Programs

Traditional advertising remains the cornerstone of any marketing program. The various licensing trade publications, which include *License!*, *Total Licensing*, *Licensing Book*, *The Licensing Report* and

Royalties, are all geared toward accommodating a property owner's advertising needs and requirements. Many of these publications also include electronic versions such as, for example, the *License! Global* email newsletter.

Some of these publications publish "dailies" during each of the various licensing shows that are distributed to attendees and exhibitors. For example, *License! Global* publishes a daily for the Licensing Expo held in Las Vegas, NV in June of each year as well as at Brand Licensing held in London, England September of each year. Each of these dailies offers a unique advertising opportunity to help promote a property.

There are also a number of directories of licensing properties as well as trade show directories that accept advertising. The advantage of advertising in a directory rather than a periodic publication is that, at least theoretically, the directory is used all year long and, as such, the advertiser's exposure is greater. Again, these are excellent opportunities to convey a message to a targeted group.

When designing an advertising program, consideration should also be given to running ads in industry specific publications where they can be seen and read by potential licensees and retailers. For example, dedicated toy industry publications include *The Toy Book*, *The Toy Report*, *Specialty Toys and Gifts*, *Toy Wishes, Toys 'N Playthings* and *TDMonthly*. *KidScreen* is a trade publication that services kids' entertainment professionals while *Gifts & Decorative Accessories* and *Gift Shop* both focus on the gift industry. The fashion industry has a host of industry specific publications that accept advertising, including *Fashion Market* and *Women's Wear Daily*. For the music industry *Billboard* is perhaps the leading publication, while *PCGamer* is a publication directed to the video game market. *Brandweek* and *Advertising Age* are excellent vehicles for reaching the advertising industry and corporate markets, which also regularly publish licensing-focused feature articles.

On-line advertising cannot be overlooked, particularly on industry specific sites. Many of the above mentioned publications include on-line editions that accept some form of advertising. In addition, there are a number of blogs and websites devoted to specific industries that carry advertising and these should be explored as well.

Obviously, advertising is a highly developed industry and there are a number of excellent advertising agencies that have extensive experience in all forms of advertising. These agencies can provide able assistance to property owners in not only developing their advertising strategy, but in creating excellent copy and advising on its placement so as to maximize exposure.

11.3 Direct Marketing

Reaching manufacturers, licensees, retailers and consumers has never been easier or, for that matter, cheaper. The Internet has opened up a new market for disseminating one's message at a fraction of what it once cost. The day of the catalog that is sent via snail mail to millions of people has been replaced by electronic newsletters in .pdf files or e-blasts that accomplish the same thing, only they reach their recipients in a fraction of the time and at a far lower cost than a printed publication.

Many property owners regularly create and distribute their own electronic newsletters that not only highlight the property but trumpet the success of their licensing activities. These are distributed far and wide via the Internet.

In addition, single page e-blasts are being used with increased frequency to reach targeted markets and to not only promote their property but to help drive recipients to their websites where they can learn more about the property and the licensing program.

11.4 Effective Public Relations[7]

"Public relations" is defined as: the "business of inducing the public to have an understanding of and the goodwill for a person, firm or institution."

Some people believe that because the public generally has a short memory, good public relations merely consists of a story or article that spells the company's name correctly and includes a URL to an active website. An added bonus, in some cases, would be if the story contained enough detail for the public to know what the company employees actually do for a living. Obviously, that's not enough.

The objective of a good public relations program is *ubiquity*, which means conveying one's message everywhere or at least to as many places as possible, preferably simultaneously. While that is probably an impossible goal, the closer a publicist gets to that goal, the more effective the program.

---

[7] Based on a presentation made by Dean Bender of Bender/Helper Impact at a 2008 CLS Program entitled, *Innovative Promotions and Creative Public Relations.*

The basic requirements for a good publicist are to:

- Know your audience

- Know your message

- Know your objective

Today's media world offers infinitely more opportunities than ever before because of the virtually endless types of media that are available. In addition to traditional media outlets, e.g., newspapers, magazines, television and radio, the online and mobile worlds have opened up an almost unlimited number of new possibilities, not only on traditional websites but through blogs, social networks, digital advertising, and smart phones. Moreover, the list is not a static one—it gets broader and more diverse by the minute. Five years ago, who would have thought that Facebook or Twitter would become the promotional vehicle that they have?

At a recent seminar on the subject sponsored by LIMA, Dean Bender provided an example of one effective public relations program involving a licensed game called Karaoke Revolution American Idol ("KRAI") that was operating under an AMERICAN IDOL license. KRAI was a music-themed, rhythm-action game that was based on the *American Idol* phenomenon and Dean Bender's firm, Bender/Helper Impact, created and executed a comprehensive public relations strategy that was designed to maximize awareness for the game by capitalizing on the huge appeal of the television show.

The overriding objective of the program was to generate publicity for the product throughout the entire *American Idol* television season by taking advantage of specific events, including the selection of the final 24 contestants and the final episode. The specific objectives of the program were to:

- Position the KRAI game as a must-own game for the target consumer;

- Establish recognition of the franchise among all media;

- Take advantage of the television phenomenon to generate coverage in non-traditional media outlets; and

- Reach pop culture and features writers about the *American Idol* phenomenon and its influence on various forms of entertainment.

In executing the program, the publicists faced a number of challenges, most notably:

- They did not have any access to talent;

- There was only limited access to the product;

- There was only limited synergy with the television show;

- Other publishers had released AMERICAN IDOL games in the past;

- The popularity of the *American Idol* television show had reached its maturity; and

- Paula Abdul was not a part of the game.

The following four tiered strategy was chosen:

- Time period #1--street date/premiere of the television season;

- Time period #2--final 24 party;

- Time period #3--season finale;

- Time period #4--holiday gift guides.

The campaign surrounding the premiere of the television season included a number of individual elements, including: the issue of a press release announcing the product; a mailing to a host of individuals and retailers describing the product; the placement of reviews for the game with notable publications; specific mentions of the game in television stories about the new season and broadcast features in segments about the new season.

A Final 24 Party was staged in Los Angeles with kiosks featuring the KRAI games in order to promote it. "Talent" was invited to and actually attended the Final 24 Party to try their hands at the game and broadcast crews and photographers were invited to shoot the talent playing the game so that the videos and photographs could be used at a later date. Finally, video game journalists were invited to attend the event to generate enthusiastic coverage.

The season finale for the *American Idol* series is always the most viewed show of the season and frequently results in *American Idol* "withdrawal" on the part of its viewers. In order to combat this, the PR program pitched both broadcast and weekly entertainment magazines with stories about what to do after the season ended and how to combat this withdrawal symptom, including the idea of playing the KRAI video game while waiting and getting ready for the next season.

Some of the other "pitches" that were used included:

- When the season ends, the fun still goes on;

- Music Games Roundup;

- Roundup of Games Based on Television Shows (*TV Guide*);

- The Business of *American Idol*; and

- *American Idol* Marketing Story.

The PR program was coordinated with Fox Media Synergy for the *American Idol* show and was targeted at all Fox owned media outlets, e.g., Fox News Channel, Fox News Feed, *NY Post*, etc. It included game reviews, piggyback stories on *American Idol* coverage, product roundups and stories and segments on all games, including KRAI. It resulted in about 10 weekly hits on Fox Baltimore as well as mentions on a number of other Fox stations, including Chicago and Phoenix, who did one-off competitions.

One of the features of the program was the first-ever, virtual video game competition that took place in highly trafficked malls in major markets where each competitor recited a song on KRAI. The top finishers by score in each market had videos posted on the Internet with the public voting who would become the "Virtual American Idol." Publicity was run on a local, national and trade level.

The results of the program were excellent, generating a total consumer reach of approximately 150 million impressions. It achieved top tier placements in *Disney Adventures*, *Business Week*, the Associated Press, Gannett, *USA Today* (3 hits), *New York Times*, *San Francisco Chronicle*, *Dallas Morning News*, *Washington Post*, *LA Times*, *Chicago Tribune*, *Extra*, *Fox News Channel*, *Morning Show w/Mike & Juliet*, foxnews.com, E! Online, yahoo.com, ew.com, KOL, maxim.com, and ivillage.

Effective PR can be accomplished in a number of different non-traditional ways. One particularly effective (although typically accidental) way is to simply not produce sufficient quantities of the product to meet customer demand, i.e., to create a shortage of the products. For example, when Coleco first introduced its original CABBAGE PATCH dolls, it could (or would) not supply the products fast enough to retailers to meet demand for that product. As lines began forming at various retail establishments so consumers could quickly buy up their meager supply of the product, the story hit the newspapers which further fueled the demand for the CABBAGE PATCH dolls.

Apple Computer had a similar experience when they introduced the iPad and then the 4G version of their iPhone. People lined up to snatch up the product, resulting in literally a mountain of media that served to further drive up the demand for and ultimately sales of the products.

Fisher-Price tried a different approach when it introduced its ELMO dolls for the first time.[8] It is reported that they made a conscious decision to keep the design of the dolls a secret, even after they introduced the product at Toy Fair. Mattel even kept its sales force in the dark as to what the product would actually look like. They chose to use closed boxes so that people couldn't actually see what the dolls looked like. Speculation as to the appearance of the product ran rampant which generated a score of newspaper and trade journal articles. The actual unveiling of the product on Good Morning, America resulted in yet another media event that further hyped sales of the product.

When the product was first offered for sale at Toys R Us in New York, it sold out in three hours which, again, generated further publicity. The fact that it would ultimately become TIA's Toy of the Year should come as no surprise, since the die had been cast more than a year before by the planning of a creative PR program.

11.5   Innovative Promotions[9]

Many property owners regularly rely on the development and staging of creative promotional programs to further enhance the visibility of and demand for their properties. The combination of an effective public relations program with a creative promotions program can be a killer one-two punch.

Fox Sports, which features an on-air robotic "mascot" that is displayed before many of its sports telecasts, conducted an extremely successful "Name the Robot" contest as a promotion for its shows. The contest embraced and empowered their fans and made them "decision makers." The contest was promoted both on-air as well as online and

---

[8] Based on a presentation made by Bruce Maguire, CEO of Freeman Public Relations, 16 Furler St., Totowa, NJ 07512 during LIMA's 2008 CLS program titled *Promotional Strategies and Buzz Marketing.*

[9] Based on a program by Howard Nelson, Fox's Vice-President of Worldwide Promotions at a 2008 CLS Program entitled, *Innovative Promotions and Creative Public Relations.*

received more than 50,000 entries and attracted individuals to whom Fox could market permission-based initiatives in the future.

The Fox promotions involving *The Simpsons* television show and related licensed products has similarly met with enormous success. The show has run continuously since 1989 and is the longest running prime time show in television history. The winner of 23 Emmy Awards, the show is seen in over 60 different countries and is broadcast in more than 20 languages.

A SIMPSON's ride opened at Universal Studios Parks in both Orlando and Hollywood in May 2008. Guests are placed in the middle of Krustyland that showcases the back story and humor of THE SIMPSONS. Fox developed a number of promotions surrounding this ride which have helped both promote the television series as well as the licensing program. The characters featured in the ride all had the voices of the original actors. It also included a motion simulator called the "Krusty Mobile" where the rider could twist and turn, plummet and soar, without ever moving more than a couple of feet. The cars even simulate 360 degree barrel rolls. Universal made a financial investment in the ride at a cost about $40 million per ride.

Fox also did a promotion involving its show *Family Guy* which has broadcast more than 100 episodes, sold more than 5 million DVD's and attracted millions to its website every day. The campaign coordinated a national FAMILY GUY promotion with the restaurant chain, Subway. Over 22,000 Subway restaurants participated in this promotion, which featured a fully branded 32oz. collector cup and a sweepstakes. The promotion had two unique elements:

- An interactive web experience featuring the characters from *Family Guy*; and

- A unique animated television commercial featuring Peter Griffin.

The promotion certainly aided Subway. Subway restaurants that had been open for more than a year increased sales by 11%. The campaign was considered one of the best of 2007 by the Subway Franchise Advertising Fund Trust Board and the licensing revenue generated for Fox made it the highest grossing promotion in the brand's history.

The use of a licensing property to help advertise or promote the sales of an unrelated product, particularly in a television commercial, can be very effective. For example, Coca-Cola used the STEWIE character from *Family Guy* in a television commercial that it ran during the 2008

Super Bowl which turned out to be the most-watched football game in history, capturing an average of 97.5 million viewers. *USA Today* rated the commercials that were run during the game as the top commercials for the year. The Coca-Cola commercial, which cost millions of dollars to create, was perhaps the most popular. The *Wall Street Journal* described it as, "Awesome and exactly what a Super Bowl commercial should be... It's big, epic, funny and beautiful." While it certainly helped advertise and promote the COCA-COLA products, it also generated a significant license fee for Fox.

Tips for a successful promotion include:

- **Consider the Consumer and Retail Needs.** Where is the opening in the market? Consider different character styles, wardrobe, production design, props, etc. Know your competition and point of difference.

- **Think about Niche Marketing.** Navigating the world beyond Wal-Mart is essential. It's OK to start small to measure consumer demand.

- **Walk the Retail Aisles.** Think like a consumer and retail buyer. Ask questions.

- **Collaborate with Licensors and Licensees.** Be open minded, but pay attention. Provide access to writers and producers.

- **The World is Competitive....So be Competitive.** Promotion is as competitive as the television industry. Licensees and retailers are increasingly taking a wait and see approach before committing, so be bold and challenge the *status quo.*

11.6 How to Use Buzz Marketing[10]

"Buzz Marketing" or "Social Marketing" is a low cost, but extremely powerful, way to promote a property. Because of the ease of communicating online, it is a grassroots way to make the world aware of your property and help form relationships with the consuming public. Buzz marketing focuses primarily on such social networks as Facebook,

---

[10] Based on a presentation made by Chas Salmore of MarketingWorks, Inc. 7000 Romaine St. West Hollywood, CA 90038-2304 during the 2007 CLS Program on *Promotional Strategies and Buzz Marketing* and a 2009 LIMA webinar by Sheryl Victor Levy of Savvy Strategy, New York, NY entitled *How Social Media Can Help Build Your Business.*

MySpace and LinkedIn as well as blogs and micro blogs, such as Twitter chat rooms and message boards.

In the past decade, buzz marketing has become a very powerful tool for property owners to promote their properties as well as for licensees to promote their products. This is due, in large measure, to the interconnectivity of the Internet. Property owners and manufacturers have come to understand and recognize that they need to communicate with consumers in an interactive way. Candid, transparent communication between the property owner and consumers is the key.

Property owners who want to engage in this type of promotion need first to identify where they want to go and then how they want to get there. Not unlike traditional marketing strategies, property owners and their licensees who want to utilize buzz marketing need to first identify the demographics and life styles of their potential markets and then target the promotions to that demographic. For example, the owner of a property such as PLAYBOY should be targeting an adult, male audience rather than a children's market.

To be useful, the property owner needs to be respectful of the people already on the network or blog, lest the messages be viewed as spam or a fake blog. There should be full disclosure, e.g., telling those on the blog or network that "I represent..." or "I am part of...", etc. The watchword is "respectful," lest you are viewed as a shill which could negatively impact the effectiveness of your message.

The advantage of the Internet is that people who go online are generally not shy or reserved, rather they will typically tell you what they are thinking and why. For a property owner or a manufacturer, that type of consumer feedback is invaluable. People on these blogs are typically honest, sometimes brutally so. If channeled properly, however, such feedback can be almost as effective as a focus group at a significantly lower cost.

Chat rooms are another way to go because they are highly interactive. One problem with chat rooms, however, is that they are like a grain of sand on the beach in a windy day—participants in the chat room come and go hourly and, as such, there is no lasting legacy. Because of the transient nature of the participants, it may be necessary to view these conversations over a relatively long time period in order to reach a broader group of people.

Social networks like Facebook, Twitter, MySpace, YouTube and LinkedIn, etc., have become a very popular way to spread one's message to a wide group of people and every property owner and licensee should consider taking advantage of their broad appeal. Each has a relatively stylized theme, purpose and engagement channel. Interestingly, the first social network was Classmates which launched in 1995 and currently has 40+ million subscribers.

Why are social networks so popular? In 2009, it was estimated that one third of all adults in North America visited a social network at least once per month. While many think that the typical user of Facebook is the teen set, its biggest growth in 2009 was in the 35-54 demographic. More than a third of the U.S. population is on Facebook and more than 50 million Americans use Twitter.

The more you "buzz market," the greater awareness you create for your property and the more you drive traffic to your website where you can control the messages that you want to convey. There is an organic benefit to the property owner because it improves its communication with the ultimate consumer about its property.

Buzz marketing has become enormously popular because:

- It's cheap and helps reduce your marketing expenses;

- It's a direct driver to a company's website and helps build traffic;

- It helps grow your underlying business;

- It allows you to give consumers insights into things that you may not be able to convey any other way;

- It permits you to directly and repeatedly tell consumers about the benefits of your property or product, versus a few seconds on a television advertisement;

- It allows you to build lists which can be used for subsequent marketing or future promotions;

- It permits you to get consumer insights or feedback on various things;

- It permits you to do trend spotting, e.g., to learn what's happening, what people are thinking, etc.; and

- If need be, it's great for crisis management.

It is important to track the results of any buzz marketing program to both measure its effectiveness and determine what to do for future campaigns. Some of the established buzz marketing agencies, such as

MarketingWorks, have developed specialized software for doing just that and provide such reports to their clients.

Chapter 12

The Retailer's Role in Licensing

12.1   Introduction

A "retailer" is any business that sells goods to the consumer, versus wholesalers or suppliers which typically sell their goods to other businesses or to retailers for re-sale to the consumers. The retail industry is the second largest industry in the United States and employs approximately 12% of its total workforce. Total sales of all retail products in the United States are more than $4.2 trillion.

Mention the word retailer and most people immediately think of WalMart—the world's largest big box store. However, in fact, retailers fall into a number of different categories, starting with independently owned, "mom & pop" shops that actually make up about 90% of the total market. While these small stores constitute the vast majority of the total, they account for less than half of all retail sales which shows that consumers like to shop at the big box stores.

The retail market is actually divided into a number of categories or sectors, including:

- High-End Department Stores, e.g., Saks Fifth Avenue, Neiman Marcus, Bloomingdales, etc.;

- Mid-Tier Department Stores, e.g., Macy's, Kohl's, J.C. Penney, etc.;

- Big Box or Mass Market Stores, e.g., WalMart, Target, etc.;

- Off-Price Retailers, e.g., TJ Maxx, Marshall's, Ross, etc.;

- E-commerce or on-line retailers, including Amazon.com and eBay.com.

- Specialty Stores, broken down by type of merchandise:

    - Apparel, e.g., The Gap, Abercrombie & Fitch, Ann Taylor, J. Crew, Old Navy, etc.;

    - Cosmetics & Pharmaceuticals, e.g., CVS, Walgreens, Rite Aid, etc.;

    - Electronics, e.g., Best Buy, Radio Shack, etc.;

- Footwear, e.g., Foot Locker, The Athlete's Foot, etc.;

- Home Improvement, e.g., Home Depot, Lowes, etc.;

- Home Products, e.g., Bed Bath & Beyond, Pier 1 Imports, etc.;

- Jewelry, e.g., Tiffany, Cartier, Zales, etc.;

- Office Supplies, e.g., Staples, Office Depot, etc.;

- Sporting Goods, e.g., Modell's, Dick's Sporting Goods, Sports Authority, etc.;

- Toys, e.g., Toys 'R Us; FAO Schwartz, etc.; and

- Grocery Stores, e.g., Krogers, Safeway, etc.

According to *Deloitte's 2010 Global Power of Retailing* report, the ten largest global retailers by total sales were:

1. WalMart (United States), hypermarket/superstores with $401.2 billion in sales;

2. Carrefour (France), hypermarket/superstores with $127.9 billion in sales;

3. Metro AG (Germany), cash & carry/warehouse clubs with $99 billion in sales;

4. Tesco (United Kingdom), hypermarket/superstores with $96 billion in sales;

5. Schwarz Unternehmens Treuhand (Germany), discount stores with $79.9 billion in sales;

6. Kroger (United States), supermarkets with $76 billion in sales;

7. Home Depot (United States), home improvement stores with $71.3 billion in sales;

8. Costco Wholesale Club (United States), warehouse club with $70.98 billion in sales;

9. Aldi GmbH (Germany), discount stores with $66 billion in sales; and

10. Target (United States), discount department stores with $62.9 billion in sales.

Licensing is all about selling licensed products and retailers sell products. As such, they are critical to the success of a licensing program and, at times, responsible for its failure. For this reason, retailers have a special place in the hearts of both licensors and licensees.

Over the years, retailers have wielded enormous power over licensors and their licensees since they control the shelf space and, without shelf space, a product is doomed. Retailers, thus, have become accustomed to setting the terms of any relationship with property owners and their licensees, particularly when it involves lesser known properties. While the owners of hot properties and their licensees may be able to set some, or all, of the terms of the relationship, the owners of lesser known properties and their licensees will have a much harder time with retailers.

12.2   What Are Retailers Looking For?

The answer to this question is straight forward. Retailers want to pay the lowest possible price for the highest quality product that has the most appeal to their customers and, therefore, the greatest potential to generate strong sales. The goal of most retailers is to stock their shelves with targeted merchandise that meets the needs of their customers—at the right price. It's that simple.

Every retailer prefers, if possible, to be the exclusive supplier of a particular product, because exclusivity gives them an advantage over the competition. It is a way that smaller retailers can compete with the big box stores who have historically outsold them. If the smaller retailer has exclusivity, a big box store cannot beat them on price, simply because they cannot carry the product. Even limited windows of exclusivity are good, since this allows a retailer to promote the products as only being available at their store, which gives them a marketing advantage. While any retailer would obviously prefer exclusivity, they recognize that in most cases that is simply not possible. Nevertheless, there is no harm in asking and most retailers will.

Since lead times for the delivery of products are important to every retailer, having an established track record for reliability can be invaluable, particularly if the manufacturer had previously helped the retailer fill an order on short notice. Thus, property owners and licensees who maintain such relationships hold a significant advantage over competitors that have never worked with the retailer in the past or, worse yet, at one point may have dropped the ball.

Licensors need to be highly conscious of this dynamic. As discussed in previous chapters, most licensees work on a tight schedule in order to meet deadlines established by retailers. The fastest way to derail that schedule is for the licensor to delay in acting on the licensee's product submissions. If the licensee is unable to meet the retailer's schedule, it can have an enormously detrimental impact on the licensee's ability to effect the sale of those licensed products. Moreover, it can damage the licensee's relationship with the retailer and, potentially, even cast a shadow on the overall program since the retailer may be reluctant to deal with any of the property owner's other licensees.

Retailers are also concerned about the quality of the products that they carry and don't want to sully their reputation by carrying inferior products. More specifically, they don't want to have to deal with handling excessive numbers of returns, a factor that can also have a damaging impact on the property's whole licensing program. Again, this is where a good track record or, at the very least, a great set of references who will attest to the great quality of your products is important.

At the end of the day, however, retailers do not want to take on products that won't sell or where the turnover will be slow. That is why most will expect that the property owner and its licensees provide some form of marketing or promotional assistance with respect to their products, typically in the form of promotions that will get the attention of potential purchasers.

When it comes to promotions, the key is "cool" and the cooler the better. As shown by the examples cited in Chapter 11, interactive promotions that offer prizes or rewards are very popular because they involve the potential customer and make them more inclined to actually spend money to buy the products. Over the years, on-line sweepstakes have also proven very successful.

Hosting celebrity appearances at a retailer's flagships stores is another successful type of promotion, particularly if the products are actually licensed by that celebrity. Everyone wants to get to meet their favorite sports hero or pop singer. If they also happen to give away autographed baseballs or actually sing the National Anthem to open the store for the shoppers, it just adds more excitement—which retailers love because it brings in traffic and, therefore, helps sell more products.

12.3   Think Smaller—Limited Distribution

Since it is critical for a property owner and its licensees to get a retailer to carry its licensed products, the process starts by first getting in the retailer's door and, thereafter, communicating effectively with its decision makers towards ultimately closing the deal. In many instances, that is easier said than done.

In the "old days," property owners and their licensees thought "big." They wanted to see their licensed products sold at all stores in national chains and were frequently unhappy with anything else. The recent recession changed that. Retailers have become more conservative and are reluctant to roll out a line of products on a store-wide basis without first knowing that customers will actually buy them. Obviously, they do not want to build up large inventories of products that simply don't sell.

The current trend among retailers is limited distribution rather than all-store buys. In today's market, retailers are more willing to take on new products on a test program, or special project basis, because these approaches are far less risky. A further trend in retail is the opening of smaller stores, i.e., stores with smaller footprints. The advantages of these smaller stores are that they serve as testing "labs" for the retailer, who can use them to determine whether a particular product will sell and whether it's worth rolling out on a larger scale.

Retailer-conscious manufacturers have recognized these developments and have begun working with retailers to accommodate their more conservative tendencies. Manufacturers who are willing to accept limited distribution, versus all-store distribution are looked upon more favorably by retailers. A manufacturer's willingness to play ball with the retailer on more limited distribution can ultimately lead to larger distribution, should the product perform well.

12.4   Retailer Strategies beyond the Top Ten[11]

There is a world beyond the Top Ten global retailers identified at the beginning of this chapter. This is particularly true as the retail landscape continues to change and as the number of retailers shrinks almost daily, with many actually going into bankruptcy never to be heard from again. Between 2008 and 2010 alone, more than seventy-eight retail chains declared bankruptcy while another twenty-six announced major store closings. All told, more than 16,500 brick and mortar retail stores in the U.S closed their doors during this period. Strip malls regularly display "For Rent" signs.

---

[11] Based on a 2009, 2010 & 2011 LIMA CLS presentation entitled Retailer Strategies Beyond The Top 10 by Sean Heitkemper and Todd Donaldson, IMC, 200 York Street Louisville, KY 40203 and Michael Slusar, Brandar Consulting, LLC, 27 Southgate Drive, Annandale, NJ 08801.

This shrinking landscape has impacted property owners and their licensees because of the fear of partnering with a retailer who is suddenly no longer in business by the time the program is expected to take hold.

The larger concern, for some, is that these bankruptcies are indicative of a trend signaling major shifts in the entire retail marketplace. While the brick and mortar retail model worked well in the twentieth century, it remains to be seen whether it will be as viable in the current one. Many retail experts believe that the time has passed for this model, an outlook being shaped by very real changes in the buying habits of consumers that they expect will only continue. Some, in fact, believe that this last recession ushered in the biggest transformation in consumer behavior to have occurred over the past seventy years.

One also must wonder about whether the explosion of the large chains at the expense of the smaller retailers is healthy....for anyone. If the "too big to fail" concept didn't work for investment banking firms such as Lehman Brothers, how will it work with retailers? The concern is that if one of the mega-chains should fail, it will not only impact its investors and employees, but could well have a dramatic impact on its suppliers and vendors.

If sales of a licensed product to a single retailer represent a significant part of a manufacturer's selling season and that retailer should go bankrupt, it will not only kill that selling season, but it could even shutter the manufacturer as well. Licensors and licensees also face a similar fate in the event that they fall victim to SKU rationalization. This outlook is not intended to stir anxiety, but rather to show that property owners and licensees would be well advised to look beyond the Top Ten as a way of hedging their future security and building momentum for their programs.

The good news is that there is a life outside the Top Ten and it can, in fact, be a good life. While it's far easier to make one sale to a major retailer than 10 sales to different smaller retailers or a thousand sales on a direct basis, spreading sales around to a broader group of customers can offer significantly more security in tough times. Brand and license exclusives at retailers such as Kohl's, Hot Topic and the TJX companies are proof that successful programs outside of the big box setting abound for retailers, licensors and licensees alike. Even regional retailers like Meijer and Belk have found continued success in licensing exclusives.

More importantly, property owners and licensees need to understand that brick and mortar retail may never return to pre-recession levels. Business always tends to gravitate toward efficiency, while consumers tend to gravitate toward convenience. When looking through this lens, it is easy to see that brick and mortar stores are not the most efficient or most convenient way to buy goods.

In actuality, the most efficient and convenient way for consumers to buy goods is through e-commerce. Some economists believe that there will be a further decline in brick and mortar store sales as the economy picks up, but a rapid acceleration of share gain in e-commerce sales. New malls are not being opened and existing malls are experiencing their highest vacancy rates in decades. In the last few years, Government statistics all show across-the-board declines in the volume of sales by brick and mortar stores, but an increase in the number of e-commerce sales. Property owners and their licensees should recognize this and prepare for the likely shift in marketing channels that is taking place. Observe the emergence of companies like Amazon and Zappos. Watch the major retailers continue to develop their online presence. See DRTV giants QVC and HSN continue to launch new channels. Success for retailers and marketers alike will rely on multi-channel strategies.

If, in fact, the future of retailing is through e-commerce rather than conventional brick and mortar retail channels, the possibilities are endless for property owners and licensees. Some may actually begin to consider the formerly unheard of, i.e., becoming their own retailer by creating their own e-commerce sites and selling direct to consumers.

While property owners can, of course, allow their licensees to open up their own e-commerce site, an alternative approach might be for the property owner to simply create its own site and offer distribution through that site to its licensees as a benefit. Some property owners who have already done this actually charge their licensees to use the infrastructure of their e-commerce site. The creation of such sites is not difficult and if a property owner lacks the resources or expertise to do so, it is something that can easily be outsourced.

Due to the efficiency of both warehousing and mass distribution of products from a single location, licensed products can be sold directly to the consumer at much lower prices than by a brick and mortar store, which must be leased, staffed, heated and powered. That price advantage can and should be passed on to the consumer. One retail consultant, when asked how direct e-commerce sales should be priced, counseled, "Cut the price in half and then lower it."

There are other advantages of selling licensed products through e-commerce. For starters, such sales are typically more profitable for the property owner and its licensees because they absorb both the wholesale and retail margins.

Another advantage of e-commerce selling is that because of the reduced selling costs and the lower resultant retail price, licensed products are actually able to favorably compete with private label brands even though they are typically sold by brick and mortar stores at prices below that of licensed products. It actually may be possible to even undersell a private label brand because of the reduced distribution costs.

It is also possible to use e-commerce to test a new product that may never make it to a retailer's shelf, or as a viable alternative distribution method for products that have had difficulty meeting (often rigid) brick and mortar retail requirements. E-commerce has provided the high-end collectibles category with the means of providing their customers with considerable information about the product, and a significant amount of product exposure. These are factors that make it much easier to sell such merchandise, and which traditional retailers cannot normally provide due to limitations on shelf space.

12.5   Direct to Retail Licenses[12]

There has been a growing trend in licensing of "direct to retail" ("DTR") licenses, where the property owner by-passes the manufacturer and grants a license directly to a particular retailer for distribution of a line of licensed products. Typically, these licenses are "exclusive," hence the phrase "retail exclusive" licenses. In virtually all cases, they are intended to be sold throughout the entire chain of stores for the retailer.

In such a relationship, the retailer is responsible for sourcing out the manufacture and supply of the licensed products, typically through factories that it has previously worked with in the Far East. The design and actual manufacture of these licensed products are subject to the same quality control reviews and approvals requirements as would be the case in a conventional licensor-licensee relationship.

When one thinks of direct to retail licensing, they generally think of entertainment and celebrity licenses. Early examples of direct to retail licenses include the WINNIE THE POOH program between Disney and Sears that goes back to the 1970's and the JACQUELINE SMITH line of apparel with K-Mart, which started in the 1980's. Direct to retail licenses are not, however, limited to entertainment properties. This approach has

---

[12] Based on LIMA's panel on *Retail Exclusive Licensing*, conducted at the 2010 Licensing University.

also been used, for example, with corporate properties such as Staples, which carries a line of co-branded OXO office products.

It should be appreciated that direct to retail exclusive licenses don't necessarily have to be for the whole property—it can simply be for a particular version or treatment of the property. For example, Nickelodeon partnered with K-Mart to do an exclusive line of DORA LOVES PUPPIES products. The property looked like DORA, but with a "slight twist." One fear was that if K-Mart carried this version, it would cannibalize its basic DORA sales. Not only did that not happen, but it actually enhanced the sales of the original DORA products. Nickelodeon worked collaboratively with K-Mart on its promotion, which included running a series of television commercials, while K-Mart featured it in a series of flyers and other promotions were also done with Shutter-Fly. What made it work were the in-store activations that were viewed by the millions of people walking through K-Mart every day, as well as online activation generated through its web site.

Of the major retailers, Kohl's is one of the leaders in direct to retailer licenses, having exclusive DTR deals with VERA WANG for a line of SIMPLY VERA products as well as DTR licenses for a wide variety of products bearing some of the Iconix brands like MUDD and CANDIE'S. Quick to follow the lead was J.C. Penney's, with brands such as ONE KISS BY CINDY CRAWFORD for jewelry and CONCEPTS BY CLAIBORNE for more than 30 different products. They also incorporated a store-within-a-store concept for the branded line of SEPHORA cosmetics.

DTR licenses offer many advantages to the parties. For the property owner, it virtually guarantees distribution of the licensed products in a specific market with the assurance that the retailer will make a commitment to help support marketing and promotion. Since they have a financial interest in the property, the retailer has a strong incentive to do whatever it takes to help move the products. Retailers will frequently make a "statement" for the product line and dedicate significantly more floor space for such products than they might otherwise have done if they were simply selling another licensee's products.

Direct to retail licenses offer a number of advantages to the retailer as well. By eliminating the traditional licensee and their profit incentive and going directly to the factory, they are able to obtain the licensed products at a lower cost than if they had purchased them from a traditional licensee. Similarly, by dealing directly with the factories, they are usually in a better position to control the design and manufacture of the products. Finally, most DTR licenses are retailer-exclusive deals. This gives the retailer a clear competitive advantage over their competition, since such products are only available through that retailer.

No licensing arrangement is perfect, however, and even DTR exclusives can be risky. By granting exclusive distribution to a single retailer, the property owner is prevented from seeing its property widely commercialized by multiple retailers throughout that channel of distribution. Depending on the arrangement, the property owner may even be prevented from entering other channels of distribution since exclusive retailers will not want to see similarly branded products at other stores. Another potential problem for a property owner with exclusive DTR licenses is that their fate is solely in the hands of one retailer. Should the retailer undergo tough times or, worse yet, be forced to close its doors, the property owner would be directly impacted.

DTR licenses also present a number of potential problems for retailers as well. Apart from the financial commitments that a retailer must make under the DTR license agreement, e.g., advances, guarantee, etc., it is the retailer who is responsible for financing the design and manufacture of the products in addition to creating sufficient inventory to meet potential demand. Should the products not sell as well as expected, the retailer is faced with the challenge of disposing of any existing inventory.

Chapter 13

Accounting, Auditing & Tax Considerations[13]

13.1   Introduction

The royalty audit, also referred to as either a royalty "inspection" or a royalty "examination," is the primary method used by a licensor to confirm that its licensees are being compliant with the material terms of their license agreements. The term "audit" referred to throughout relates to the "audit provision" as contained in the license agreement and does not constitute an audit performed on financial statements as a whole. The purposes for conducting a royalty audit include the following:

- To determine whether the licensee is reporting and paying the full contractual amount due on a timely basis;

- To determine whether the licensee is adhering to the provisions of the license agreement, including advertising commitments, distribution channel requirements, territorial limitations and insurance requirements;

- To determine whether the licensee is paying royalties on all products exploited ("sold") which use the licensed property;

- To determine whether all licensed products have received required approvals prior to production and distribution; and

- To determine whether the licensee is selling unauthorized or unapproved products.

13.2   Audit Provisions in the License Agreement

In order to be able to able to actually audit or otherwise inspect the books of a licensee, the licensor must make sure that an appropriate

---

[13] Written by Brian J. Harris, Andrew B. Koski, Michael J. Quackenbush, and Charles Schnaid, partners in the Royalty Compliance Div. of Miller, Kaplan, Arase & Co., LLP 4123 Lankershim Blvd. North Hollywood, CA 91602-2828.

audit provision is included in the license agreement. In the absence of such a provision, a licensee may be able to successfully challenge the licensor's right to conduct such an audit short of actual litigation.

Consequently, most license agreements include provisions that give the licensor the right to conduct a complete royalty inspection of the licensee. Such provisions provide the licensor with a mechanism to conduct an audit and confirm that the licensee is fully complying with all the provisions of the agreement. This not only ensures that the licensor will receive all of the royalties due, but that the licensee is not selling unauthorized or unapproved products and is otherwise in compliance with the provisions of the agreement. A licensor truly interested in protecting its intellectual property must insist on full compliance with the terms of the agreement by the licensee. Accordingly, most license agreements include the following provisions:

[A] "Right to Audit" Provision

A "Right to Audit" provision allows the licensor to inspect the books and records of the licensee and is typically limited to a specific period of time. Ideally the provision should provide:

- The licensor has the right to conduct the inspection itself or by someone of the licensor's choosing.

- How and when notice of the audit will be given to the licensee and the minimum notice that is required, e.g., at least five business days (most licensors seek to keep the notice period as short as possible to make it difficult for a licensee to alter or destroy relevant records).

- The royalty auditor has the right to make and retain copies of pertinent documents and records, thereby allowing the auditor to retain relevant information or materials to support its findings.

- The licensee is required to cooperate with the licensor or its representative.

- The licensee, if so requested by the licensor or its representative, will provide the transactional data supporting its royalty statements in electronic format.

- The auditor may access the licensee's general ledger and any reports that document monthly activities, particularly those relating to manufacturing, inventory, sales, returns and inventory destruction (having access to such reports will help the auditor tie together a licensee's financial data and verify that the information the licensee had provided was complete and accurate).

- The auditor has access to all of the licensee's books and records, not only those that pertain to the licensed products.

- The auditor has the right to communicate with the licensee's current or former employees as well as its vendors and customers, all of whom may provide independent third party confirmation of purchases and sales.

- The auditor may examine the records of the licensee's related entities, e.g., parents, subsidiaries or affiliates in order to confirm that the licensee has not sold licensed products to related companies at sub-market prices.

It should be appreciated that the above is a "wish list" of requests. Many licensees will find some of these requests objectionable and could be reluctant to giving the licensor such broad access to their business operations.

[B] "Record Keeping" Provision

The "Record Keeping" provision typically specifies the type of records that the licensee is required to retain and for how long. The purpose of this provision is to avoid a situation where the licensee has destroyed relevant records rather than making them available to the auditor, particularly where the production of such records will not support the royalty statements that the licensee had previously submitted.

Most licensors will require that the licensee retain all companywide records for a set period of time both during and *after* termination of the license agreement. Retention of records in the following categories are particularly important: sales, invoices, promotions, shipping information, bills of lading, catalogs, price lists, price changes, inventory records, destruction records, manufacturing records, purchase orders, vendor invoices, customs documents, as well as quality control and manufacturing approval documents.

The provision should also state the manner in which the documents should be retained, i.e., paper or electronic. Electronic documents are preferable because they allow for efficient and easy manipulation and analysis of the data.

In some cases, a licensor may want to perform a royalty audit covering a period of several years or may decide to perform a royalty audit subsequent to the termination of the license agreement. Thus, the license agreement should also provide for how long the licensee is required to maintain relevant records, preferably at least one to three years subsequent to the expiration or termination of the license agreement, including successor license agreements.

The provision should also prevent the licensee from destroying any records during the pendency of any royalty audit, i.e., the records shall not be destroyed until after the royalty audit (or litigation, if applicable) is settled or finalized.

[C] "Interest on Findings" Provision

The "Interest on Findings" provision will require the licensee to pay interest on any underpayments. The provision should state that interest will be calculated commencing from the date the amount would have been due if the amount had been properly reported. It should also state the method for determining the interest rate to be used, e.g., the base prime lending rate in effect for the territory, or use of a stated interest index plus a percentage. Providing for a high interest rate can discourage a licensee from underreporting or late reporting of royalties.

[D] "Extrapolation" Provision

The Agreement should permit the extrapolation of findings using the error percentage for the tested selection as compared to the overall royalties reported.

[E] "Recovery of Audit Fees" Provision

The "Recovery of Audit Fees" provision requires the licensee to pay the cost of the audit, in the event that the audit findings show an underpayment above a certain threshold. To determine whether the threshold is exceeded, the auditor will compare the audit findings to the total royalties reported or paid. If the amount of underpayment exceeds the threshold (usually 5-10%), the licensee will bear the responsibility of reimbursing the licensor for the cost of the audit. If the threshold amount is based on paid royalties, the license agreement should state whether advances and minimum guarantees are to be included in the amount or whether it is based on earned royalties only. The term "Deficiencies" should also be defined in the license agreement to include all amounts due to the licensor, including findings, interest due on findings, interest due on late payments, and penalties for selling unapproved products.

This provision is intended to encourage licensees to accurately account for and pay royalties in accordance with the contractual provisions, in order to avoid having to bear the costs of the royalty audit. Furthermore, this provision promotes cooperation with the royalty auditors, since additional costs are incurred when a licensee is uncooperative and does not provide (or has not retained) the records to support the amounts on the royalty statement.

13.3   When Should an Audit Be Performed?

At the very least, the licensor should pay careful attention to the licensee's royalty reports submitted during the early years of the license term and, ideally, conduct a royalty examination early in the initial term and certainly prior to the expiration of the licensor's right to audit all periods. Follow-up royalty examinations should be periodically performed thereafter. It should be noted that licensee audits can be expensive and, as such, should be selectively applied to those licensees that generate a reasonable level of royalties or are suspected of underreporting royalties.

By following such a procedure, the licensor should be able to confirm that the licensee has adequate royalty accounting systems and procedures in place to facilitate accurate reporting. It also confirms that the licensee understands what it is required to do under the agreement.

In many cases, the licensor does not have a complete understanding of how a licensee operates its business. This can result in the parties having a different understanding of such contract terms as "Net Sales," which should be defined in the license agreement. By discovering these ambiguities early in the term, the licensor and licensee can get on the same page before a small problem becomes a much larger one.

It is very common to wait several years after the start of the license agreement, or until the termination of the license agreement, to decide to perform a royalty audit. Other times, a royalty audit may be performed sooner due to a concern that there have been royalty underpayments. It should be appreciated that it is much more difficult to perform a royalty audit several years into the term of the license agreement, because individuals involved in the drafting of the license agreement may no longer be with the licensor or licensee and/or the licensee may have changed accounting software, thus making access to earlier records potentially more difficult—particularly if the licensee has not retained the conversion matrix ("interface") used to migrate the data between systems. Other records may be lost, misfiled or buried deep in storage. As a result, the royalty auditor may not be able to determine the precise amount of underpayment, if any.

In addition, the results of the findings may indicate that the licensee owes a substantial amount that they are simply not able to pay at the time of the royalty audit. This can result in the licensor accepting less than the full amount due or having to litigate in order to collect the full amount.

13.4   Selecting the Royalty Auditor

While many licensors believe that any accountant should be able to conduct a royalty audit, experienced royalty auditors can mean the difference between one that simply verifies the licensee's arithmetic to one that actually finds willful underreporting.

The royalty auditor should have solid experience in accounting, auditing and financial matters as they relate to the business of licensing, including standard terminology, industry practice and the possible legal issues which may arise during the course of an examination. They should also have expertise in the specific field in which the license is granted, because different industries operate in different ways. What might be a common allowable discount or allowance in one industry may not be acceptable in another.

A licensor may have someone on staff or an internal audit department that can perform the royalty inspection. In many cases, however, the licensor elects to engage an outside firm for specialty purposes or, at times, because there are issues with the licensee that may require a truly independent party.

An outside royalty auditor will typically start by preparing an engagement letter which covers the terms of the royalty audit to be performed. The letter normally includes an identification of the parties involved, the license agreement(s) and license term(s) that form the basis of the royalty audit, estimated fees for the royalty engagement and payment terms. The engagement letter will also include a preliminary list of procedures that will take place.

In order to be able to prepare an engagement letter, most auditors will typically want, at the very least, to review the following:

- License agreement(s);

- A description of the licensee's royalty reporting and accounting systems; and

• The licensee's royalty reports or statements.

The actual procedures to be followed by the auditor should be discussed between the licensor and royalty auditor. In some instances, the licensor may only want the auditor to inspect certain aspects of the licensee's operations or accounting system, e.g., sales but not inventory transactions, with the understanding that if the audit reveals underpayments on those specific focal areas, the scope of the audit will be expanded in a subsequent audit.

Due to the confidential nature of the information being transmitted between the licensor, licensee and the royalty auditor, the auditor is frequently asked to sign a non-disclosure agreement prior to beginning fieldwork.

13.5 Preparing for the Royalty Audit

The audit procedure typically starts with the licensor sending the licensee a notice of its intention to audit the licensee's books and records. The notice will typically cite that portion of the license agreement which gives them the right to conduct such audit, as well as an identification of the auditor and the date, time and place of such audit. The date of the actual audit can always be changed, but it is important to pick one to get the process started.

The licensor should provide the royalty auditor with all relevant information regarding the licensee and the engagement. The quality of such document production is important and may ultimately minimize audit costs. Such items include:

• License agreement(s)

• Royalty reports submitted by the licensee

• Date and amount of payments made by the licensee

• Relevant correspondence between the licensor and licensee

• Issues and concerns

• Listing of approved products

• Results of any prior royalty audits

The royalty auditor will want to review this information prior to actually visiting the licensee. The auditor may also use tools such as the Internet to gather information about the licensee. Through the Internet, the royalty auditor may be able to see licensed products offered for sale through the licensee's website. This is very helpful in determining, for instance, whether the licensee is selling any of the licensor's products but not including them on the royalty reports. Tracking the sales of the licensee's products through the websites of its customers can also be a useful tool.

Once engaged, the royalty auditor will contact the licensee and make arrangements to begin the royalty audit process. At this point, the auditor and the licensee will establish the timing and location of the fieldwork. The royalty auditor will also typically provide the licensee with a list of documents and records that it will want to review during fieldwork, as well as those documents that it might want in advance of the actual inspection.

Most auditors will request that the licensee provide information in electronic format, so that they can perform data sorting and data mining procedures. In addition, the royalty auditor may look to interview the licensee's personnel to gain an understanding of how its accounting and royalty reporting systems work, as well as how the licensed product is produced, transported and distributed.

13.6   Information Required From the Licensee

The royalty auditor will typically prepare an initial document request listing those items that the auditor will want the licensee to make available during the royalty inspection process. These records should be available for the entire period under audit. The royalty auditor may limit the request to specific test periods.

The initial document request does not prevent the auditor from requesting additional items during the course of fieldwork as a result of its findings, additional areas of interest or the unavailability of certain records. Commonly, the books and records requested by the royalty auditor include the following:

[A] Sales Journals, Invoices and Cash Receipts

The royalty auditor will compare sales totals from the sales journals to the information reported in the royalty reports, as well as look for unreported items. The procedures generally include a request for a sample of sales invoices to compare the statement information against the transactional details, thus supporting the quantities or amounts appearing on the royalty statement. They will also use sales information gathered from the sales journals and sales invoices to determine if the licensee accurately reported its net sales in accordance with the terms of the license agreement. The auditor may inspect the cash receipts and compare them to the invoice amounts to ascertain whether the amounts received agree with the sales invoice.

[B] Manufacturing and Purchasing Records

The royalty auditor will use these records to determine the number and quantity of items that were produced for sale under the license. These records may indicate whether additional approved or unapproved products were manufactured or distributed but were not reported on the royalty statements. These records almost always generate more questions.

In some cases, products manufactured at an outside facility may be shipped directly ("drop shipped") to the licensee's customers and no entry is made in the licensee's inventory system. The royalty auditor may also seek to confirm that the licensee had been using approved manufacturers.

[C] Inventory Records

The royalty auditor will complete a reconciliation of inventory, by SKU (stock-keeping unit number), as follows:

- Beginning Inventory
  - Add: Inventory additions (items manufactured or purchased)
  - Subtract: Inventory sales
  - Add/Subtract: Inventory adjustments (samples, returns and destroys)
- Should equal: Ending Inventory

The auditor may also compare the licensee's sales and manufacturing/ purchase information to its perpetual inventory records.

[D] Credit Memo Journals

The auditor will need to determine if there are any returns of inventory. If so, the auditor will compare the amount credited to the original sales amount and ascertain whether the items were placed back into inventory or were classified as damaged and unsalable. They will also confirm that any reduction in net sales for returns is authorized by the license agreement. The auditor will also test for excess returns which could be an indicator of quality problems.

[E] General Ledgers, Tax Returns and Financial Statements

To establish completeness, the auditor will compare information from the sales journals, manufacturing/purchase records and the inventory records to the general ledger as well as the licensee's tax returns and financial statements.

[F] Product Catalogs

Auditors should review the licensee's product catalog to confirm that all licensed products were included in the royalty reports. In some cases, the licensee may be selling a generic product that includes the property and, therefore, is royalty bearing. The auditor will also review the licensee's website and, if possible, its showroom and warehouse. Some auditors even visit stores where licensed products are sold.

[G] Price Lists

Auditors typically look at a licensee's price lists or schedules to determine whether the gross prices recited on a customer's invoice reflect a true gross selling price or whether the licensee has built into the gross price otherwise impermissible discounts or allowances, or made sales to a related third party at a greatly reduced wholesale price.

13.7 Royalty Audit Procedures

Royalty audit procedures are generally tailored to each engagement, based on the license agreement, the licensed product, and the licensee's royalty reporting and accounting systems. Royalty auditors generally start with a standard procedure that they adjust for the specific engagement. Common preliminary procedures include:

- Read the license agreement(s) to gain an understanding of its key provisions.

- Review the royalty reports and other information provided by the licensor.

- Research the licensee and licensed products through the Internet and other sources.

- Speak with licensee's personnel to:

  - Gain an understanding of the licensee's accounting and royalty reporting systems.

- Determine how the products are manufactured (on-site or purchased from an outside vendor).

- Determine how the products are sold.

• Request product catalogs.

The following steps are typically performed in the course of the fieldwork:

• Review the licensee's accounting and royalty reporting systems to determine whether they are operating as described and can provide accurate information.

• If the product is manufactured on-site, tour the facility and observe its manufacture.

• Perform sales tests by dollars and units, including a review of sales invoices and shipping information.

• Perform tests of pricing, including discounts and allowances.

• Examine sales reports for samples, free goods and close-outs.

• Determine whether any sales were made outside of the normal sales system.

• Determine whether there are any related party sales or purchases.

• Review sales for territorial restrictions and compliance with approved distribution channels.

• Prepare a trend analysis to look for unusual sales patterns.

• Review product returns, including damaged products.

• Reconcile inventory, including tests of manufacturing or purchases.

• Compare products available for sale to what was reported on the royalty reports to confirm that all licensed products are being properly reported.

• Review all royalty reports and determine that the royalty rates used are appropriate.

13.8   The Royalty Audit Report

Upon completion of the fieldwork, the auditor will prepare a draft report for the licensor's review and comments. Once the licensor's comments have been addressed or resolved, a final royalty report will be issued by the auditor to the licensor. The royalty report will usually contain the following:

- A listing of procedures, which may be in summary form.

- A summary of the amounts owing to the licensor, including findings, interest and penalties.

- Details of each finding, along with supporting schedules.

- Calculation of any interest on the findings.

- Recitation of any audit fees chargeable to the licensee.

- Details of the auditor's findings of the licensee's non-compliance with other terms of the license agreement, e.g., sales outside of authorized territories or channels, failure to maintain required insurance, etc.

- Identification of items requested, but not provided by the licensee.

Once the royalty report is issued, the licensor must determine how best to proceed. Licensors typically forward the report to the licensee and give it an opportunity to review and, if appropriate, dispute any of the audit findings. It is not uncommon for a licensee to refute some or all of the findings or attempt to provide an explanation or other documentation in support of its actions.

Most audit disputes are resolved between the parties through negotiation although, in some cases, litigation or arbitration may become necessary.

13.8.1 Common Monetary Findings

The purpose of an audit is to find unreported or underreported amounts, which occur for a number of reasons, including administrative errors, systematic errors in a variety of accounting and reporting programs, misinterpretations of the terms of the license agreement including definitions, failure to use the applicable royalty rates and, on occasion, misreporting sales amounts or quantities. The following are common monetary findings uncovered during royalty audits:

- Unreported product sales;

- Use of incorrect interpretation of the definition of "Net Sales;"

- Unallowable deductions from sales;

- Excessive allowable returns;

- Excessive allowable discounts;

- Excessive reserves;

- Non-reporting of promotional giveaways and samples;

- Sales to related parties at less than an arm's-length price;

- Failure to properly report sales for bundles and assortments; and

- Penalties for selling unapproved products.

13.8.2 Common Non-Monetary Findings

The following are common non-monetary findings:

- Sales in unapproved territories;

- Sales through unapproved product distribution channels;

- Failure to properly account for damaged goods;

- Failure to obtain product approvals;

- Failure to carry required insurance; or

- Failure to include required "sold under license" verbiage on packaging

13.9 Accounting Provisions in License Agreements

How the accounting provisions in a license agreement are drafted is particularly important since the language in these provisions will be relied on quite heavily by the royalty auditors.

During the initial negotiations with any potential licensee, the licensor should try to obtain a full understanding of how that licensee conducts its business operations, particularly the manner in which it actually sells or intends to sell its licensed products. Earlier chapters of this book have explained in great detail the different types of royalty rates used in licensing, e.g., domestic landed rates, F.O.B. rates, direct sales rates, etc. The more the licensor knows about how the licensee will actually sell the licensed products, the easier it will be to define the applicable royalty rates.

Royalty auditors will pay particular attention to those provisions in the license agreement that explain or identify:

- Whether a licensee may include freight in the cost of the product. For these cases, an agreed-upon freight allowance can be provided for in the definition of net sales.

- Unforeseen transactions, such as a large sale to a discounter, which may result in unallowable discounts. In these instances, the licensee should try to obtain a one-time waiver from the licensor.

Communications between the licensor and its licensees are critical during the licensing program. As new accounting and royalty reporting issues arise (and they always do), they should be discussed and, if possible, resolved between the parties so as to avoid surprises in any subsequently issued audit report. If there is a change of conditions or something unforeseen occurs that necessitates a change in the license agreement, the agreement should be amended accordingly.

13.9.1 Definition of Terms

Some of the more important terms used in a license agreement that royalty auditors pay particular attention to are:

[A] Net Sales, Discounts and Allowances

Most royalty calculations are based on a percentage of net sales. Therefore, it is very important that the agreement precisely define how the licensee is to compute its net sales figure. Each item in the calculation of net sales should be specifically defined, including any limitations.

Agreements that simply define net sales as "gross sales less returns, discounts and allowances" are too ambiguous and may result in lost royalties to the licensor. Most licensees will read such a provision very expansively in order to lessen the amount of royalties payable.

Royalties due to a licensor may also be computed on a flat fee, per unit rate as opposed to a percentage of sales. In those cases, the licensor should make sure that the license agreement provides the licensor and its auditor full and unfettered access to the licensee's manufacturing records, including purchase orders, manufacturing invoices, supporting payment documentation and unit quantities received into inventory at the distribution warehouse.

Care should also be taken to define exactly what is meant by "gross sales" which should, ideally, be the higher of either the selling price recited on the licensee's list price or the highest price charged to any third-party customer.

Sales prices may vary widely depending on the type of customer and the distribution channel. For example, licensees may sell directly to consumers through their website at prices significantly above the sales price to wholesale. The license agreement should also define when the product is considered sold, e.g., at the earlier of invoicing, shipment or payment.

Many licensors elect to cap a licensee's returns, discounts and allowances as a percentage of its gross sales. The license agreement should specify how that limitation is computed, e.g., calculated quarterly or annually and whether the cap applies to individual SKUs or all products being reported.

The license agreement should also specify what types of allowances may be taken and, in some cases, what deductions may not be taken, e.g., cash discounts that do not benefit the licensor, write-offs for bad debts, or deduction of marketing and advertising expenses. Some common allowances that may be permitted are allowances for co-op advertising and new store stocking.

Many licensors require that the licensee approve all distribution agreements, particularly those that provide for discounts above a pre-determined threshold. The objective of such an approval requirement is to generate a discussion between the licensor and licensee to, hopefully, bring the parties into agreement on how to treat these discounts.

It is also advisable to provide for situations where the licensee may elect to bundle the licensed products with other products and if done, how royalties are to be calculated in such a situation. It is also advisable to address other issues in the agreement including: how to treat consignment sales; whether samples and other free giveaways are royalty bearing; and whether a royalty is due on employee and close-out sales and, if so, at what rate.

[B] Payment Terms

The license agreement should specify when the licensee is required to report its sales and pay its royalties as well as any advances or guarantees. Most merchandising agreements provide for quarterly reporting, with royalty statements and payments typically due 30 to 45 days after the end of the calendar quarter.

The agreement should also specifically state that late payments are subject to a specified interest rate (including the method for calculating the rate) since the absence of such a provision may prevent the licensor, as a matter of law, from charging interest on late payments.

Some license agreements require that the minimum guaranteed royalty be calculated and, if due, submitted on a quarterly or yearly basis, rather than at the end of the license term.

[C]   Royalty Reports

The license agreement should specify what items must be included in the royalty report. Some licensors even provide its licensees with a sample of the type of report that it expects the licensee to submit and may even attach it as part of the license agreement. In some cases, the licensor will want the reports provided in electronic format to facilitate entry into the licensor's licensing administration package.

Many licensees report the gross sales and number of units sold by SKU numbers. It is preferable that the sales price for each SKU be listed separately so that the licensor can review the royalty report for any discounts. Such discounts, along with returns and allowances should be separately recorded in the royalty report. In addition, some licensors may require further breakdown with respect to territory, brand and/or product line.

[D]   Sublicense Agreements

Although most merchandising agreements do not permit sublicensing, there are exceptions. In those cases, the sublicensee is typically required to pay its royalties directly to the licensee who must then account to the licensor. Most licensors in sublicensing situations will require that the licensee submit all sublicense agreements to it for approval prior to their execution. Such sublicense agreements should incorporate the terms and definitions that are included in the original license agreement.

The license agreement should state how sublicensing royalties will be computed and paid to the licensor. In most instances, the sublicensing revenue received from the sublicensee is divided between the licensor and licensee according to a formula stated in the original license agreement.

When sublicensing is allowed, the licensor should make sure that it retains the right to audit the sublicensee or require the licensee to perform such an audit. The licensor should also be entitled to receive a copy of any royalty audit that the licensee may perform on a sublicensee, including the final settlement of any dispute.

13.10 Tax Considerations

Depending upon the licensee's country and the type of licensed product, governmental taxes may apply on the royalty being paid from an overseas based licensee to a United States based licensor. Many countries, including Germany, China, and South Korea, require withholding tax to be levied on royalties paid by a licensee. Other countries, such as Japan and Taiwan, do not normally require such withholding although it may be required if certain conditions are met. For example if the licensor applies for a waiver of the tax withholding by filing a waiver request, withholding may be required. The United States maintains tax agreements with a number of countries that address the issue of double taxation so as to avoid such situations.

If taxes are withheld in another country, corporate licensors will need to collect from its licensee proof that the taxes were actually paid in the other country. A tax payment stamped receipt from the other government generally constitutes proof of the actual payment of such taxes. The licensor may then be able to claim the foreign tax credit on its U.S. income tax return by filing a Form 1118 with the Internal Revenue Service. It is worth noting that the process for obtaining such forms of proof from governmental agencies tends to be quite slow. As such, the parties should plan accordingly.

Where the licensor knows that a problem may arise, it is advisable to address this issue in the license agreement lest the licensor be restricted from benefitting from this tax credit in certain instances. The agreement should clearly indicate the intentions of the parties so that the licensor is not "out-of-pocket" from the receipt of the net amount after deducting withholding taxes.

It may be possible to structure the agreement so that the licensee advances the full royalty and is reimbursed to the extent the licensor is refunded the foreign tax credit, although this may not, in certain situations, be the full amount of the withholding. This can be a relatively complex issue and licensors are well advised to consult their tax advisors as to how best to address it.

Royalties, other than mineral, oil, gas or copyright royalties, are considered personal holding company (PHC) income. Any corporation (unless specifically exempted) is a PHC if more than five individuals from the U.S. own more than 50% of its outstanding stock *and* at least 60% of its adjusted gross income, which *includes* royalty income (unless specifically exempted). Because of this fact, care should be taken since penalties can be imposed on PHC income under certain circumstances.

Again, this is a fairly complex issue and licensors should seek tax advice if this is applicable.

Chapter 14

Infringements & Counterfeits

14.1 Introduction

While Ben Franklin may have believed that there were only two certain things in the world, i.e., "death and taxes," if merchandising had been popular in the 18th century, he would have added a third—someone will always try to knock off a successful property. We live in a world where infringements are a way of life because counterfeiting it is a lucrative business. The owner of every successful property will, undoubtedly, face the problem at some point in time.

The drill for every property owner is to take appropriate steps toward protecting its property, to be aware of what is happening in the marketplace and, if it discovers that its property has become a target for counterfeiters, to take prompt and aggressive action. In the licensing industry, the reality is that licensees are usually closest to the problem since they are the ones who are actually in the marketplace facing competition from unlicensed products every day. As such, property owners can be assured that its licensees will quickly bring these issues to their attention as soon as they become apparent.

Counterfeiting is the deliberate unauthorized use of another's intellectual property, e.g., trademarks, product designs and copyrights, including, the use of a false trademark that is identical to, or substantially indistinguishable from, a registered trademark. It can also encompass the passing off of a product whose design is similar or identical to the design of the authentic product, or the act of copyright piracy where an audio-visual work is copied and distributed on an unauthorized basis.

It should be appreciated that counterfeiting is not simply the infringement of another's intellectual property rights. It is the blatant duplication of such property with the intent to have consumers believe that their product is genuine—even though it is usually being sold at a small fraction of the cost.

For a successful property owner, the job of trying to stay ahead of infringers and counterfeiters can be a full time burden. Because of the profit potential that counterfeiting offers, counterfeiters have become very good at their trade and generally, unless property owners take swift, aggressive action, the problem will only escalate. A property owner who believes that it can simply kick back and let its licensees fend for themselves against unlicensed competition, will soon have few, if any, royalty paying licensees. Thus, protecting the licensee's right to sell its products free from competitors that are not paying royalties or taxes is not simply an obligation, it is in the licensors own best interest. Successful property owners understand this very basic issue.

14.2 The Counterfeiting Industry–a Growing Market

How big a problem is counterfeiting? It's huge and, sadly, it's growing despite the best efforts of property owners and governments around the world to stem the tide. The reason for this is simple—it's extraordinarily lucrative for the counterfeiter. They have the ability to sell a massive amount of product without any of the implied costs associated with originating design, maintaining regulatory compliance, brand building, etc., to say nothing of compensating the property owner. The counterfeiter simply skips to the last two steps in the process: it knocks-off the product and sells it for a fraction of the price charged by licensed manufacturers, typically through less than reputable channels of distribution.

The overall problem is getting worse. For example, in 2008 the U.S. Customs and Border Protection ("CBP") and U.S. Immigration and Customs Enforcement ("ICE") announced the seizure of more than $272.7 million of counterfeit and pirated goods, which represented a 38% increase over the prior year. More significantly, it represented almost a 300% increase since 2002. The most frequently seized product was footwear, which accounted for 38% of the total seizures. Almost 98% of this counterfeit footwear originated in China which is, by far, the leading source of all counterfeit merchandise. Counterfeit products from China, India and Hong Kong constituted about 94% of all counterfeit product seized by ICE over the same period.

The United States is not the only country having a problem with counterfeit merchandise. In 2008, 178 million counterfeit items were seized by European Customs authorities, an increase of 79 million from 2007. Pirated CDs and DVDs accounted for 44% of all products seized; 23% were counterfeit cigarettes and 10% were articles of counterfeit clothing. Of all counterfeit goods seized, 54% originated from China, although a majority of the seized counterfeit food and beverage products came from Indonesia and most of the counterfeit pharmaceuticals came from India.

Counterfeiting is not, as some believe, a victimless crime—it clearly harms both the property owner and the consumer. Counterfeiting steals the identity and goodwill that the property owner has go to great lengths to establish and robs the consumer of the comfort and reliability that it has when it buys a presumably branded product. Furthermore, counterfeiting produces economic damage on multiple levels. It deprives municipalities, states and countries of tax revenues derived from the sale of genuine products, on top of the revenues lost by property owners and its licensees. More important, it can pose a danger to consumers, particularly if the counterfeit product is not manufactured up to the quality levels of the genuine article, as is often the case.

When licensing executives think of counterfeiting, they focus mainly on designer brands, apparel and toy products, which are certainly areas of significant counterfeiting activity. Unfortunately, however, the problem is far more widespread than that. Counterfeiting is also alive and well in the entertainment, automotive, aircraft, food and pharmaceuticals industries as well.

The problem is particularly noticeable though when it comes to licensed apparel and accessories. In the world of designer brands, those most often copied consistently include: Burberry, Louis Vuitton, Gucci, Chanel, Lacoste, Cartier, Nike and Abercrombie & Fitch, along with Adidas and Puma in the footwear category.

Major events and celebrity properties also spawn a wave of counterfeit products. For example, U.S. Customs seized 15,653 counterfeit items at the 2009 Super Bowl in Tampa, FL worth $1,826,562, which was up significantly from the prior year in Arizona, where they seized 10,212 counterfeit items worth $542,120. It has also been estimated that of the $596 million of Bob Marley products sold in a given year, only $4 million of it is authorized or licensed.

One of the largest seizures of counterfeit clothing occurred when $7 million of knock-off t-shirts and sweatshirts were seized from the home and warehouse of William Haskell Farmer, who had been selling the products to 191 stores throughout the United States. Farmer eventually pled guilty to a felony count of trafficking.

The counterfeiting of toy products can not only hurt toy companies economically, but it can actually injure the children who play with the cheap, counterfeit substitutes. While legitimate toy companies spend millions in making sure that their products comply with all governmental regulations concerning child safety, those subtleties are usually lost on the counterfeiters who regularly manufacture products with unacceptable levels of lead and phthalates, frequently exceeding the acceptable limits by 100 times or more. Moreover, counterfeiters have little regard for requirements issued by the Consumer Products Safety

Commission regarding the use of small, sharp and/or breakable parts that can pose a choking hazard to children. The presence of these toys in the marketplace has damaged the entire toy industry, without question.

The entertainment and software industries also are regularly impacted by counterfeiting, from the early release of bootlegged motion picture DVD's, music recordings and computer programs even before these products reach theatres or stores.

John Sankus Jr., was sentenced to 46 months in prison for leading an international piracy ring called DrinkorDie, which included 60 members from numerous countries and was responsible for copying and distributing software, games and movies. Their biggest claim to fame was distributing copies of Windows' operating system software two weeks before the official release.

While counterfeiting is an economic problem for merchandisers and software developers, it is downright dangerous in other industries. For example, it was reported that a mother and her child were killed in an automobile accident when a counterfeit brake pad made out of wood chips failed. A faulty clutch made of counterfeit parts caused a helicopter crash that killed a traffic reporter. It was subsequently discovered that more than 600 helicopters had been equipped with counterfeit parts, putting literally thousands of people at risk. A Norwegian plane crash killing 55 people was caused by the failure of counterfeit bolts in the plane.

The food industry is another target for counterfeit products that put consumers at grave risk. For example, authorities discovered that a counterfeit version of Similac baby formula being sold at Safeway and Pak n' Save stores in more than 16 states was actually responsible for causing rashes and seizures in a number of infants.

Likewise, the pharmaceutical industry is plagued by counterfeiting, where the use or ingestion of inferior knock-offs can prove deadly. For example, it was reported that a liver transplant recipient received a counterfeit version of Epogen to treat anemia. Because it was at only 5% of regular strength, instead of improving the boy's condition, it caused excruciating aches and spasms. In two other instances, the FDA recalled $7 million worth of pumps used during open-heart surgery that contained malfunctioning counterfeit parts and Searle discovered that over a million counterfeit birth control pills had been distributed to unsuspecting women, resulting in unwanted pregnancies and irregular bleeding.

Counterfeiting also has a serious political impact. Investigators have found that Chinese organized crime syndicates regularly rely on counterfeiting as a source of tax-free income and that some terrorist organizations derive a portion of their funding through trafficking in counterfeit goods. Raids of counterfeit operations in New York and New Jersey resulted in the seizure of counterfeit designer handbags that contained heroin, establishing a clear tie between drug smuggling and counterfeiting.

Just in economic terms, the impact of counterfeiting is staggering. The International Chamber of Commerce estimates that 7% of the world trade is in counterfeit goods, which means and that the counterfeit market is worth some $350 billion. In 2009, U.S. companies lost an average of 22% in revenue as a result of counterfeiting. The annual drain on the United States as a result of counterfeiting has been estimated at $2 billion and 100,000 lost jobs. Fortune 500 companies spend an average of between $3.5 million every year to combat counterfeiting, with some spending as much as $10 million.

Certain industries are harder hit than others. For example, the software industry looses between $12-16 billion a year because of counterfeiting, equal to more than 40% of all software industry sales. In some countries, more than 90 percent of computer software sales are illegitimate copies. U.S. automobile manufacturers and suppliers lose $12 billion a year in revenue worldwide, due to the sale of counterfeit parts and the FTC estimates that this industry could hire 210,000 more workers by eliminating the presence of counterfeits.

14.3   Identifying Counterfeit Products

Since one of the principal attractions of a counterfeit product is cost, the easiest way to identify it is to use that same yardstick. The old adage, "if something is too good to be true, then it usually is," applies. If the selling price of a product is so far below that of what the genuine product typically sells for, the red flags should start to go up.

Since counterfeit product is most often cheaply manufactured, a close inspection of the product should also reveal whether an item is real or fake. Tell tale signs that a product is counterfeit are:

- Packaging with blurred lettering or labeling;
- Misspelling of words or altered product names;
- No placement of legal notices on the product or packaging;

- Drastic changes in product content, color, smell, or packaging;

- Products or packaging that lacks manufacturer's codes, trademarks and/or copyrights; and

- Products with unusual claims and warranties.

Also, counterfeit products are typically sold through "non-traditional" channels of distribution since the better retailers will not normally carry such products. Many property owners regularly employ private investigators and even set up "sting" operations to locate counterfeiters. These investigators visit major retail stores, canvas street vendors in known counterfeiting areas, attend trade shows, review magazines and trade publications and regularly monitor the Internet to find dealers who are selling counterfeit merchandise. Similarly, they target those markets most notorious for trafficking such products, e.g., Canal Street and Times Square in New York City.

14.4   Steps to Take Against Infringers

Step one is to make sure that your intellectual property protection is in place, as was discussed in Chapter 5. A particularly effective measure that many property owners regularly utilize is to record their trademark and copyright registrations with the U.S. Customs Service. Customs will cooperate with owners of registered trademarks and copyrights in attempting to stop counterfeit merchandise from entering the United States and will often seize the bogus products at their port of entry and retain them. If the products are determined to be infringing or counterfeit, Customs may require removal of infringing content prior to their release and, in some instances, actually order the destruction of the offending merchandise. The cost for registering an item with Customs is relatively inexpensive—in 2010 it was $190.

14.4.1 Cease and Desist Letters

An alternative to initiating a lawsuit against any infringer or counterfeiter is the sending of a cease and desist letter. Although such letters are not a prerequisite for litigation, they may be appropriate, particularly if the property owner believes that the alleged infringer was innocent. For example, a small retail shop that is innocently selling infringing items is likely to cooperate with the property owner upon receipt of such a letter, thereby saving the cost of defending a full-blown litigation.

Such letters are not, however, terribly effective against major counterfeiters or anyone who may otherwise believe that they have a valid defense to infringement. In fact, in the latter case, the sending of such a letter can actually create a problem of its own.

Cease and desist letters that include a threat of litigation if the demands made in the letter are not followed, can actually give the accused party a right to initiate a court action against the property owner for a declaration that there is no actual infringement, or that the property owner's property is not valid. This gives the alleged infringer a procedural advantage, since it allows them to choose the forum in which the dispute will be heard, typically a court closer to home or one that may have a more favorable attitude toward defendants. Psychologically, such action also turns the accused infringer into the aggrieved plaintiff.

14.4.2   Keeping a Perspective on Litigation

When all is said and done, in order to halt infringing or counterfeiting activities, the property owner may have no alternative but to litigate. Once the decision has been made to initiate litigation, it should move forward as quickly as possible since delay can adversely affect the property owner's ability to obtain pre-trial relief, i.e., a temporary restraining order or preliminary injunction. In order to be entitled to pre-trial relief, the moving party must demonstrate that it would be irreparably harmed if the infringement continued until trial. Courts may find that a delay in initiating such an action by a property owner is an indication that there was no irreparable harm looming if the infringement continued through trial.

There are other reasons for prompt action. Sales of infringing products can result in lost sales for a licensee and, as a consequence, lost royalty income for the licensor. Also, the presence of infringing or counterfeit products in the marketplace can diminish the exclusivity and goodwill associated with the property.

A greater concern arises when a counterfeit product of inferior quality causes injury to a consumer. Even if the property owner can ultimately avoid liability when an infringing product is shown to be counterfeit, there is always some attendant harm to the property owner as a result of the adverse publicity that inevitably follows.

In making the decision to litigate, the property owner needs to be mindful that litigation is merely a means to an end, namely, protection of the licensed property. It should never be pursued thoughtlessly since, at the very least, it provides the accused infringer with the opportunity to challenge the validity of the licensed property and the owner's rights in

213

such property. Litigation for litigation's sake is never the appropriate course. Moreover, it is expensive and time consuming.

Care should be taken so that litigation does not spin out of control and take on a life of its own. As long as the objective remains the protection of the licensed property and the licensing program, litigation can be a useful tool in this pursuit. Maintaining this perspective will also enable the property owner to continue to pursue settlement negotiations during the litigation, with a view toward resolving the dispute short of an actual trial. The achievement of a settlement on solid business grounds is almost always preferable to allowing a judge or jury to decide the matter since they generally lack the knowledge or appreciation of how the business works. While many judges and juries "get it right" MOST of the time, a surprisingly high number do not.

14.4.3 Theories of Litigation

If a property owner decides to pursue litigation, there are a number of possible theories that it may rely on, depending on the type of property, how it has been protected, and how it is being used by the alleged infringer or counterfeiter.

[A]   Trademark Infringement

When the property has been registered as a trademark with the USPTO and the defendant is using a mark that is confusingly similar to the registered mark on like or similar goods, the federal trademark laws (the "Lanham Act") provide very strong and enforceable remedies. While an action for the infringement of a registered trademark can be brought in either state or federal court, most are brought in federal court which has original jurisdiction over such cases.

In order to prevail in such actions, the property owner must first establish that it is the owner of the trademark registration. This is usually satisfied by simply presenting a copy of the registration and, as such, is the easy part. The harder part is establishing that the mark is valid and protectable and that the accused infringer is using the mark in a manner that is likely to create consumer confusion, i.e., the accused infringer's use of the trademark is likely to cause confusion in the marketplace.

The first element, i.e., that the mark is valid and protectable becomes an issue in most litigations. If the owner has used the mark in commerce for more than five consecutive years and has filed a declaration to such effect with the USPTO, that will aid greatly in meeting that test. The issue of whether the accused infringer is using the mark in such a manner as to be likely to cause consumer confusion is, however, the real issue in most cases.

Most courts have adopted certain tests or standards to determine what actually constitutes a likelihood of confusion and these tests vary slightly, depending upon the court applying them. Generally speaking, however, courts will look at the relative strength of the registered trademark; the differences between the registered mark and the accused mark; the differences, if any, between the goods or services on which the marks are being used; and the channels in which the respective goods are being sold or used.

The issue of likelihood of confusion is far too complex to discuss in a book of this type. It has actually been the subject of a number of books or, at least, sections of books, devoted to that issue alone. The property owner would be well advised to consult with its intellectual property counsel to assess the strength or weakness of its claim.

Section 43(a) of the Lanham Act also provides relief for the infringement of a property owner's unregistered trademarks and trade dress or where another party makes false advertising claims. The standard under section 43(a) is whether such actions by the alleged infringer are likely to create a false designation of origin of their product or service or whether it results in a false or misleading description of fact. The courts have broadly interpreted this section to provide protection against a variety of acts of unfair competition.

The specific advantage of a section 43(a) action is that the property owner does not need to have a federal trademark registration in order to prevail. In order to prevail on such a claim, the property owner must establish that it is likely to be damaged by such false designation, etc., and that the accused party has affixed the mark to products or containers that are sold or used in commerce.

The standard for determining a claim under section 43(a) is the same as for trademark infringement, namely, whether the false designation, description or representation is likely to cause confusion. The property owner must establish: 1) that it owns the property; 2) that the property is capable of functioning as a mark or other indication of source, origin or sponsorship and 3) that the accused activity is likely to cause confusion. The same standards are typically used in determining the issue of likelihood of confusion.

In addition to federal actions for trademark infringement and counterfeiting, a number of remedies also exist under state and common law. The standard of proof for such causes of action is essentially the same as for federal Lanham Act claims, i.e., whether the infringer's use is likely to cause consumer confusion.

[B]   Dilution

The federal and state anti-dilution laws provide another means of protecting a property owner's trademarks. These laws are intended to protect against the gradual whittling away or dispersion of the distinctive quality of trademarks through their use by third parties and are primarily aimed at protecting well-known or famous trademarks—the very type of marks that are typically licensed. Unlike infringement claims where it is necessary to prove that the infringer's mark is likely to cause confusion in the marketplace, in order to prevail on a dilution claim the property owner must only establish that the accused infringer's use would blur the mark's product identification or tarnish the goodwill associated with the mark.

The remedies available for a successful party in a Lanham Act case include a nationwide injunction against use of the mark by the accused party as well as an award of damages, typically measured by the trademark owner's lost profits. Frequently, that means that the property owner will be awarded the infringer's profits from its use of the mark in question.

[C]   Counterfeiting

Counterfeiting actions are a special breed. Where the infringer has intentionally used the identical mark that the property owner had registered for the same goods as recited in the trademark registration, the line between infringement and counterfeiting has been crossed and the property owner can bring the action under the Trademark Counterfeiting Act. This act provides both civil and criminal penalties for persons who knowingly use a counterfeit mark when intentionally trafficking in goods or services.

Civil counterfeiting actions are brought by the trademark owner in federal court. If the trademark owner is able to convince a court of the merits of its case and the urgency of the matter, a court can order the seizure of counterfeit goods without notice to the counterfeiter. The party seeking the order must post an adequate bond. If the owner prevails in such an action, it is entitled to an award of three times the counterfeiter's profits, plus recovery of its attorney fees, unless the counterfeiter can show extenuating circumstances.

Criminal actions for counterfeiting are federal prosecutions brought by the applicable U.S. Attorneys' Offices. In order to establish a criminal cause of action, the accused party must have intentionally trafficked in the goods or services and must have knowingly used the counterfeit mark in connection with such goods or services. It must be shown that the accused party: 1) knew the mark was counterfeit; 2) that it was spurious; 3) that it was used in connection with trafficking in goods and services; 4) that it was identical or virtually indistinguishable from another mark; and 5) that it is likely to cause confusion. An individual found guilty under the Act is liable for a fine or imprisonment or both and there have been numerous instances of counterfeiters that are actually sent to jail for significant periods of time. While many courts take trademark counterfeiting quite seriously, the challenge can be in trying to convince a U.S. Attorney to put them at the head of their criminal dockets.

[D]   Copyright Infringement

The copyright laws can also be used to enforce copyrighted properties. Actions for copyright infringement are brought exclusively in the federal court that has jurisdiction over an accused infringer. Obtaining a copyright registration is a prerequisite to filing a suit for copyright infringement. If the copyright was registered with the Copyright Office within three months after it was first published, the copyright owner can seek an award of either actual or statutory damages as well as a recovery of its attorneys' fees. Thus, there is a strong incentive for owners of copyrightable materials to seek early registration.

The property owner must establish that it owns the copyright in the property and that the infringement occurred while it was the owner of the work. In addition, it must establish that it had obtained a copyright registration in the work and that the accused infringer violated such rights by making and distributing copies thereof.

In order to prevail in an action for copyright infringement, the owner must prove that the alleged infringer actually copied the copyrighted work since, in the absence of actual copying, there can be no infringement. Consequently, independent creation of the accused work by the alleged infringer is an absolute defense to any claim. This factor sets this type of action apart from patent or trademark infringement claims, where independent adoption or creation is not a defense.

Proving that someone actually copied a work can, of course, be a difficult task and, as such, courts will allow the copyright owner to establish copying by circumstantial evidence, i.e., that the accused infringer had access to the copyrighted work and that the two works are substantially similar.

One defense available to anyone accused of copyright infringement is that its use of the work was "fair use." Fair use will typically involve use of the copyrighted work for purposes of criticism, comment, and news reporting or teaching. Use of the copyrighted work as a parody may also constitute a fair use although it must be a legitimate attempt at parody and not merely a justification to exploit the copyrighted work.

[E]   Right of Publicity Violations

As noted in Chapter 5, celebrity properties are protectable under the celebrity's right of publicity which protects their name or likeness against unauthorized use. The right of publicity is solely a creature of state law and, consequently, the scope of protection of such right can vary widely from state to state. Some states do not even recognize the right and, of those that do, the scope of relief accorded celebrity rights is anything but uniform.

14.4.4 Litigation Strategies

Most actions for trademark and copyright infringement and virtually all actions for counterfeiting start with a bang. The property owner, in addition to simply filing the complaint and waiting for the case to proceed in the normal fashion (which could take years before reaching an ultimate conclusion), will seek immediate pre-trial relief by asking the court to enjoin the defendant's use of the property during the pendency of the case. This is done by seeking either a temporary restraining order (which the court can grant immediately and based solely on the proof presented by the property owner) or a preliminary injunction (which typically involves a hearing where both sides present their respective cases). Either type of motion will result in fairly swift action by the court.

In counterfeiting actions, immediacy is critical. Virtually all counterfeiters operate in secrecy, use fictitious names, and keep minimal business records. Thus, if the property owner waited for a normal civil action to run its course, the counterfeiter would have likely disappeared along with the evidence needed to convict them. As a consequence, most property owners will not only seek a temporary restraining order but also ask the court to issue an order to require the seizure of all counterfeit merchandise.

Where there is a serious issue that evidence will be destroyed by the alleged counterfeiter, a court may permit the property owner to have a U.S. Marshall or other designated representative enter the premises of the accused party and seize counterfeit merchandise along with pertinent books and records. Any seized items will be maintained in the custody of the U.S. Marshall's Office until the hearing on the motion for preliminary injunction.

Seizure orders will issue against known counterfeiters and various "John Does" who are likely to be selling counterfeit merchandise during a specific time and at a specific location on the day of the event. "John Doe" seizure orders are an effective tool at concerts and sports venues where history has shown that counterfeiting will likely take place, although the actual identity of the counterfeiters will not be known in advance. The seizure orders will authorize the seizure of such merchandise—much to the delight of legitimate licensees, who have spent time and money in producing royalty-bearing, authorized merchandise for sale at the event.

In order to prevail on any of these "pre-trial" remedies, the property owner needs to be able to demonstrate that it would be irreparably harmed if the infringement (or counterfeiting) continued and that it is likely to prevail on the merits at trial. Meeting the first prong of that standard, i.e., irreparable harm, is fairly easy if a trademark is involved since the courts have long recognized that the infringement of a party's trademark can cause irreparable harm to the owner.

Meeting the second prong, however, can be more challenging since the property owner must establish that it will likely win the case. The greater the similarity of the products, trademarks and copyrighted elements, the greater the likelihood of success. Any evidence of actual instances of consumer confusion, or of willful or intentional conduct by the accused party, will also go a long way to support the issuance of a preliminary injunction.

Another effective tool for obtaining expedited relief or, at the very least, for narrowing the issues at trial is a motion for summary judgment. A court will enter a summary judgment in favor of either party if there are no genuine questions of material fact existing as to any claim and it can, therefore, be decided as a matter of law.

Since any contested factual issues will always be resolved in favor of the nonmoving party, the facts should be clearly developed before seeking summary judgment. Thus, the motion is only appropriate where the act of counterfeiting or infringement is clearly evident.

Summary judgment motions can be brought at any time prior to trial and, if there are any factual issues potentially in dispute, they should be resolved during the course of discovery so as to make the case ripe for summary disposition at a time closer to trial. A grant of full or partial summary judgment will avoid the expense of time and money in trying the issues disposed of in advance by summary judgment. It is, therefore, a useful litigation tool.

Should the case ultimately go to trial, there are three critical elements to an effective trial presentation: preparation, preparation and preparation. The job of the property owner at trial is to convince the trier of fact, whether a judge or a jury, why it's claim has merit. Given the heavy case loads in most courts, the property owner will likely be given only a limited amount of time to make its case but, with careful preparation of witnesses and exhibits, this can be done. The purpose of a trial should be to educate, not to confuse or bore the trier of fact.

The elements of a claim for trademark and copyright infringement have been set forth above. Each of these elements should serve as a road map for trial preparation and presentation. Omissions of evidence on a critical point could result in dismissal of the complaint and the close of the property owner's case.

The end goal of the property owner is to stop infringement of its licensed property, which can be accomplished post-trial by a permanent injunction. Even where a temporary restraining order or preliminary injunction has issued, these must be ultimately converted into a permanent injunction, either by settlement or a final judgment.

Trial courts can, and frequently have, awarded a property owner damages based on the infringer's actions. In some instances, a court may also require recall of infringing products or the placement of corrective advertising.

Appendix-1

LICENSING AGENT AGREEMENT

THIS AGREEMENT is made this ____day of _____, by and between _____ with offices at _____ (the "Owner") and _____ with offices at _____ (the "Agent").

WITNESSETH:

WHEREAS, the Owner is in the business of and has developed certain trademarks, brands, designs, artwork, and intellectual property identified more fully in the attached Schedule A (the "Property");

WHEREAS, the Owner is desirous of retaining the services of an experienced licensing agent to commercialize or otherwise license the Property to third party Manufacturers (the "Manufacturer") for a line of Licensed Products bearing the Property (the "Licensed Products"); and

WHEREAS, Agent is willing to represent the Owner with respect to commercialization of the Property;

NOW, THEREFORE, in consideration of the promises and agreements set forth herein, the parties, each intending to be legally bound hereby, do promise and agree as follows:

1. AGENT GRANT

A. The Owner hereby grants to Agent, during the Term of this Agreement, the exclusive right (to the exclusion of others as well as the Owner representing itself) to represent the Owner in the countries identified in Schedule A attached hereto (the "Territory") with respect to the commercialization or licensing of the Property to Manufacturers.

B. With respect to agreements with Manufacturers, Owner hereby empowers Agent to negotiate the terms of such agreements within the parameters agreed upon between Agent and Owner prior to the commencement of such negotiations and to present such agreements to Owner for execution. All such agreements shall be in the name of Owner. Owner may not unreasonably refuse to execute an agreement presented by Agent.

C. In the event that the Owner is approached directly by a Manufacturer within the Territory during the Term of this Agreement, it shall refer such Manufacturer to Agent. Owner agrees that during the Term of this Agreement, it will not negotiate with any other person or entity within the Territory to represent it in any capacity in connection with the manufacture or sale of the Property.

2. TERM OF THE AGREEMENT

This Agreement and the provisions hereof, except as otherwise provided, shall be in full force and effect commencing on the date of execution by both parties and shall extend for an Initial Term as recited in Schedule A attached hereto (the "Term"). This Agreement shall be automatically renewed for additional "Extended Terms" as provided for in Schedule A unless either party notifies the other in writing of its intention not to renew the Agreement, such notification to be provided at least sixty (60) days prior to the expiration of the then in-effect Term.

3. DUTIES AND OBLIGATIONS

A. Subject to the conditions herein specified, Agent shall use reasonable efforts during the Term of this Agreement to find and conclude business arrangements with licensees for the Property that are advantageous to the Owner and, thereafter, to reasonably service such arrangements during the term thereof. In furtherance of Agent's duties as herein specified, Agent will:

1. Periodically meet and confer with the Owner to discuss the state of the merchandising industry;

2. Develop a merchandising plan for the Property in the Territory and provide a copy of same to Owner within thirty (30) days of the date of execution of this Agreement by both parties;

3. Implement the merchandising plan by contacting those prospective licensees best able to produce licensed products of the type and quality for the Property;

4. Negotiate all agreements with third party licensees in the name of the Owner and subject to the approval of the Owner;

5. Provide record keeping and billing services to the licensees as reasonably requested by Owner and monitor and oversee the licensing program with such third-party licensees to ensure that the licenses, royalties, minimums, and sales reports are promptly submitted;

6. Make appropriate recommendations to the Owner with respect to seeking and maintaining appropriate intellectual property protection for the Property; and

7. Investigate all potential infringements of Owner's intellectual property rights in the Territory and report to the Owner.

B. In addition to the foregoing, Agent shall be responsible for the enforcement of the quality control provisions of the third party license agreements which shall include periodic inspection of all Licensed Products.

C. The Agent shall engage in other such activities as the parties may mutually agree and, in general, use its best efforts consistent with sound business practices to maximize revenue generated from the exploitation of the rights granted hereunder and to enhance the value and reputation of the Property.

D. While the Agent is empowered to propose all necessary art, design, editorial, and other related approvals for the creation of the Licensed Products as well as to enforce the appropriately high standard of quality for all such Licensed Products created and produced pursuant to licensing and promotional agreements entered into pursuant to this Agreement, the Owner retains the right to grant final approval on art, design, and editorial matters. The Agent agrees to submit to the Owner, for final approval, drafts, prototypes and finished samples of all Licensed Products and any and all advertising, promotional and packaging material related to said Licensed Products. Owner will respond to the Agent regarding approval within ten (10) business days after receipt of such samples. Failure to respond within said period shall be deemed disapproval.

E. Agent shall oversee the payment by the licensees of all royalties and other payments due under this Agreement. F. It is understood that the Owner may have concepts and properties other than the Property and such concepts and properties do not form part of this Agreement.

G. The Owner recognizes that Agent performs similar services for its other clients and that the Owner's retention of the Agent is subject to such understanding.

H. The Owner shall be solely responsible for all costs and expenses associated with the protection of the Property, including the costs for obtaining and maintaining patent, trademark, and copyright protection.

4. COMPENSATION

A. In consideration for the services rendered by Agent, the Owner agrees to and shall pay Agent a Retainer Fee in the amount of and in accordance with the terms recited in Schedule A attached hereto. Such Retainer Fee is non-refundable and non-creditable against any other compensation owed Agent under this Agreement.

B. In addition to the aforementioned Retainer Fee, Owner agrees to pay Agent a Commission in the amount recited in Schedule A attached hereto based on the Net Revenues received by the Agent from the Manufacturers based on the Manufacturer's sales or other use of Licensed Products bearing the Property.

C. "Net Revenues" shall include all income received by Agent (prior to the deduction of Agent's commission) from such third party Manufacturer within the Territory pursuant to any contract or agreement for the sale, lease, license or other disposition of the Property resulting directly from the efforts of Agent including, but not limited to, advances, royalties, guarantees, fees and payments (whether in cash, barter or other form of consideration) less any payments made or expenses incurred by Agent for or on behalf of the Owner with the prior approval of Owner.

D. After termination or expiration of this Agreement for any reason, Agent shall be entitled to continue to receive its full Commission based on those contracts or agreements entered into by Owner with Manufacturers in the Territory during the Term of this Agreement or within one (1) year from the date of termination or expiration of this Agreement resulting from presentations made or negotiations conducted by Agent during the Term of this Agreement for which Agent would have received a Commission had the Agreement not been terminated or expired. Agent shall be entitled to such post-termination Commission for so long as the Owner continues to receive revenues under such agreement with a Manufacturer as well as from any renewals, modifications, continuations or extensions thereof.

5. WARRANTIES AND INDEMNIFICATIONS

A. The Owner represent and warrant that it is the owner of all rights in and to the Property, that it has the right and power to license and/or sell such Property, that the use of the Property on the Licensed Products shall not infringe upon the rights of any third party, and that it has not granted anyone else the right or authority to act for it in a manner which would conflict with Agent.

B. The Owner hereby agree to defend, indemnify and hold Agent, its shareholders, directors, officers, employees, agents, parent companies, subsidiaries, and affiliates, harmless from and against any and all claims, liabilities, judgments, penalties, and taxes, civil and criminal, and all costs, expenses (including, without limitation, reasonable attorneys' fees) incurred in connection therewith, which any of them may incur or to which any of them may be subjected, arising out of or relating to a breach of the Owner' representations and warranties. During the pendency of any indemnified claim against Agent, Agent shall have the right to withhold any monies then owed Owner to help defray any costs or expenses that Owner may incur as a result of such claim.

C. Agent hereby agrees to defend, indemnify and hold the Owner, their shareholders, directors, officers, employees, agents, parent companies, subsidiaries, and affiliates, harmless from and against any and all claims, liabilities, judgments, penalties, and taxes, civil and criminal, and all costs, expenses (including, without limitation, reasonable attorneys' fees) incurred in connection therewith, which any of them may incur or to which any of them may be subjected, arising out of or relating to any action by Agent.

6. STATEMENTS AND PAYMENTS

A. Owner agrees that Agent shall receive all royalty reports and collect all royalties and payments from the Manufacturers both during and after termination or expiration of this Agreement. Such royalties and payments shall be deposited in an account which the parties mutually agree upon. Agent shall remit all royalties, inclusive of copies of all royalty reports, less Agent's Commissions, on a quarterly basis based on revenues received by Agent during the previous calendar quarter. Such payments and statements reflecting the basis for such payments shall be made within forty-five (45) days after the close of each calendar quarter.

B. Agent agrees to keep accurate books of account and records at its principal place of business covering all transactions relating to the agreements with the Manufacturers. Owner or its designee shall have the right, at all reasonable hours of the day and upon at least ten (10) business days notice, to examine Owners books and records as they relate to the subject matter of this Agreement only. Such examination shall occur at the place where the Owner maintains such records.

C. All books and records pertaining to the obligations of the Agent hereunder shall be maintained and kept accessible and available to Agent for inspection for at least three (3) years after the date to which they pertain.

7. NOTICE AND PAYMENT

A. Any notice required to be given under this Agreement shall be in writing and delivered personally to the other designated party at the above stated address or mailed by certified, registered or Express mail, return receipt requested or by Federal Express and/or UPS.

B. Either party may change the address to which notice or payment is to be sent by written notice to the other under any provision of this paragraph.

8. TERMINATION

A. This Agreement may be terminated by either party upon thirty (30) days written notice to the other party in the event of a breach of a material provision of this Agreement by the other party, provided that, during the thirty (30) days period, the breaching party fails to cure such breach.

B. The Owner shall have the right to terminate this Agreement immediately in the event that the Agent fails to enter into at least ____ license agreements with third parties with _____ months after execution of this Agreement and generates at least $_____ of licensing revenue from such third parties within _____ months after execution of this Agreement.

C. In the event that Agent is unable to meet its obligations when they become due or make an assignment for the benefit of its creditors, Owner shall have the right to either immediately terminate this Agreement, or alternatively, convert it to a non-exclusive agreement.

9. EFFECT OF TERMINATION

A. Upon termination or expiration of this Agreement as it relates to the Property, all rights granted to Agent relative to the Property shall forthwith revert to the Owner who shall be free to contract with others to commercialize such Property subject to the provisions of this Agreement subject to the post-termination provisions of this Agreement. Agent shall, thereafter, refrain from further efforts to commercialize the Property.

B. Upon termination or expiration of this Agreement, Owner may request that Agent provide it within sixty (60) days of such notice with a complete schedule of all prospective Manufacturers contacted on behalf of the Owner relative to the Property as well as returning all materials relating to the Property.

10. JURISDICTION/DISPUTES

This Agreement shall be governed in accordance with the laws of [State]. All disputes under this Agreement shall be resolved by litigation in the courts of the State of [State], including the federal courts therein and the parties all consent to the jurisdiction of such courts, agree to accept service of process by mail, and hereby waive any jurisdictional or venue defenses otherwise available to it.

11. AGREEMENT BINDING ON SUCCESSORS

The provisions of the Agreement shall be binding upon and shall inure to the benefit of the parties hereto, their heirs, administrators, successors and assigns.

12. ASSIGNABILITY

A. Neither party may assign this Agreement or the rights and obligations thereunder to any third party without the prior express written approval of the other party which shall not be unreasonably withheld.

B. In the event that anytime during the Term of this Agreement, the Owner intends to sell, assign, transfer or abandon some or all of its rights in the Property, it shall provide Agent with written notice to such effect at least thirty (30) days prior to the actual sale, assignment, transfer or abandonment of the Property. Upon receipt of such notice, the parties shall promptly meet and negotiate an arrangement under which this Agreement shall be assigned to and assumed by the acquiring party who will agree to assume all obligations thereunder with the Owner agreeing to guarantee the acquiring party's performance thereof. In the event that the acquiring party does not intend to receive an assignment of the Agreement and/or the Owner is unwilling to guarantee the acquiring party's performance thereof, the Owner and Agent shall agree to a termination of the Agent Agreement. In such event, the parties will negotiate in good faith a mutually acceptable termination package for the Agent in an amount to be mutually agreed upon between the Parties to compensate the Agent for lost potential revenues caused by such termination. In the event that the Parties are unable to mutually agree to what constitutes fair compensation, the Parties agree to binding arbitration before a single arbitrator under the then current rules of the American Arbitration Association in the AAA office closest to the Agent.

13. WAIVER

No waiver by either party of any default shall be deemed as a waiver of prior or subsequent default of the same of other provisions of this Agreement.

14. SEVERABILITY

If any term, clause or provision hereof is held invalid or unenforceable by a court of competent jurisdiction, such invalidity shall not affect the validity or operation of any other term, clause or provision and such invalid term, clause or provision shall be deemed to be severed from the Agreement.

15. INDEPENDENT CONTRACTOR

Agent shall be deemed an independent contractor and nothing contained herein shall constitute this arrangement to be employment, a joint venture or a partnership. Agent shall be solely responsible for and shall hold the Owner harmless for any and all claims for taxes, fees or costs, including but not limited to withholding, income tax, FICA, workman's compensation.

16. INTEGRATION

This Agreement constitutes the entire understanding of the parties, and revokes and supersedes all prior agreements between the parties and is intended as a final expression of their Agreement. It shall not be modified or amended except in writing signed by the parties hereto and specifically referring to this Agreement. This Agreement shall take precedence over any other documents which may conflict with this Agreement.

IN WITNESS WHEREOF, the parties hereto, intending to be legally bound hereby, have each caused to be affixed hereto its or his/her hand and seal the day indicated.

OWNER   **AGENT**

By:_____   By:_____

Title:_____   Title:_____

Date:_____   Date:_____

SCHEDULE A
TO LICENSING AGENT AGREEMENT

1.   **PROPERTY & TRADEMARK NOTICE:**

2.   **TERRITORY:**

3.   **TERM:**

4.   **RETAINER FEE:**

5.   **COMMISSION:**

6.   **ADDITIONAL SERVICES:**

Appendix-2

SUB-AGENT AGREEMENT

THIS AGREEMENT is entered into this _____ day of _____ by and between _____ with offices at _____ (the "Agent") and _____, with offices at _____ (the "Sub-Agent").

WITNESSETH:

WHEREAS, Agent, pursuant to an agent agreement dated _____ between _____ (the "Owner") and the Agent (the "Agent Agreement"), the Property Owner has granted certain rights to the Agent to develop and conduct a licensing program for the property described in Schedule A attached hereto (the "Property"); and

WHEREAS, Agent would like to retain the services of Sub-Agent to commercialize or license the Property to third-party licensees in the Sub-Agent's territory as defined in Schedule A (the "Territory") for a line of licensed products (the "Licensed Products"); and

WHEREAS, Sub-Agent is willing to represent the Agent in such Territory with respect to the licensing of the Property within the Territory;

NOW, THEREFORE, in consideration of the promises and agreements set forth herein, the parties, each intending to be legally bound hereby, do promise and agree as follows.

1. SUB-AGENT APPOINTMENT

A. Agent hereby appoints the Sub-Agent, for the Term of this Agreement, its exclusive representative in the Territory for the purpose of commercializing or licensing the Property to third-party licensees, subject to the approval of Agent and the Owner.

B. In this regard, Sub-Agent shall be authorized to present, negotiate, and conclude licensing arrangements with third-party licensees using a form agreement approved by Agent and Owner and pursuant to terms and conditions previously approved by Agent and Owner.

C. All third-party license agreements shall be in the name of Owner and shall be signed by Owner, although Sub-Agent shall be a party to all such agreements as agent for Owner. All payments from third parties shall be directed to Sub-Agent.

D. It is understood and agreed that this Agreement shall relate only to the enumerated Property and to no other properties owned or controlled by Agent and/or Owner. Agent and Owner shall be free to commercialize such other properties to the exclusion of Sub-Agent.

E. Agent agrees not to retain the services of any third party to represent Agent with respect to the Property in the Territory. However, Agent may retain the services of other subagents with respect to merchandising of the Property in countries outside the Territory.

F. Sub-Agent agrees to refrain from licensing the Property to third party licensees who intend or are likely to sell the Licensed Products outside the Territory.

2. TERM OF THE AGREEMENT

This Agreement and the provisions hereof, except as otherwise provided, shall be in full force and effect commencing on the date of execution by both parties and shall extend for a Term as recited in Schedule A attached hereto (the "Term").

3. DUTIES AND OBLIGATIONS OF PARTIES

A. Subject to the conditions herein specified, Sub-Agent shall use reasonable efforts during the Term of this Agreement to find and conclude business arrangements with licensees for the Property that are advantageous to Agent and Owner and, thereafter, to reasonably service such arrangements during the term thereof. In furtherance of Sub-Agent's duties as herein specified, Sub-Agent will:

1. Periodically meet and confer with Agent to discuss the state of the merchandising industry;

2. Develop a merchandising plan for the Property in the Territory and provide a copy of same to Agent within thirty (30) days of the date of execution of this Agreement by both parties;

3. Implement the merchandising plan by contacting those prospective licensees best able to produce licensed products of the type and quality for the Property;

4. Negotiate all agreements with third party licensees in the name of the Owner and subject to the approval of Agent and Owner;

5. Provide record keeping and billing services to the licensees as reasonably requested by Agent and monitor and oversee the licensing program with such third-party licensees to ensure that the licenses, royalties, minimums, and sales reports are promptly submitted;

6. Remit all Advances paid by licensees within ten (10) days after receipt thereof and all other payments made by licensees within twenty (20) days of receipt thereof. All payment shall be made in U.S. Dollars by wire transfer.

7. Make appropriate recommendations to the Agent with respect to seeking and maintaining appropriate intellectual property protection for the Property; and

8. Investigate all potential infringements of Owner's intellectual property rights in the Territory and report to Agent.

B. In addition to the foregoing, Sub-Agent shall be responsible for the enforcement of the quality control provisions of the third party license agreements which shall include periodic inspection of all Licensed Products and conducting personal visits to the third-party licensees' manufacturing facilities to ensure that the quality control provisions of the license agreements with the licensees are being complied with. Sub-Agent shall submit to Agent a written report after each of said reviews and visits.

C. Sub-Agent shall engage in other such activities as the parties may mutually agree and, in general, use its best efforts consistent with sound business practices to maximize revenue generated from the exploitation of the rights granted hereunder and to enhance the value and reputation of the Property.

D. While Sub-Agent is empowered to propose all necessary art, design, editorial, and other related approvals for the creation of the Licensed Products as well as to enforce the appropriately high standard of quality for all such Licensed Products created and produced pursuant to licensing and promotional agreements entered into pursuant to this Agreement, Agent retains the right to grant final approval on art, design, and editorial matters. Sub-Agent agrees to submit to Agent, for final approval, drafts, prototypes and finished samples of all Licensed Products and any and all advertising, promotional and packaging material related to said Licensed Products. Agent will respond to Sub-Agent regarding approval within thirty (30) business days after receipt of such samples. Failure to respond within said period shall be deemed disapproval.

E. Sub-Agent shall oversee the payment by the licensees of all royalties and other payments due under this Agreement. If necessary, Sub-Agent shall conduct periodic royalty investigations of the licensee's books and records to ensure that all payments have been made. The cost of such royalty investigations shall be borne by the Sub-Agent. However, any recoveries received as a result of such royalty investigation shall be applied against the cost of conducting such investigation. The Sub-Agent shall provide the Owner and the Agent with copies of any reports rendered as a result of such investigations.

F. It is understood that Agent and Owner may have concepts and properties other than the Property and such concepts and properties do not form part of this Agreement.

G. Agent recognizes that Sub-Agent performs similar services for its other clients and that Agent's retention of Sub-Agent is subject to such understanding.

H. Agent and Owner shall be solely responsible for all costs and expenses associated with the protection of the Property, including the costs for obtaining and maintaining patent, trademark, and copyright protection.

4. LICENSE AGREEMENTS

A. All proposed license agreements presented by Sub-Agent under this Agreement shall be subject to the express written approval of Agent and Owner, such approval not to be unreasonably withheld. It is understood that Sub-Agent will submit all such proposed agreements to Owner through Agent for consideration, approval, and execution and Agent will, thereupon, advise Sub-Agent within thirty (30) business days after receipt of the proposed agreement as to whether Agent and Owner agree or disagree to the terms thereof and whether Owner will execute same. Failure to act within said thirty (30) day period shall be deemed a disapproval of any such agreement. No agreement shall be binding on Agent or Owner until signed by Owner.

B. All such license agreements with third-party licensees shall be between Owner and the third-party licensee presented by Sub-Agent. The basic form license agreement that is to be used by Sub-Agent in negotiating license agreements with third-party licensees has been deemed approved by Agent and Owner as in form only -- all prospective licenses, even if in this form, must be submitted for approval by Agent and Owner. Any and all additions, deletions and changes to this basic form agreement shall be subject to the absolute, unfettered express written approval of Agent and Owner and notification of approval or disapproval shall be provided to Sub-Agent within ten (10) business days after receipt of same by Agent. The lack of response from Agent within such ten (10) day period shall be deemed a disapproval of any proposed addition, deletion and/or change.

5. COMPENSATION

A. In consideration for the services rendered by Sub-Agent, Agent agrees to and shall pay Sub-Agent, during the Term of this Agreement, a commission in the amount recited in Schedule A attached hereto (the "Commission").

B. In addition to the Commission recited in Schedule A, Agent agrees to reimburse Sub-Agent for all reasonable expenses incurred on behalf of Agent, provided that such expenses have been previously approved by Agent.

C. Agent further agrees to pay Sub-Agent, during the Term of this Agreement, a Subagent Fee in the amount recited in Schedule A attached hereto.

D. "Gross Revenues" shall include all income generated as a result of any commercialization, sale, or licensing of the Property in the Territory (prior to deduction of Sub-Agent's Commission) from such third-party licensee(s), due solely to the efforts of Sub-Agent.

E. In the event that this Agreement should expire or terminate for reasons other than a breach of any provision herein by Sub-Agent, Sub-Agent shall be entitled to post-termination compensation based on gross income received by Owner from any third-party license agreement, for the life of such third party agreement, entered into through Sub-Agent during the Term of this Agreement and for which Sub-Agent would have received compensation had this Agreement not expired, subject to the schedule recited in Schedule A attached hereto.

F. Sub-Agent shall not be entitled to any post-termination compensation in the event that this Agreement is expressly terminated by Agent in the event of a material breach by Sub-Agent of the terms of this Agreement. Sub-Agent shall not be entitled to such post-termination compensation for any other agreements subsequently entered into by Agent or Owner.

G. All payments due hereunder shall be made in United States currency drawn on a United States bank, unless otherwise specified between the parties.

H. All fees payable hereunder shall be based on the official exchange rate on the date on which such payment is due and Sub-Agent shall provide detailed conversion calculations with every payment submitted hereunder. If, by any reason of any governmental or fiscal restrictions affecting the convertibility, payment cannot be made in U.S. funds, then Sub-Agent shall take such reasonable actions with respect to the payment due as Agent shall direct.

6. WARRANTIES AND INDEMNIFICATIONS

A. Agent represents and warrants that it has the right and power to enter into this agreement and, further, that it has not granted anyone else the right or authority to act for it in a manner that would conflict with Sub-Agent.

B. Agent hereby agrees to defend, indemnify, and hold Sub-Agent, its shareholders, directors, officers, employees, agents, parent companies, subsidiaries and affiliates, harmless from and against any and all claims, liabilities, judgments, penalties, and taxes, civil and criminal, and all costs and expenses (including, without limitation, reasonable attorney's fees) incurred in connection therewith, which any of them may incur or to which any of them may be subjected, arising out of or relating to a breach of Agent's representation and warranty or of any actions or inactions of Agent.

C. Sub-Agent hereby agrees to defend, indemnify, and hold Agent and any of its related entities harmless from and against any and all claims, liabilities, judgments, penalties, and taxes, civil and criminal, and all costs and expenses (including, without limitation, reasonable attorney's fees) arising out of or relating to a breach of Sub-Agent's representation and warranty or that may arise out of any action or inaction by Sub-Agent, other than as it may relate to Agent's warranty, as above stated.

D. Sub-Agent hereby agrees to comply with all laws and regulations in each country in the Territory.

7. STATEMENTS AND PAYMENTS

A. All payments from licensees based on agreements for the Property shall be paid directly to Owner. Within thirty (30) days after receipt by Agent of its commission from Owner, Agent shall transmit to Sub-Agent its Commission.

B. Agent agrees to keep accurate books of accounts and records at its principal place of business covering all transactions relating to the agreements with the licensees. Sub-Agent, through an independent certified public accountant acceptable to Owner, shall have the right, at all reasonable hours of the day and upon at least five (5) days' written notice, to examine Agent's books and records as they relate to the subject matter of this Agreement only. Such examination shall occur at the place where Agent maintains such records.

C. All books and records pertaining to the obligations of Sub-Agent hereunder shall be maintained and kept accessible and available to Agent for inspection for at least three (3) years after the date to which they pertain.

8. NOTICES

A. Any notice required to be given under this Agreement shall be in writing and delivered personally to the other designated party at the above-stated address or mailed by certified or registered mail, return receipt requested, or delivered by a recognized national overnight courier service.

B. Either party may change the address to which notice or payment is to be sent by written notice to the other under any provision of this paragraph.

9. TERMINATION

A. This Agreement may be terminated by either party upon thirty (30) days' written notice to the other party in the event of a breach of a material provision of this Agreement by the other party, provided that, during the thirty (30) day period, the breaching party fails to cure such breach.

B. Agent shall have the right to terminate this Agreement immediately in the event that Sub-Agent fails to enter into at least _____ license agreements with third parties with _____ months after execution of this Agreement and generates at least _____ of licensing revenue from such third parties within _____ months after execution of this Agreement.

C. The Agent shall have the right to immediately terminate this Agreement in the event that the Sub-Agent should be unable to meet its obligations when they become due, make an assignment for the benefit of its creditors or should there be a change in the existing management of Sub-Agent.

D. This Agreement shall terminate automatically in the event that the Agent Agreement between Agent and Owner shall terminate or expire.

E. In the event that this Agreement shall terminate or expire, Sub-Agent shall turn over to Agent all records relating to each license entered into under this Agreement. All rights granted to Sub-Agent shall revert to Agent and Sub-Agent shall refrain from any further use of the Property.

233

10. JURISDICTION AND DISPUTES

This Agreement will be governed by, and construed and enforced in accordance with the laws of [State] without regard to conflicts of law principles. All disputes under this Agreement shall be resolved by the courts of the state of [State], including the United States District Court for the District of [State]. The parties all consent to the jurisdiction of such courts, agree to accept service of process by mail, and hereby waive any jurisdictional or venue defenses otherwise available to it.

11. SUBORDINATION

The parties recognize that Agent's rights with respect to the Property are governed exclusively by the Agent Agreement. In the event there are conflicts between the Agent Agreement and this Agreement, the provisions of the Agent Agreement shall govern.

12. AGREEMENT BINDING ON SUCCESSORS

The provisions of the Agreement shall be binding on and shall inure to the benefit of the parties hereto, their heirs, assigns, and successors.

13. WAIVER

No waiver by either party of any default shall be deemed as a waiver of prior or subsequent default of the same or other provisions of this Agreement.

14. SEVERABILITY

If any term, clause, or provision hereof is held invalid or unenforceable by a court of competent jurisdiction, such invalidity shall not affect the validity or operation of any other term, clause, or provision and such invalid term, clause, or provision shall be deemed to be severed from the Agreement.

15. INDEPENDENT CONTRACTOR

Sub-Agent shall be deemed an independent contractor and nothing contained herein shall constitute this arrangement to be employment, a joint venture, or a partnership. Sub-Agent shall be solely responsible for and shall hold Agent harmless for any and all claims for taxes, fees, or costs, including but not limited to withholding, income tax, FICA, and workmen's compensation.

16. ASSIGNABILITY

This agreement and the rights and obligations thereof are personal to Sub-Agent and shall not be assigned by any act of Sub-Agent or by operation of law unless in connection with a transfer of substantially all of the assets of Sub-Agent or with the consent of Agent and Owner.

17. GOVERNMENTAL APPROVAL

Sub-Agent agrees to submit copies of this Agreement to any governmental agency in any country in the Territory where approval of this Agreement is necessary, and agrees to promptly prosecute any such application diligently. This Agreement shall become effective in such country or countries only upon receipt of appropriate approval from the applicable governmental agency.

18. GOVERNING LANGUAGE

This Agreement is in the English language. No translation of this Agreement into any language other than English shall be considered in the interpretation thereof, and in the event that any translation of this Agreement is in conflict with the English language version, the English version shall govern.

19. BLOCKED CURRENCY

A. In the event that any payment required to be made to Owner pursuant to this Agreement cannot be made when due because of the exchange control of any country in the Territory and such payment remains unpaid for twelve (12) months, Agent and/or Owner may, by notice served to Sub-Agent, elect any of the following alternative methods of handling such payment:

1. If the currency can be converted into currency other than U.S. Dollars for purposes of foreign remittance, Owner may elect to receive such payment in any such currencies as it may specify and, in such case, the amount payable in the foreign currency so selected shall be determined by reference to the then existent legal rate of exchange which is most favorable to Owner.

2. Owner may elect to have payment made to it in the local currency, deposited to the credit of Owner in a bank account in such country designated by Owner, in which event Sub-Agent shall furnish to Owner evidence of such deposit.

B. All expenses of currency conversion and transmission shall be borne by Sub-Agent and no deduction shall be made from remittances on account of such expense. Sub-Agent from time to time may prepare all applications, reports or other documents which may be required by the government of the applicable country in order that remittances may be made in accordance with this Agreement.

20. INTEGRATION

This Agreement constitutes the entire understanding of the parties, and revokes and supersedes all prior agreements between the parties and is intended as a final expression of their Agreement. It shall not be modified or amended except in writing signed by the parties hereto and specifically referring to this Agreement. This Agreement shall take precedence over any other documents that may conflict with this Agreement.

IN WITNESS WHEREOF, the parties hereto, intending to be legally bound hereby, have each caused to be affixed hereto its or his/her hand and seal the day indicated.

AGENT   SUB-AGENT

By:_____   By:_____

Title:_____   Title:_____

Date:_____   Date:_____

SCHEDULE A

TO SUB-AGENT AGREEMENT

1. LICENSED PROPERTY:

2. TERRITORY:

3. TERM:

4. COMMISSION:

5. SUB-AGENT FEE:

6. POST TERMINATION COMPENSATION:

Appendix-3

Licensee Application

Date:	
Property:	
Licensee:	
Street Address:	
City, State & Zip Code	
Telephone No.	
Fax Number:	
E-Mail Address	
Business Contact/Phone: Product Dev Contact/Phone:	
Legal Contact & Phone:	
Finance/Royalty Contact & Phone:	
Proposed Licensed Products:	
Proposed Term:	
Exclusive or Non-Exclusive	
Proposed Royalty Rates Domestic/ F.O.B./ Direct Sales:	
Proposed Advance:	
Proposed Guarantee(s):	
Proposed Channels of Distribution:	

Appendix-3/Licensee Application

Proposed Territory:	
Proposed Sell-Off:	
Sales Projections:	Year 1 -
	Year 2 -
	Year 3 -
Top 4 Retailers:	1)
	2)
	3)
Proposed Marketing Date:	
Proposed First Sale Date:	
Proposed Product Category:	Attach sheet to describe
Marketing Strategy:	Attach sheet to describe
Retail Strategy:	Attach sheet to describe
Current Licenses Held:	Attach list.
Main Product Lines:	List on separate sheet
Stipulations:	List on separate sheet
Public or Private:	
Dun & Bradstreet #:	
Two references & contact info	
Please send the following items:	

This document does not constitute a legal agreement but is a summary of the deal points being discussed. No agreement will exist until execution of a formal license agreement by both parties.

By:_____   Date:_____

238

Appendix-4

License Deal Memo

LICENSEE:

ADDRESS:

CITY/STATE:

PHONE:

FAX:

E-MAIL:

CONTACT:

LICENSOR:

PROPERTY:

TYPE OF LICENSE: Exclusive or Non-Exclusive

LICENSED PRODUCTS:

DISTRIBUTION RIGHTS:

ADVANCE: $_____ due upon execution of a formal license agreement

GUARANTEE: 20XX $_____

                                 20XX $_____

                                 >20XX $_____

MEDIA SPENDING:

ROYALTY RATES: _____%

                               _____% on FOB Sales

                               _____% on Direct to Consumer Sales

TERM:

RENEWAL OPTIONS:

ASSIGNMENT:

TERRITORY:

DISTRUBUTION:

SPECIAL PROVISIONS:

EFFECTIVE DATE:

Upon signature of the Deal Memo, both parties undertake to negotiate in good faith and agree upon a long form license agreement the ("License Agreement") incorporating the terms set forth in this Deal Memo. Neither this Deal Memo nor any agreements otherwise reached between the parties relating to this proposed transaction shall be binding on either party unless and until a formal Licensed Agreement is executed by both parties. If no formal License Agreement is executed within sixty (60) days from the date of this Deal Memo, this Deal Memo shall automatically expire and any offer being made by Licensee shall expire.

LICENSOR   **LICENSEE**

By:_____   By:_____

Title:_____   Title:_____

Date:_____   Date:_____

Appendix-5

LICENSE AGREEMENT

WITNESSETH:

THIS AGREEMENT is made this ____ day of _____ , by and between _____ with offices at _____ (the "Licensor") and _____ with offices at _____ (the "Licensee").

WHEREAS, Licensor is the sole and exclusive owner of the Property or Properties identified more fully in Schedule A attached hereto (the "Property") including, but not limited to, those trademark and service marks identified in Schedule A attached hereto (the "Trademarks"); and

WHEREAS, Licensor has the power and authority to grant to Licensee the right, privilege and license to use, manufacture and sell those types of products that incorporate or are otherwise based on the Property as identified in Schedule A attached hereto (the "Licensed Products"); and

WHEREAS, Licensee has represented that it has the ability to manufacture, market and distribute the Licensed Products in the distribution channels (the "Channels of Distribution") and the countries both of which are identified in Schedule A attached hereto (the "Territory"); and

WHEREAS, Licensee desires to obtain from Licensor a license to use, manufacture, have manufactured and sell Licensed Products in the Territory and to use the Trademark on or in association with the Licensed Products; and

WHEREAS, both Licensee and Licensor are in agreement with respect to the terms and conditions upon which Licensee shall use, manufacture, have manufactured and sell Licensed Products and to use the Trademark on or in association with the Licensed Products.

NOW, THEREFORE, in consideration of the promises and agreements set forth herein, the parties, each intending to be legally bound hereby, do promise and agree as follows.

1. License Grant.

A. Grant of Limited License. Licensor grants to Licensee for the term of this Agreement as defined in Schedule A attached hereto (the "Term"), subject to the terms and conditions herein contained, and Licensee hereby accepts, the non-exclusive right, license and privilege to utilize the Property and Trademarks solely and only in connection with the manufacture of the Licensed Products as well as for the advertising, promotion, distribution, offering for sale and sale of such Licensed Products within the Channels of Distribution and within the Territory to those Approved Customers identified in Schedule A attached hereto or who are otherwise approved in writing by Licensor under the terms and conditions stated herein.

B. Individuals. Licensee expressly acknowledges that this license grant does not convey any rights to the Licensee with respect to the individuals and athletes who compete or participate in Licensor's events, whose rights are not controlled by Licensor.

Licensee shall not use the names, images or likenesses of such individuals and athletes without first obtaining permission directly from such individuals and athletes.

  C. No Sublicensing. Licensee may not grant any sub-licenses to any third parties without the prior express written permission of Licensor, which permission may be withheld in Licensor's sole discretion.

  D. Non-Authorized Use. Licensee agrees that it will not utilize the Property in any manner not specifically authorized by this Agreement.

  E. Grant of Other Rights. Nothing in this Agreement shall be construed to prevent Licensor from granting other licenses for the use of the Property in any manner whatsoever. Licensor specifically reserves all rights not herein granted, including, without limitation, premium and promotional rights.

  F. Distribution Outside of Authorized Channels. It is understood and agreed that the Licensee may, with the prior express written approval of Licensor, manufacture and/or have manufactured the Licensed Products outside the Territory provided that all sales are within the Territory. Licensee agrees that it will not make, or authorize, any use, direct or indirect, of the Licensed Products or Property in any distribution channel other than the approved Channels or Distribution or in any country other than the Territory without the prior express written permission of the Licensor nor shall Licensee knowingly offer to sell or sell Licensed Products to persons who intend or are likely to resell them in distribution channels or than the approved Channels of Distribution or any country other than the Territory.

2. Consideration.

  A. Royalty. In consideration for the licenses granted hereunder, Licensee agrees to pay to Licensor during the Term of this Agreement (as defined in Schedule A attached hereto), a royalty in the amount provided in Schedule A attached hereto (the "Royalty") based on Licensee Net Sales of Licensed Products. If any amount payable to Licensor is subject to any non-US tax, charge or duty, Licensee shall furnish to Licensor official proof of such payment, including official proof of receipt of Licensee's payment from the government entity imposing such tax, charge or duty. If Licensor does not receive full and complete U.S. tax credit for any such tax, charge or duty, then the amount payable by Licensee shall be increased to provide to Licensor such amount as would be payable to Licensor in the absence of any such tax, charge, duty or impost.

  B. Royalty Period. The Royalty owed Licensor shall be calculated on a quarterly calendar basis (the "Royalty Period") and shall be payable no later than thirty (30) days after the termination of the preceding calendar quarter.

  C. Marketing Fee. During each Royalty Period on the dates specified in Schedule A, Licensee shall pay to Licensor a Marketing Fee in the amount recited in Schedule A. Licensee's obligation to pay the Marketing Fee is absolute and independent of the Royalty. Licensee shall no right to set off, compensate or make any deduction from payments of the Marketing Fee for any reason whatsoever. Any amount that Licensee may directly spend on advertising (as previously approved by Licensor) in excess of the amount required herein shall not be used to offset the required Marketing Fee for the subsequent Royalty Period. Licensor may use or expend all Marketing Fees paid by Licensee hereunder in its sole discretion.

  D. Royalty Statement. With each Royalty Payment, Licensee shall provide Licensor with a written Royalty Statement in a form acceptable to Licensor. Such Royalty Statement shall be certified as accurate by a duly authorized officer of Licensee, reciting: (1) gross sales of all Licensed Products for the applicable Royalty Period, itemized by SKU; (2) Net Sales on which the Royalties are based; (3) all related party sales, employee sales, parking lot, warehouse or similar sales, and any other unusual sales transactions; (4) allowed deductions or credits taken against gross sales; and (5) quantity and dollar amount of Licensed Products sold to each customer, broken down by month and each country and Channel of Distribution within the Territory, if applicable, as well as any other information relating to the Licensed Products that may be reasonably requested by Licensor. Failure to deliver statements and reports in a timely manner as provided by this Section shall constitute a material breach of this Agreement. Such statements shall be furnished to Licensor whether or not any Licensed Products were sold during the Royalty Period.

    E.   Advance and Guaranteed Minimum Royalty. Licensee agrees to pay to Licensor a Guaranteed Minimum Royalty in accordance with the terms of Schedule A attached hereto (the "Guaranteed Minimum Royalty"). As recited in Schedule A, a portion of the Guaranteed Minimum Royalty for the first year shall be payable as a non-refundable Advance against royalties (the "Advance"). The actual royalty payments shall reflect the amount of all Guaranteed Minimum Royalty payments including any Advances made. Licensee shall only be permitted to carry forward any unused credit for the Advance or Guaranteed Minimum Royalty for the subsequent year.

    F.   Net Sales Defined. "Net Sales" shall mean Licensee gross sales (the gross invoice amount billed customers) of Licensed Products, less any *bona fide* returns (net of all returns actually made or allowed as supported by credit memoranda actually issued to the customers). In no event shall the total credits taken by Licensee for returns exceed 10% of the total gross sales for any Royalty Period. No other costs incurred in the manufacturing, selling, advertising, and distribution of the Licensed Products shall be deducted nor shall any deduction be allowed for any uncollectible accounts or allowances.

    G.   Sale of a Product. A Royalty obligation shall accrue upon the sale of the Licensed Products regardless of the time of collection by Licensee. For purposes of this Agreement, a Licensed Product shall be considered "sold" upon the date when such Licensed Product is billed, invoiced, shipped, or paid for, whichever event occurs first.

    H.   Invoices. Upon the request of Licensor, Licensee shall submit to Licensor copies of invoices, credit memoranda, price lists, line sheets and customer lists related to the sale of Licensed Products. All payment terms discounts and trade discounts must appear on the face of each invoice; each such discount must be itemized as a percentage reduction in Licensee's published wholesale list price.

    I.   Off-Sale Pricing. If Licensee sells any Licensed Products to any party at a price less than the regular price charged to other parties, the Royalty payable Licensor shall be computed on the basis of the regular price charged to other parties. In the event that Licensee combines or bundles any Licensed Product with non-licensed goods or services, the Royalty due Licensor will be based on the proportional value of the cost of goods of the Licensed Products as a percentage of the cost of goods of the bundled product including the Licensed Products.

    J.   No Bar. The receipt or acceptance by Licensor of any Royalty Statement, or the receipt or acceptance of any royalty payment made, shall not prevent Licensor from subsequently challenging the validity or accuracy of such statement or payment.

    K.   Acceleration. Upon expiration or termination of this Agreement, all Royalty obligations, including any unpaid portions of the Guaranteed Minimum Royalty, shall be accelerated and shall immediately become due and payable.

L. <u>Survival of Termination.</u> Licensee obligations for the payment of a Royalty and the Guaranteed Minimum Royalty shall survive expiration or termination of this Agreement and will continue for so long as Licensee continues to manufacture, sell or otherwise market the Licensed Products.

M. <u>U.S. Currency.</u> All payments due hereunder shall be made in United States currency drawn on a United States bank, unless otherwise specified between the parties.

N. <u>Interest.</u> Late payments shall incur interest at the rate of ONE PERCENT (1%) per month from the date such payments were originally due.

3. Time of the Essence.

Time is of the essence with respect to timely delivery of Royalty Statements and payments as herein provided and Licensee's failure to comply shall constitute a material breach of the Agreement. If any such breach is not cured within five (5) days of receiving written notice of such breach by Licensor, or if Licensee shall receive written notice of such breach more than twice times in any twelve (12) month period, such shall be grounds for automatic termination without a further opportunity to cure.

4. Audit.

A. <u>Right to Audit.</u> Both during and after termination or expiration of this Agreement, Licensor shall have the right, upon at least five (5) days written notice and no more than once per calendar year, to inspect the books and records of both Licensee and any of Licensee's related or affiliated entities, e.g., parents, subsidiaries, etc., and all other documents and material in the possession of or under the control of Licensee with respect to the subject matter of this Agreement at the place or places where such records are normally retained by Licensee. Licensee shall provide access to such records in electronic format, if possible, and shall fully cooperate with the Licensor or its representative in connection with such audit and Licensor and/or its representative shall have free and full access thereto for such purposes and shall be permitted to make copies thereof and extracts therefrom.

B. <u>Discrepancies.</u> In the event that such inspection reveals a discrepancy in the amount of Royalty owed Licensor from what was actually paid, Licensee shall pay such discrepancy, plus interest, calculated at the rate of ONE PERCENT (1%) per month. In the event that such discrepancy is in excess of the lesser of TEN THOUSAND UNITED STATES DOLLARS ($10,000.00) or THREE PERCENT (3%) of the monies owed Licensor, Licensee shall also reimburse Licensor for the cost of such inspection including any attorney's fees incurred in connection therewith. If it is determined that Royalty payments due are in excess of TWENTY PERCENT (20%) of the Royalties paid for the period covered by such audit, then, in addition to any and all other rights, legal and/or equitable, of Licensor, Licensor shall have the right to immediately terminate the Term upon notice to Licensee.

C. <u>Record Retention.</u> This audit right shall survive termination or expiration of the Agreement. All books and records relative to Licensee obligations hereunder shall be maintained and kept accessible and available to Licensor for inspection for at least three (3) years after expiration or termination of this Agreement.

D. <u>Periodic Financial Statements.</u> Within ninety (90) calendar days after the end of each of its fiscal years Licensee shall provide Licensor (all in English) with: (1) an annual audited financial statement of Licensee (audited by an accounting firm satisfactory to Licensor); (2) an annual composite statement, certified by its chief financial officer, showing the aggregate gross sales, trade discounts, returns, allowances, payment term discounts and closeout discounts and any other deduction taken to arrive at the Net Sales price of all Licensed Products sold by Licensee; and (3) an annual inventory reconciliation, certified by a certified public accountant, confirming actual reconciliation of the inventory to Licensee's general ledger and including computer reports summarizing inventory by SKU.

5. Marketing.

A. Commercially Reasonable Efforts. At all times during the Term, Licensee shall use commercially reasonable efforts to generate the maximum possible level of sales of the Licensed Products within the Channels of Distribution in the Territory including, without limitation, the design and development of unique retail displays to include "exclusive" styles, designs, powerful point of purchase visual display and minimum square footage requirements at each of its locations that desires to sell the Licensed Products. Licensee acknowledges that Licensor is entering into this Agreement not only in consideration of the payments to be made by Licensee, but also in consideration of the promotional value to Licensor of the widespread marketing, distribution, advertising, promotion, offer for sale and sale of the Licensed Products. Accordingly, Licensee shall use commercially reasonable efforts to seek to procure the greatest volume of sales of the Licensed Products consistent with high quality and shall diligently and continuously make and maintain timely and adequate arrangements for their manufacture, marketing, distribution, advertising, promotion, offering for sale and sale.

B. Sufficient Inventory. Licensee shall use commercially reasonable efforts to maintain sufficient on-hand inventory to support market demand for the Licensed Products.

C. Marketing Plan. No later than September 1st of each calendar year during the Term, Licensee shall provide to Licensor Licensee's proposed marketing plan and budget ("Marketing Plan") for the promotion and distribution of the Licensed Products for the ensuing calendar year.

D. Marketing Budget. Licensee shall establish a marketing budget, and shall expend an amount, for advertising and related sales promotion activities, for each year during the Term, equal to a percentage of all Net Sales in the amount recited in Schedule A attached hereto. Licensee shall provide Licensor within sixty (60) days after the end of each calendar year with an accounting signed and certified by an officer of Licensee, reflecting the amounts expended by Licensee on advertising the Licensed Products.

E. Manner of Sale. Licensee shall sell and distribute the Licensed Products in the Territory and Channels of Distribution outright and not on approval, consignment, guaranteed sale or return basis, or as a premium, promotional tie-in, or give-away.

F. Licensor's Assistance in Marketing Efforts. Licensor shall provide reasonable assistance to Licensee in marketing the Licensed Products, at Licensee's request, but shall not be required to expend material amounts of time or money in doing so.

6. Approval of Products and Promotional Materials.

A. Quality of the Licensed Products. The licenses granted hereunder are conditioned upon Licensee's full and complete compliance with the marking provisions of the patent, trademark and copyright laws of the United States. The Licensed Products, as well as all promotional, packaging and advertising material relative thereto, shall include all appropriate legal notices as reasonably required by Licensor.

245

B. <u>Approval of Preliminary Material.</u> Licensee agrees to submit to Licensor, for final approval, sketches, prototypes and production samples of all Licensed Products and any and all advertising, promotional and packaging material related to said Licensed Products. Licensor shall provide Licensee with written approval or disapproval within ten (10) business days after receipt of such sketches, prototypes and production samples. Licensor hereby agrees that any item submitted will not be unreasonably disapproved and, if it is disapproved, that Licensor will give the Licensee specific grounds therefore. Once such samples have been approved by Licensor, the Licensed Product shall not materially depart there from without Licensor's prior express written consent, which shall not be unreasonably withheld. Should Licensor fail to provide such written approval or disapproval within ten (10) business days, such failure shall be deemed to be disapproval of such submission. Licensee shall thereafter have the right to demand, in writing, such written approval or disapproval from Licensor. Should Licensor fail to provide such written approval or disapproval within three (3) business days thereafter, such failure shall be deemed to be approval.

C. <u>Compliance with Standards.</u> The Licensed Products manufactured by or for Licensee, shall comply in all respects with Licensor's standards, specifications, directions and processes and shall be in substantial conformity with the production sample of the Licensed Product approved by Licensor. Once Licensor has approved the Production Sample(s), Licensee will manufacture Licensed Products only in accordance with such approved Production Sample(s) and will not make any changes without Licensor's prior written approval.

D. <u>Pre-Production Samples.</u> Prior to the commencement of manufacture and sale of the Licensed Products, Licensee shall submit to Licensor, at no cost to Licensor two (2) sets of samples of all Licensed Products which Licensee intends to manufacture and sell and one (1) complete set of all promotional and advertising material associated therewith.

E. <u>Annual Samples.</u> At least once during each calendar year, Licensor may require that Licensee shall submit to Licensor an additional two (2) sets of samples.

F. <u>Compliance with Laws.</u> Licensed Products will, at all times, be manufactured, sold and distributed with labels, tags, packaging, and sales promotion materials that are appropriate for merchandise of such quality; and will at all times be manufactured, sold and distributed in accordance with all applicable federal, state and local laws and regulations, and shall in no manner reflect adversely upon the good name of Licensor.

G. <u>Failure of Quality.</u> If the quality of a particular Licensed Product falls below such a production-run quality, as previously approved by Licensor, Licensee shall use commercially reasonable efforts to restore such quality. In the event that Licensee has not taken appropriate steps to restore such quality within thirty (30) days after notification by Licensor, Licensor shall have the right to delete such Licensed Product from the Agreement. Such deletion shall have no effect on the remaining terms of the Agreement and the Agreement shall remain in full force and effect.

H. <u>Seconds</u>. If, in the reasonable discretion of Licensor and Licensee, any Licensed Product(s) is not in conformity with Licensor's approval as set forth herein, but is suitable for sale as a non-first quality product ("Seconds"), then Licensee may sell such Seconds in a way which shall not reduce the value of the Trademarks or Property or detract from Licensor's reputation in any major respect, provided, however, that (1) Licensee's sales of Seconds shall not exceed five (5%) of its total Net Sales for any Royalty Period; (2) Licensor shall have a right to approve such Licensed Products sold as

246

Seconds, such approval not to be unreasonably withheld; and (3) a full Royalty shall be due on all such sales of Seconds.

I. Inspections. The Licensee agrees to permit Licensor or its representative to inspect the facilities where the Licensed Products are being manufactured and packaged.

J. Quality of Promotional Materials. The quality, contents and workmanship of all promotional and advertising material containing the Property (the "Ancillary Materials") shall at all times be of a high standard, and of such style, appearance and quality as to be adequate and suited to their exploitation to the best advantage and to the protection and enhancement of the Licensor and the Trademarks and the goodwill pertaining thereto; no less than the best quality of similar ancillary material used by Licensee.

K. Approval of Ancillary Materials. Licensee shall, in sufficient time for review and consideration, submit to Licensor, for Licensor's approval, all Ancillary Materials relating to the Licensed Products. Licensor shall provide Licensee with written approval or disapproval within ten (10) business days after receipt of such Ancillary Materials. Any submission not approved in writing by Licensor Group within such ten (10) day period shall be deemed disapproved. Licensee shall thereafter have the right to demand, in writing, such written approval or disapproval from Licensor. Should Licensor fail to provide such written approval or disapproval within three (3) business days thereafter, such failure shall be deemed to be approval. Licensee shall not use or disseminate any Ancillary Materials without the prior express written approval of Licensor. Licensor hereby agrees that any item submitted will not be unreasonably disapproved and, if it is disapproved, that Licensor will give the Licensee specific grounds therefore.

L. Advertising Material and Placement. All media advertising and media advertising placements with respect to the Licensed Products shall be mutually acceptable to both parties. Licensor hereby agrees that any item submitted will not be unreasonably disapproved and, if it is disapproved, that Licensor will give the Licensee specific grounds therefore.   .

M. Intellectual Property Notices. Licensee agrees to affix to the Licensed Products, and to any Ancillary Materials which depict the Property and/or Trademarks, such legal notices as required and approved by Licensor in writing. In addition, wherever appropriate and required by Licensor, Licensee shall affix the appropriate symbol ® or ™ as well as any such material, such other reasonable notice or notices of trademark and copyright as requested by Licensor. The Licensed Products shall also contain the following copyright notice, which Licensor can change from time to time by notice to Licensee:

> © 20__ (or year introduced)
> All Rights Reserved.

Such notices shall appear on the Licensed Products, or on any label or tag affixed to the Licensed Products, as Licensor may approve. The parties recognize and agree, however, that there will be instances where it will not be possible to contain a full copyright or trademark notice. In such event, they will agree upon an appropriate "short form" or abbreviated version of such notice.

N. Approval of Third Party Manufacturers. In the event that the Licensee elects to have the Licensed Products manufactured by a party other than itself, Licensee shall promptly identify the party or parties that will be manufacturing the Licensed Products and obtain the written approval of the Licensor prior to having such party commence the manufacture of such Licensed Products who shall enter into a written Manufacturing Agreement with the Licensee in a form acceptable to the Licensor.

O. <u>Compliance with Labor Compliance Rules.</u> The manufacture, packaging and storage of the Licensed Products shall be carried out only at premises approved by the Licensor or its nominee in writing from time to time. The Licensor or its nominee shall be entitled at any time on reasonable notice to the Licensee to enter, during regular business hours, any premises used by the Licensee or its manufacturers for the manufacture, packaging or storage of the Licensed Products, to inspect such premises, all plant, workforce and machinery used for manufacture, packaging or storage of Licensed Products and all other aspects of the manufacture, packaging and storage of Licensed Products. The Licensee shall, and shall insure that its manufacturers shall make any changes or improvements to its premises, plant, workforce, machinery and other aspects of the manufacture, packaging and storage of Licensed Products as the Licensor or its nominee may reasonably request. Licensee shall comply in all material respects with the LIMA Code of Business Practices attached hereto as Exhibit A.

7.   Intellectual Property Rights.

A. <u>No Challenges by Licensee.</u> The parties agree that Licensee will not take any action or fail to take any action inconsistent with the ownership, title or any rights of Licensor in and to the Property or Trademarks or attack the validity of this Agreement or the Property or Trademarks.

B. <u>Trademark Registrations.</u> The parties acknowledge and agree that Licensor has the right, but not the obligation, to apply for any and all registrations in the United States and elsewhere for the Trademarks under its own name. Licensee agrees to provide reasonable assistance to Licensor with respect to tiling such applications and obtaining and maintaining the resulting registrations for the Trademarks.

C. <u>Trademarks Unique and Original.</u> Licensee acknowledges Licensor's rights in the Property and Trademarks and, further, acknowledges that the Property and Trademarks are unique and original to Licensor and that Licensor is the owner thereof. Licensor, however, makes no representation or warranty with respect to the validity of any trademark or copyright which may issue or be granted therefrom.

D.   <u>Secondary Meaning.</u> Licensee acknowledges that the Property and Trademarks have acquired secondary meaning.

E. <u>Trademarks Inure to Benefit of Licensor.</u> Licensee agrees that its use of the Property and Trademarks inures to the benefit of Licensor and that the Licensee shall not acquire any rights in the Trademarks.

F.   <u>Works Created by Licensee.</u> All intellectual property rights, whether copyrights, trademark rights, or patent rights, in the Licensed Products and/or relating to the Property or Trademarks or used in the packaging, advertising or promotion thereof, shall be deemed the property of Licensor. In the case of copyrightable materials, such materials shall be considered to be "works made for hire" under the Copyright Act. In the case of trademarks (including trade dress) all use of such trademarks and trade dress relating to the Licensed Products and/or Trademarks, whether now in existence or developed by Licensee during the Term of this Agreement, shall be deemed owned by Licensor and all use thereof by the Licensee, including all good will relating thereto, shall inure to the exclusive benefit of Licensor. In the case of patentable inventions and concepts as well as copyrightable materials that do not constitute "works made for hire," Licensee hereby assigns to Licensor all of Licensee rights in and to such patentable inventions and concepts and such copyrightable materials, without further compensation from Licensor. Under no circumstances shall Licensee continue to use any intellectual property rights approved for use with the Licensed Products after termination or expiration of this Agreement or any trademarks, trade dress, designs, artwork or graphics that could reasonably be considered to be associated with the Licensed Products or the Trademarks. In the event this Agreement is terminated or expires, Licensee shall promptly execute such documents as may be required to assign any and all rights in and to such Property, including all copyrights in any artwork relating thereto to Licensor. Artwork shall include all works which Licensee proposes to and/or does use in connection with the manufacture, sale promotion, advertising, marketing and/or distribution of a Licensed Product, and shall include, but not be limited to, pictorial, graphic, sculptural and literary works as well as software and textual material. Artwork further includes works embodied in all forms and media, including sketches or such other definition of the use of Property or Trademarks as Licensor requires for evaluation and approval. No Licensed Products shall be approved by Licensor unless its artwork has been approved.

8. Representations and Warranties.

A. <u>Licensor Representations and Warranties.</u> Licensor represents and warrants that (1) no third party owns any right, title or interest in the Property and Trademarks; (2) the Property and Trademarks do not interfere with, infringe upon, misappropriate or otherwise conflict with any intellectual property rights of any third party when used on or in association with the Licensed Products; (3) it has full right, power and authority to convey the right, title and interest described herein; and (4) it has not taken, and will not take, any action in conflict with this Agreement.

B. <u>Licensee Representations and Warranties.</u> Licensee represents and warrants that: (1) it shall comply with all applicable laws and regulations in connection with the manufacture, use, sale, distribution, advertising and promotion of the Licensed Products; (2) it will use its best efforts to promote, market, use, sell, and distribute the Licensed Products and will maintain sufficient inventories of Licensed Products to reasonably fulfill orders; (3) it shall be solely responsible for the manufacture, production, sale, and distribution of the Licensed Products and will bear all related costs associated therewith; (4) it will conduct itself in a business-like and professional manner so as not to bring disrepute to the Property and Trademarks; and (5) it will manufacture or have manufactured all Licensed Products in compliance with the LIMA Code of Business Standards, a copy of which is attached hereto as Exhibit A.

C. <u>Introduction of Licensed Products.</u> It is the intention of the parties that Licensee shall introduce the Licensed Products in the Licensed Territory on or before the Product Introduction Date recited in Schedule A and commence shipment of Licensed Products in the Territory on or before the Initial Shipment Date recited in Schedule A. Failure to meet either the Product Introduction Date or the Initial Shipment Date shall constitute grounds for immediate termination of this Agreement by Licensor.

9. Termination

The following termination rights are in addition to the termination rights provided elsewhere in this Agreement:

A. <u>Immediate Right of Termination.</u> Licensor shall have the right to immediately terminate this Agreement by giving written notice to Licensee in the event that Licensee does any of the following:

(1) fails to meet the Product Introduction Date or the Initial Shipment Date as specified in Schedule A; or

(2) after having commenced sale of the Licensed Products, fails to continuously sell Licensed Products for three (3) consecutive Royalty Periods; or

(3) fails to obtain or maintain product liability insurance in the amount and of the type provided for herein; or

(4) files a petition in bankruptcy or is adjudicated a bankrupt or insolvent, or makes an assignment for the benefit of creditors, or an arrangement pursuant to any bankruptcy law, or if the Licensee discontinues its business or a receiver is appointed for the Licensee or for the Licensee business and such receiver is not discharged within thirty (30) days; or

(5) breaches any of the provisions of this Agreement relating to the unauthorized assertion of rights in the Trademarks; or

(6) after receipt of written notice from Licensor, fails to immediately discontinue the distribution or sale of the Licensed Products or the use of any Ancillary Materials that do not contain the requisite legal legends; or

(7) fails to make timely payment of Royalties when due two or more times during any twelve-month period;

(8) fails to meet the Minimum Sales requirement in any calendar year;

(9) fails to make the Minimum Advertising Expenditure in any calendar year;

(10) fails to comply with the Marketing Requirements as provided for in Schedule A attached there; or

(11) sells Licensed Products to an unapproved customer;

(12) undergoes a change of control of more than 50% of its outstanding shares, or merge, consolidate with or into any other corporation or other entity, or directly or indirectly sell or otherwise transfer, sell or dispose of all or a substantial portion of its business or assets;

(13) understates Royalties as provided in Paragraph 4B., makes any unreported sales or cash sales, or intentionally reports incorrect or false manufacturing, sales or financial information;

(14) itself, or any of its manufacturing subcontractors or sub-subcontractors, manufactures, offers for sale, distributes, uses or sells any Licensed Product or Ancillary Material incorporating the Property, without the express permission of Licensor as herein provided, or manufacture or sell any disapproved products; or

(15) offers to sell, sells or ships the Licensed Products to customers or distributors outside the Channels of Distribution or the Territory or to non-Approved Customers, or to customers or distributors whom Licensee knows or should know will resell or ship the Licensed Products outside the Channels of Distribution or the Territory;

Notwithstanding the foregoing, if Licensor elects to provide Licensee with notice and an opportunity to cure any breach described in this Sections (in Licensor's sole discretion), such action will not constitute a waiver of or bar to Licensor's right to strictly enforce immediate termination in the future, without any right to cure, in the event of the same or any other breach.

      B. Immediate Right to Terminate a Portion. Licensor shall have the right to immediately terminate the portion(s) of the Agreement relating to any Trademark and/or Licensed Product(s) in the Territory if Licensee, for any reason, fails to meet the Product Introduction Dates or the Initial Shipment Dates specified in Schedule A or, after the commencement of manufacture and sale of a particular Licensed Product, ceases to sell commercial quantities of such Licensed Product for three (3) consecutive Royalty Periods.

      C. Right to Terminate on Notice. This Agreement may be terminated by either party upon thirty (30) days written notice to the other party in the event of a breach of a material provision of this Agreement unrelated to Licensee payment obligations by the other party, provided that, during the thirty (30) day period, the breaching party fails to cure such breach. With respect to Licensee payment obligations hereunder, Licensor may terminate this Agreement upon five (5) days written notice to Licensee in the event of a breach by Licensee of its payment obligations hereunder, provided that during this five (5) day period, Licensee fails to cure such breach.

10. Post Termination Rights

      A. Inventory upon Termination. Not less than thirty (30) days prior to the expiration of this Agreement or immediately upon termination thereof, Licensee shall provide Licensor with a complete schedule of all inventory of Licensed Products then on-hand (the "Inventory").

      B. Sell-Off Period. Upon expiration or termination of this Agreement except for reason of a breach of Licensee duty to comply with the quality control or legal notice marking requirements, Licensee shall be entitled, for an additional period of three (3) months and on a nonexclusive basis, to continue to sell such Inventory. Such sales shall be made subject to all of the provisions of this Agreement and to an accounting for and the payment of a Royalty thereon. Such accounting and payment shall be due and paid within thirty (30) days after the close of the said three (3) month period. Licensee shall not be permitted to sell Licensed Products during this period at a price point discounted more than 50% of its traditional wholesale selling price.

      C. Discontinuance of Use of the Property. Upon the expiration or termination of this Agreement, all of the rights of Licensee under this Agreement, except for Licensee rights under paragraph 10B., shall forthwith terminate and immediately revert to Licensor and Licensee shall immediately discontinue all use of the Trademarks, at no cost whatsoever to Licensor.

      D. Return of Materials. Upon termination of this Agreement for any reasons whatsoever, Licensee agrees to immediately return to Licensor all material relating to the Trademarks including, but not limited to, all artwork, color separations, prototypes and the like, as well as any market studies or other tests or studies conducted by Licensee with respect to the Trademarks, at no cost whatsoever to Licensor.

      E. Continued Sale of Similar Products. The parties understand and agree that the Licensed Products will have acquired a particular look and feel and association with the Trademarks and Property. Accordingly, Licensee recognizes and agrees that the continued use of any similar trademark, trade name, trade dress or other industrial or intellectual property has the potential to cause significant consumer confusion after termination or expiration of this Agreement should Licensee continue to use or adopt the use of any trademark, trade name, trade dress or other industrial or intellectual property that was not a "safe distance" from the Property, Trademark or any trade name or trade dress associated therewith and Licensee hereby agrees to maintain such "safe distance" upon the termination or expiration of this Agreement.

11.   Infringements

A.   Initiation of Infringement Actions.   Licensor shall have the right, in its discretion, to institute and prosecute lawsuits against third persons for infringement of the rights licensed in this Agreement.

B.   Cost of Litigation.   Any lawsuit shall be prosecuted solely at the cost and expense of Licensor and all sums recovered in any such lawsuits, whether by judgment, settlement or otherwise, shall be retained by Licensor.

C.   Cooperation of Parties.   Upon request of Licensor, Licensee shall execute all papers, testify on all matters, and otherwise cooperate in every way necessary and desirable for the prosecution of any such lawsuit.   Licensor shall reimburse Licensee for the expenses incurred as a result of such cooperation.

12.   Indemnification.

A.   Licensee Indemnity.   Licensee agrees to defend, indemnify and hold Licensor, and its officers, directors, employees, agents, and advisors, harmless from and against any and all costs, loses, obligations, suits, judgments, damages and costs (including reasonable attorneys' fees and costs) incurred through claims of third parties against Licensor based on the manufacture, sale, marketing, distribution, advertising or promotion of the Licensed Products including, but not limited to, actions founded on product liability or infringement of any third party intellectual property rights.   Licensor shall have the right to select counsel in connection with such actions.   No action may be settled or compromised without Licensor's prior express written approval.

B.   Licensor Indemnity.   Licensor agrees to defend, indemnify and hold Licensee, and its officers, directors, employees, agents and advisors, harmless from and against any and all claims, losses, obligations, suits, judgments, damages and costs (including reasonable attorneys' fees and costs) incurred through claims of third parties against Licensor based on any claim by any third party challenging Licensor's rights in the Property or its ability to enter into this Agreement including any claim for infringement of any third party rights based solely on Licensee's licensed use of the Property on the Licensed Products.

13.   Insurance.

A.   Product Liability Insurance.   Licensee shall, throughout the Term of the Agreement, obtain and maintain at its own cost and expense from a qualified insurance company licensed to do business in [State] with a Best rating of A- or better, standard Product Liability Insurance naming Licensor as an additional named insured.   Such policy shall provide protection against any and all claims, demands and causes of action arising out of any defects or failure to perform, alleged or otherwise, of the Licensed Products or any material used in connection therewith or any use thereof.   The amount of coverage shall be as specified in Schedule A attached hereto.   The policy shall provide for ten (10) days notice to Licensor from the insurer by Registered or Certified Mail, return receipt requested, in the event of any modification, cancellation or termination thereof.   Licensee agrees to furnish Licensor a certificate of insurance within thirty (30) days after execution of this Agreement and, in no event shall Licensee manufacture, distribute or sell the Licensed Products prior to receipt by Licensor of such certificate of insurance.

252

B. Advertiser's Insurance. Licensee shall, throughout the Term of the Agreement, obtain and maintain at its own cost and expense from a qualified insurance company licensed to do business in [State] with a Best rating of A- or better, standard Advertiser's Insurance naming Licensor as an additional named insured. Such policy shall provide protection against any and all claims, demands and causes of action arising out of any defects or failure to perform, alleged or otherwise, of the Licensed Products or any material used in connection therewith or any use thereof. The amount of coverage shall be as specified in Schedule A attached hereto. The policy shall provide for ten (10) days notice to Licensor from the insurer by Registered or Certified Mail, return receipt requested, in the event of any modification, cancellation or termination thereof. Licensee agrees to furnish Licensor a certificate of insurance within thirty (30) days after execution of this Agreement and, in no event shall Licensee manufacture, distribute or sell the Licensed Products prior to receipt by Licensor of such certificate of insurance.

14. Relationship of the Parties.

This Agreement creates no agency relationship between the parties hereto, and nothing herein contained shall be construed to place the parties in the relationship of partners or joint venturers, and neither party shall have any power to obligate or bind the other party in any manner whatsoever.

15. Severability.

If any provision of this Agreement is held by a court or arbitrator of competent jurisdiction not enforceable to its full extent, then such provision shall be enforced to the maximum extent permitted by law, and the parties hereto consent and agree that such scope may be modified by such court or arbitrator accordingly and that the whole of such provision of this Agreement shall not thereby fail, but that the scope of such provision shall be curtailed only to the extent necessary to conform to the law.

16. Assignment and Transfer.

This Agreement shall be binding upon and shall inure to the benefit of the parties hereto and their respective successors and permitted assigns. Licensee may not assign its rights or obligations hereunder without the prior written consent of Licensor; provided, however, that Licensee may assign its rights under this Agreement without the prior written consent of Licensor to any entity controlled by or controlling Licensee. No assignment shall entitle any assignee to any greater rights hereunder than those to which the assignor was entitled. For purposes of this provision, any action by Licensee that involves a change of control of Licensee or transfers of more than 50% the outstanding stock of Licensee shall be deemed an assignment and may only be made with the prior express written approval of Licensor.

17. Waivers.

The failure or delay of either party at any time to exercise any right under any provision of this Agreement shall not limit or operate as a waiver thereof.

18. No Third Party Beneficiaries.

Nothing in this Agreement is intended, or shall be construed, to give arty entity or individual other than the parties hereto any legal or equitable right, remedy or claim under or in respect of this Agreement or any of the provisions contained herein.

19. Equitable Relief.

Without limiting the right of Licensor to pursue all other legal and equitable rights available to it for violation of or failure of Licensee to comply with the terms of this Agreement, it is agreed that other remedies cannot fully compensate Licensor for such a violation or failure and that Licensor shall be entitled to injunctive or other equitable relief to prevent violation or continuing violation or to compel performance by Licensee. Licensee acknowledges that the restrictions in this Agreement are reasonable and that the consideration therefore is sufficient to fully and adequately compensate it therefore. Licensee further acknowledges that the Trademarks are special and unique property and cannot be replaced or otherwise substituted for by other property or by money damages. It is the intent and understanding of each party hereto that if, in any action before any court or agency legally empowered to enforce this Agreement, any term, restriction, covenant or promise in this Agreement is found to be unreasonable and for that reason unenforceable, then such term, restriction, covenant or promise shall be deemed modified to the extent necessary to make it enforceable by such court or agency.

20. Notices.

Any notice, consent or other communication required or permitted hereunder shall be in writing. It shall be deemed given when: (1) delivered personally; (2) sent by confirmed facsimile transmission; (3) sent by commercial overnight courier with written verification of receipt; or (4) sent by registered or certified mail, return receipt requested, postage prepaid, and the receipt is returned to the sender. Names, addresses and facsimile numbers for notices (unless and until written notice of other names, addresses and facsimile numbers are provided by either or both parties) are as follows:

If to Licensor: *With a copy to:*

If to Licensee: *With copy to:*

21. Confidentiality

A. Disclosure of Confidential Information. There may be occasions during the Term of this Agreement that either party discloses to the other certain confidential or proprietary information including, any information transmitted between the parties that relates to the transferring party's business, such as drawings, specifications, production schedules, test data, business practices and marketing strategies, prospective product concepts or ideas, or the like, or the terms of this Agreement ("Confidential Information"). The following will, however, not be considered Confidential Information:

(1) Information that is explicitly approved for release by the transmitting party,

(2) Information that is disclosed in a product marketed by the transmitting party,

(3) Information that was already known by the receiving party prior to receiving the information from transmitting party or becomes known by the receiving party independently through no wrongful act on the part of the receiving party, or

(4) Information that is known or available to the general public.

B. Use by Receiving Party. The receiving party agrees to maintain such Confidential Information received from the transmitting party in confidence, to use it only in a manner consistent with the purpose for which it was transmitted and to not disclose it to persons not having a need to know it. In the event that the receiving party needs to transmit such information to a third party, the receiving party shall safeguard the confidentiality of the information.

254

C.   Property of Transmitting Party.   All materials transmitted between the parties and containing Confidential Information shall remain the property of the transmitting party and shall be returned upon request unless previously destroyed.

D.   No License Grant.   The transmission of the material containing such Confidential Information shall not be construed to grant the receiving party a license of any type under any patents, know-how, copyrights or trademarks owned or controlled by the transmitting party.

E.   Survival of Termination.   The obligations of the parties under this section regarding confidential information shall survive termination, expiration or non-renewal of this Agreement.

22.   On-Going Cooperation.

Each party to this Agreement agrees to execute and deliver all documents and to perform all further acts and to take any and all further steps that may be requested by the other party and are reasonably necessary to carry out the provisions of this Agreement and the transactions contemplated hereby.

23.   Independent Contractor.

Licensee shall be deemed an independent contractor and nothing contained herein shall constitute this arrangement to be employment, a joint venture, or a partnership. Licensee shall be solely responsible for and shall hold Licensor harmless for any and all claims for taxes, fees, or costs arising from the manufacture, marketing, distribution or sale of Licensed Product, including but not limited to withholding, income tax, FICA, and workmen's compensation.

24.   Governing Law & Disputes.

This Agreement will be governed by, and construed and enforced in accordance with the laws of [State] without regard to conflicts of law principles. All disputes under this Agreement shall be resolved by the courts of the state of [State], including the United States District Court for the District of [State]. The parties all consent to the jurisdiction of such courts, agree to accept service of process by mail, and hereby waive any jurisdictional or venue defenses otherwise available to it.

25.   Execution in Counterparts.

This Agreement may be executed in two or more counterparts, each of which will be deemed an original but all of which together will constitute one and the same instrument. The parties may execute this Agreement and exchange counterparts of the signature pages by means of facsimile transmission, and the receipt of such executed counterparts by facsimile transmission will be binding on the parties. Following such exchange, the parties will promptly exchange original versions of such signature pages.

26.   Force Majeure.

If the performance of any part of this Agreement by either party is prevented, hindered, delayed or otherwise made impracticable because of an Act of God, riot or civil commotion, act of public enemy, terrorism, order or act of any government or governmental instrumentality (whether federal, state, local or foreign) or similar cause beyond the control of either party, that party shall be excused from such performance to the extent that performance is prevented, hindered or delayed by such causes.

255

27. Integration.

This Agreement constitutes the entire understanding of the parties, and revokes and supersedes all prior agreements between the parties, including any option agreements which may have been entered into between the parties, and is intended as a final expression of their Agreement. It shall not be modified or amended except in writing signed by the parties hereto and specifically referring to this Agreement. This Agreement shall take precedence over any other documents which may be in conflict with said Agreement.

IN WITNESS WHEREOF, the parties hereto have executed this Agreement as of the Effective Date.

LICENSOR   **LICENSEE**

By:_____   By:_____

Title:_____   Title_____

Date:_____   Date:_____

SCHEDULE A
TO LICENSE AGREEMENT

1.   PROPERTY:

2.   TRADEMARKS:

3.   LICENSED TERRITORY:

4.   LICENSED PRODUCTS:

5.   CHANNELS OF DISTRIBUTION:

6.   APPROVED CUSTOMERS:

7.   ROYALTY RATE:

   Domestic Sales Rate:

   FOB Sales Rate:

   Direct Sales Rate:

8.   GUARANTEED MINIMUM ROYALTY:

9.   ADVANCE:

10.   MARKETING FEE:

11.   PRODUCT INTRODUCTION DATE:

12.   INITIAL SHIPMENT DATE:

13   MINIMUM ANNUAL SALES:

14.   MINIMUM ADVERTISING EXPENDITURE:

15.   TERM:

16.   INSURANCE REQUIREMENTS:

17.   MARKETING REQUIREMENTS:

EXHIBIT A

TO LICENSE AGREEMENT

LIMA CODE OF BUSINESS PRACTICES

The International Licensing Industry Merchandisers' Association, Inc. ("LIMA") is committed on behalf of its member companies to the operation of factories manufacturing licensed products in a lawful, safe, and healthful manner. It upholds the principles that no underage, forced, or prison labor* should be employed; that no one is denied a job because of gender, ethnic origin, religion, affiliation or association, and that factories comply with laws protecting the environment. Supply agreements with firms manufacturing licensed products on behalf of LIMA members should also provide for adherence to these principles.

The role of LIMA is to inform, educate, and survey its members so that individual member companies can adhere to its Code of Business Practices. As an Association, it also acts to encourage local and national governments to enforce wage and hour laws and factory health and safety laws. Specific operating conditions that member companies are encouraged to meet and obtain contractor agreement in advance are as follows:

1) LABOR

a) That wages and overtime pay practices comply with the standards set by law, including the payment of compensation for overtime hours at such premium rates as is legally required in that country, but not less than at a rate equal to their regularly hourly compensation rate.

b) That working hours must exceed prevailing local work hours in the country where the work is to be performed, except with respect to appropriately compensated overtime; must not require in excess of a 60 hour week on a regularly scheduled basis; and must permit at least one day off in every 7 day period.

c) That no one under the legal minimum age is employed in any stage of manufacturing; that a minimum age of 14 applies in all circumstances, but notwithstanding the foregoing, that C138 Minimum Age Convention (1973) and C182 Worst Forms of Child Labor Convention (1999) of the International Labor Organization apply.

d) That no forced or prison labor is employed*, that workers are free to leave once their shift ends, and that guards are posted only for normal security reasons.

e) That all workers are entitled to sick and maternity benefits as provided by law.

f) That all workers are entitled to freely exercise their rights of employee representation as provided by local law.

2) THE WORKPLACE

a) That factories provide a safe and healthy working environment for their employees and comply with or exceed all applicable local laws concerning sanitation and risk protection.

b) That the factory is properly lighted and ventilated and that aisles and exits are accessible at all times.

c) That there is adequate medical assistance available in emergencies and that designated employees are trained in first aid procedures.

d) That there are adequate and well-identified emergency exits, and that all employees are trained in emergency evacuation.

e) That protective safety equipment is available and employees are trained in its use.

f) That safeguards on machinery meet or exceed local laws.

g) That there are adequate toilet facilities which meet local hygiene requirements and that they are properly maintained.

h) That there are facilities or appropriate provisions for meals and other breaks.

258

Appendix-5/License Agreement

i) If a factory provides housing for its employees, it will ensure that dormitory rooms and sanitary facilities meet basic needs, are adequately ventilated and meet fire safety and other local laws.

j) That all employees are treated with dignity and respect and that no employee shall be subjected to any physical, sexual, psychological or verbal harassment or abuse.

k) That no mental or physical disciplinary practices are employed.

l) That factories shall recognize and respect the rights of employees to associate, organize and bargain collectively in a lawful and peaceful manner, without penalty or interference.

m) That factories shall not discriminate on the basis of race, religion, age, nationality, social or ethnic origin, sexual orientation, gender, political opinion or disability.

3. COMPLIANCE

a) The purpose of this Code is to establish a standard of performance, to educate, and to encourage a commitment to responsible manufacturing, not to punish.

b) To determine adherence, LIMA member companies will evaluate their own facilities as well as those of their contractors. They will examine all books and records and conduct on-site inspections of the facilities and request that their contractors follow the same practices with subcontractors.

c) An annual statement of compliance with this Code should be signed by an officer of each manufacturing company or contractor.

d) Contracts for the manufacture of licensed products should provide that a material failure to comply with the Code or to implement a corrective action plan on a timely basis is a breach of contract for which the contract may be canceled.

e) Because of the great diversity in the kinds of licensed products manufactured and the manufacturing methods used, as well as the wide range in factory sizes and numbers of employees, a rule of reason must be used to determine applicability of these provisions.

f) This Code should be posted or available for all employees in the local language.

---

* Many countries recognize that prison labor is essential to the rehabilitation process. This provision prohibits the exportation of prison-made goods to countries that prohibit or restrict the importation of such goods.

Appendix-6

MANUFACTURER'S REPRESENTATIVE AGREEMENT

THIS AGREEMENT is made this ____ day of _____, by and between _____ with offices at _____ (the "Representative") and _____ with offices at _____ (the "Manufacturer").

W I T N E S S E T H:

WHEREAS, Manufacturer is in the business of manufacturing and marketing certain products including, but not limited to, products bearing properties licensed by third party licensors;

WHEREAS, Representative is in the business of consulting with and obtaining and developing licenses for various manufacturers;

WHEREAS, Manufacturer would like to retain the services of Representative to seek out and obtain for Manufacturer new licenses for its products.

NOW, THEREFORE, in consideration of the promises and agreements set forth herein, the parties, each intending to be legally bound hereby, do promise and agree as follows:

1. APPOINTMENT OF REPRESENTATIVE

Manufacturer hereby appoints Representative to act as its exclusive representative during the Term of this Agreement to recommend new licensed properties from third party licensors (the "New Licensed Properties") to Manufacturer and/or its affiliated and related companies for incorporation on Manufacturer's products for sale in the Territory identified in Schedule A attached hereto (the "Licensed Products") as well as to provide general consulting services relative to licensing matters. It is understood and agreed that Representative shall serve as Manufacturer's exclusive representative in its dealing with all third party licensors except for those licensors listed in Schedule A (the "Excluded Licensors"). It is understood and agreed that Manufacturer shall refer all inquiries from or contacts with third party licensors (except for the Excluded Licensors) concerning licensing matters to Representative.

2. TERM OF AGREEMENT

This Agreement shall commence upon execution by both parties and shall extend for an Initial Term as defined in Exhibit A attached hereto. This Agreement may be automatically renewed for an unlimited number of additional Extended Terms as defined in Exhibit A unless one party provides written notice to the other party at least sixty (60) days prior to the expiration of the then in-effect Term of its intention not to renew the Agreement.

3. DUTIES AND OBLIGATIONS OF PARTIES

A. Representative shall use reasonable efforts during the Term of this Agreement to find and recommend New Licensed Properties to Manufacturer that are suitable for adoption and use by Manufacturer and/or its affiliated or related companies to incorporate

261

on or in association with its products. Any New Licensed Property acquired by Manufacturer or any affiliated or related entity during the Term of this Agreement from a licensor other than an Excluded Licensor shall be deemed a New Licensed Property for purposes of this Agreement and shall be added to Exhibit B attached hereto whether or not recommended by Representative. Moreover, in the event that Manufacturer should enter into any license agreement with a licensor within one (1) year after termination or expiration of this Agreement based on negotiations initiated by Representative during the Term of this Agreement, any licensed property covered by such license agreement shall also be deemed a New Licensed Property for purposes of this Agreement and shall be added to Exhibit B attached hereto. It is understood that Exhibit B shall be periodically updated during the Term of this Agreement.

B. In the event that Manufacturer is interested in procuring any New Licensed Property, Representative will assist Manufacturer in scheduling preliminary meetings with the respective licensor(s) of such New Licensed Property, attend subsequent meetings wherever possible if requested by Manufacturer, and assist Manufacturer wherever possible in obtaining such New Licensed Property.

C. It is understood that Representative has in the past and will continue to work with other manufacturers.

D. Manufacturer shall be solely responsible for all costs and expenses associated with the obtaining of New Licensed Properties from the applicable licensor(s), including any legal fees associated with the drafting and negotiation of any agreement with such licensor.

4.   COMPENSATION

A. In consideration for the services rendered by Representative, Manufacturer agrees to and shall pay Representative, during the Term of this Agreement, a non-refundable, non-creditable monthly retainer fee in the amount recited in Schedule A attached hereto (the "Retainer Fee").

B. In addition to the foregoing Retainer Fee, Manufacturer agrees to pay Representative a Commission on Manufacturer's Net Sales of its licensed products or services bearing the New Licensed Properties or by its affiliated or related companies in accordance with the schedule recited in Schedule A (the "Commission"). The definition of Net Sales with respect to each New Licensed Property shall be governed by such definition provided in the respective license agreement with the applicable licensor.

C. Representative's right to receive this Commission shall survive termination or expiration of this Agreement for any reason. Representative shall be entitled to continue to receive its full Commission based on those contracts or agreements entered into by Manufacturer with third party licensors during the Term of this Agreement or based on any contracts or agreements entered into by Manufacturer within one (1) year from the date of termination or expiration thereof resulting from presentations or negotiations made by Representative during the Term of this Agreement for which Representative would have received a Commission had the Agreement not been terminated or expired. Representative shall be entitled to such post termination Commission for so long as the Manufacturer continues to sell such licensed products or services under such agreements and any renewals, modifications or extensions thereof.

D. Manufacturer agrees to reimburse for all reasonable expenses incurred by Representative on behalf of Manufacturer, provided that any expenses in excess of $1000 must be approved in writing by Manufacturer prior to their being incurred.

5.   STATEMENTS AND PAYMENTS

A.   The Commission owed Representative shall be calculated on a quarterly calendar basis (the "Commission Period") and shall be payable no later than thirty (30) days after the termination of the preceding full calendar quarter.

B.   For each Commission Period, Manufacturer shall provide Representative with a written Commission Statement in a form acceptable to Representative. Such Commission Statement shall be certified as accurate by a duly authorized officer of Manufacturer and shall be broken down on a Property by Property basis. With respect to each of the New Licensed Properties, Manufacturer shall further provide Representative with copies of Manufacturer's royalty statements to the respective licensor. Such Commission Statements shall be furnished to Representative regardless of whether any Licensed Products were sold during the Commission Period or whether any actual Commission was owed.

C.   The receipt or acceptance by Representative of any Commission statement or payment shall not prevent Representative from subsequently challenging the validity or accuracy of such statement or payment.

D.   All payments due Representative shall be made in United States currency by check drawn on a United States bank, unless otherwise specified by Representative.

F.   Late payments shall incur interest at the rate of ONE PERCENT (1%) per month from the date such payments were originally due.

6.   RECORD INSPECTION AND AUDIT

A.   Representative shall have the right, upon reasonable notice, to inspect Manufacturer's books and records and all other documents and material in Manufacturer's possession or control with respect to the subject matter of this Agreement. Representative shall have free and full access thereto for such purposes and may make copies thereof and Manufacturer shall fully cooperate with Representative in connection with such inspection.

B.   In the event that such inspection reveals an underpayment by Manufacturer of the actual Commission owed Representative, Manufacturer shall pay the difference, plus interest calculated at the rate of ONE PERCENT (1%) per month. If such underpayment be in excess of ONE THOUSAND UNITED STATES DOLLARS ($1,000.00) for any Commission Period, Manufacturer shall also reimburse Representative for the cost of such inspection.

C.   All books and records relative to Manufacturer's obligations hereunder shall be maintained and made accessible to Representative for inspection at a location in the United States for at least two (2) years after termination of this Agreement.

7. INDEMNIFICATION

Manufacturer hereby agrees to defend, indemnify and hold Representative, its shareholders, directors, officers, employees, Representatives, parent companies, subsidiaries, and affiliates, harmless from and against any and all claims, liabilities, judgments, penalties, and taxes, civil and criminal, and all costs, expenses (including, without limitation, reasonable attorneys' fees) incurred in connection therewith, which any of them may incur or to which any of them may be subjected, arising out of or relating to the manufacture or sale of any Licensed Products based on the New Licensed Properties including, but not limited to, actions for infringement or product liability.

8. NOTICES AND PAYMENTS

A. Any notice required to be given under this Agreement shall be in writing and delivered personally to the other designated party at the above stated address or mailed by certified, registered or Express Mail, return receipt requested or by Federal Express.

B. Either party may change the address to which notice or payment is to be sent by written notice to the other under any provision of this paragraph.

9. TERMINATION

A. This Agreement may be terminated by either party upon thirty (30) days written notice to the other party in the event of a breach of a material provision of this Agreement by the other party, provided that, during the thirty (30) days period, the breaching party fails to cure such breach.

B. Representative shall have the right to terminate this Agreement for any reason on thirty (30) days written notice to Manufacturer subject to the provisions of this Agreement and, in particular, to the post termination compensation provisions concerning commissions as provided for in paragraph 4.

10. JURISDICTION/DISPUTES

A. This Agreement shall be governed in accordance with the laws of [State].

B. All disputes under this Agreement shall be resolved by litigation in the courts of the State of [State] and the parties all consent to the jurisdiction of such courts, agree to accept service of process by mail, and hereby waive any jurisdictional or venue defenses otherwise available to it.

11. AGREEMENT BINDING ON SUCCESSORS

The provisions of the Agreement shall be binding upon and shall inure to the benefit of the parties hereto, their heirs, assigns and successors.

12. WAIVER

No waiver by either party of any default shall be deemed as a waiver of prior or subsequent default of the same of other provisions of this Agreement.

13. SEVERABILITY

If any term, clause or provision hereof is held invalid or unenforceable by a court of competent jurisdiction, such invalidity shall not affect the validity or operation of any other term, clause or provision and such invalid term, clause or provision shall be deemed to be severed from the Agreement.

14. INDEPENDENT CONTRACTOR

Representative shall be deemed an independent contractor and nothing contained herein shall constitute this arrangement to be employment, a joint venture or a partnership. Representative shall be solely responsible for and shall hold Manufacturer harmless for any and all claims for taxes, fees or costs, including but not limited to withholding, income tax, FICA, workman's compensation.

15. INTEGRATION

This Agreement constitutes the entire understanding of the parties, and revokes and supersedes all prior agreements between the parties and is intended as a final expression of their Agreement. It shall not be modified or amended except in writing signed by the parties hereto and specifically referring to this Agreement. This Agreement shall take precedence over any other documents which may conflict with this Agreement.

IN WITNESS WHEREOF, the parties hereto, intending to be legally bound hereby, have each caused to be affixed hereto its or his/her hand and seal the day indicated.

MANUFACTURER   **MANUFACTURER'S REPRESENTATIVE**

By:_____   By:_____

Title:_____   Title:_____

Date:_____   Date:_____

SCHEDULE A

TO MANUFACTURER'S REPRESENTATIVE AGREEMENT

1.   LICENSED PRODUCTS:

2.   TERRITORY:

3.   TERM:

4.   RETAINER FEE:

5.   COMMISSION:

6.   EXCLUDED LICENSORS:

INDEX